THE BEAST WITHIN

THE BEAST WITHIN
Animals in the Middle Ages

Joyce E. Salisbury

Routledge: New York & London

Published in 1994 by

Routledge
An imprint of Routledge, Inc.
29 West 35 Street
New York, NY 10001

Published in Great Britain in 1994 by

Routledge
11 New Fetter Lane
London EC4P 4EE

Copyright © 1994 by Routledge

Printed in the United States of America.

Library of Congress Cataloging-in-Publication Data

93-19168
CIP

Salisbury, Joyce E.
    The beast within: animals in the Middle Ages / by Joyce E.
    Salisbury
      p.   cm.
    Includes biographical references and index.
      ISBN 0-415-90768-3 (alk. paper)   ISBN 0-415-90769-1 (alk. paper)
      1. Animals and civilization—Europe.   2. Civilization, Medieval.
    3. Bestiality.   I. Title.
    QL85.S25   1994
    306.4—dc20

British Library Cataloguing-in-Publication Data is available.

to Nevin James Graves

Contents

Acknowledgments

Like any project that takes years to complete, this book has benefited from many conversations with colleagues and much patience from librarians. These debts are impossible to acknowledge except in the most general sense. In particular, the manuscript was much improved by the careful editing of my colleague Professor Dean Rodeheaver. Moulies Mohamed offered invaluable help in obtaining photographs and reproduction rights from libraries in France. Tena Klessig used her computer skills to produce the graphs, and Linda Gregerson was very helpful as a research assistant. The final stages of completing this work were greatly helped by the intelligent critique and patient support of Bob Balsley.

Portions of Chapter 3 were previously published as "Bestiality in the Middle Ages" in *Sex in the Middle Ages: A Book of Essays* (New York: Garland Publishing Co., 1991). This material is reprinted here with the permission of Garland.

This book is dedicated to my grandson Nevin, who was born during its preparation. Nevin's presence demonstrated beyond any doubt that while writing books is fun, grandsons are even more so. Thus, this book is dedicated fondly to him.

Introduction:
What Is an Animal?

WHAT IS AN ANIMAL, AND WHAT IS its relationship to a human? Are they distinctly separate creatures, or is humanity something that is readily lost into bestiality? Medieval thinkers reflected on these questions. The influential fourth-century church father Augustine was adamant about the separation: "And so I should not believe, on any consideration, that the body—to say nothing of the soul—can be converted into the limbs and features of animals by the craft or power of demons."[1] The early thirteenth-century chronicler, Gerald of Wales, was less certain and told the following tale:

> One evening...he happened to meet a girl whom he had loved for a long time.... He was enjoying himself in her arms and tasting her delights, when suddenly, instead of the beautiful girl, he found in his embrace a hairy creature, rough and shaggy, and indeed, repulsive beyond words. As he stared at the monster his wits deserted him and he became quite mad.[2]

These are two strikingly different views of the relationship between humans and animals. The first expresses a perception that early Christian thinkers advocated in the first centuries after the birth of Christ. The second shows that by the late Middle Ages (after the twelfth century) the paradigm of separation of species was breaking down. It was harder to determine what defined an animal and what was definitively human. In this book, I shall trace the changing attitudes towards animals that took place in the thousand years we consider the Middle Ages (from about A.D. 400 to about A.D. 1400). During that time, thinkers moved from the idea that humans and animals were qualitatively different (Augustine's view) to a notion that we have more in common with animals than we might like to admit (Gerald's view).

In the past, as now, our attitudes towards animals and our treatment of them are based largely upon how we define them relative to ourselves. Today our definition of animal is broad and biological. Animals are virtually all things organic that are not plants. As we have come to accept this definition, we accept humans as animals. We do have a few reservations about this definition: we disparagingly call someone "bestial" or "an animal" if we believe his or her behavior is not up to "human" standards. Beyond that, we by and large accept the notion that we are animals, topping a Darwinian ladder that ranks everything from the smallest protozoa to the largest whale.

This definition of animals (that includes us) means that previous boundaries between humans and animals have disappeared. As James Rachels put it, Darwinism "undermines the traditional idea that human life has a special, unique worth."[3] In our modern world, as we have accepted people as animals, we have also made animals more human, so animals shown simply as animals have virtually disappeared.[4] We portray animals in cartoons, television, and films in ways that are decidedly human. Mickey Mouse, Lassie, and Black Beauty, among many others are endowed with brains, compassion, emotion— all the characteristics that we traditionally associate with humans. We give even less famous animals almost human status: we treat pets with much the same care that we give humans, acknowledging in our care our kinship with them. In other words, contemporary humans and their animals are not clearly separate categories demanding separate treatment.

Many of our controversial animal-rights issues derive from this blurring of the boundaries between humans and animals. If there is no difference between us, should we eat animals? Subliminal issues of cannibalism have informed discussions of vegetarianism, for example.[5] Further, once we believe that animals and humans share feelings in common, should we hunt and trap animals, knowing that such treatment would cause *us* pain? Should we use animals in medical experiments when we would not use humans? I hope to provide a background for these discussions by looking at a view of animals different from our own and seeing the transformation of this view.

Our notions about animals were not uniformly acquired nor have they remained constant over time. Only in the late eighteenth and nineteenth centuries did we seem to have decided that humans and animals share feelings—thus concluding that humans should be careful of the feelings of animals.[6] Before that, we glorified human intellect and we believed that humans were set apart from animals by virtue of human reason—thus animals could have no human feelings. During this Age of Reason, some anatomists who followed Descartes "administered beatings to dogs with perfect indifference, and made fun of those who pitied the creatures as if they had felt pain. They said the animals were clocks; that the cries they emitted when struck, were only the noise of a little spring which had been touched, but that the whole body was without feeling."[7] This seventeenth-century attitude towards animals sounds at best strange to our twentieth-century ears. This is a view of animals strikingly different from our own, one that emphasizes the differences between humans and animals. This view was advocated in the first centuries after the birth of Christ by early Christian thinkers who introduced a new paradigm in the relationship between humans and animals. Their work marked a break from the classical past and became the ground from which our perspective grew. This early Christian formulation is the point of departure for my consideration of humans and animals.

In establishing their position, church fathers in part drew from an often-quoted verse of the Bible in which God says to Adam and Eve:

> Be fruitful and multiply, and fill the earth and subdue it; and have dominion over the fish of the sea and over the birds of the air and over every living thing that moves upon the earth.[8]

This command has served as a lightning rod for views of human-animal relations, as is illustrated by contemporary environmentalists. Jeremy Cohen, however, by a careful study of the history of that biblical text, convincingly argues that most churchmen did not interpret this verse as offering open season on the environment, nor in fact were most interpreters particularly interested in the meaning of "dominion" at all.[9] Cohen raises a more evocative issue for this study of people's ideas about animals: "from a Christian perspective human dominion mattered relatively little in the quest for *salvation*."[10]

If early Christians were interested in the next life more than what happens on this earth, why did they bother to formulate a new view of animals at all? Biblical authority probably was not the most influential element in forming Christian beliefs about animals. More important was the church fathers' desire to reject classical Greek and Roman ideas.

During the early centuries of Christian expansion, Christian thinkers began to define what it meant to be a Christian within a pagan world. In the course of this identity formation, they repudiated many classical beliefs, including attitudes toward sexuality, entertainment, bathing, and other social and cultural practices. In this process, they also rejected a classical view that saw humans and animals as closely related, with plenty of opportunity for crossing the borders between the species.[11] The ancient world produced a fable that expresses their belief in the close proximity of humans and animals: Zeus told Prometheus to fashion men and animals. When Zeus checked on his progress, he was displeased to see so many animals, so he told Prometheus to refashion some of the animals into men. Prometheus did so, "and so it came about that those who were not from the beginning fashioned as men have the shape and appearance of men, but the souls of wild beasts."[12] In the classical world, differences between the species were illusory.

As they distinguished Christians from pagans, the earliest church fathers rejected such species ambiguity and established a principle of a qualitative difference between humans and animals. To clarify this difference, ecclesiastical writers frequently attempted to define specifically what an animal was. Albert the Great in the thirteenth century catalogued many differences. Some of the differences he noted were obvious: animals were hairier than people; humans could laugh, and animals could not.[13] Some differences were not so obvious: unlike human sperm, animal sperm was unaffected by the movements of heavenly bodies.[14] Finally, his general summary of the characteristics of quadrupeds reveals his reasoning on all these points: "All such animals are prone to the ground, i.e. because of the weight of their head and the earthy character of their body, they tend to bear themselves in a horizontal plane, their innate heat being inadequate to maintain them in an erect posture."[15] Here we learn from Albert that animals are cooler than humans, their heads are proportionally heavier, and they are more earthy—which is why their sperm is unaffected by heavenly bodies. All these things define animals in ways that stress their differences from humans.

Animals were also defined by their behavior. The medieval scientific work on animals, the *Bestiary*, explained: "They are called Beasts because of the violence with which they rage, and are known as "wild" (ferus) because they are accustomed to freedom by nature and are governed (ferantur) by their own wishes. They wander hither and thither, fancy free, and they go wherever they want to go."[16] Here animals are marked by further differences from humans. Animals do not abide by social expectations that bind humans. They do what they want, go where they want. The *Bestiary* author also identifies a characteristic of animals that is repeated throughout the Middle Ages—violence. Thomas Aquinas wrote, "Savagery and brutality take their names from a likeness to wild beasts which are also described as savage." Therefore, he said people who act that way fall under the category of bestial.[17] One would think that people would note that humans are remarkably capable of violence, bestial or not. But apparantly human violence was understandable; it seemed to have motives and goals. It was logical violence, where animal violence was thought to be irrational. This irrationality brings us to the final and for medieval thinkers the most important characteristic of animals.

Surface differences characterized animals and marked them as different from humans, but the main principle defining animals was their perceived lack of intellect, "reason."[18] Ambrose in the fourth century defined the unbreachable difference between the two species by claiming that humans have reason and animals are irrational.[19] Augustine, too, confidently expressed humans' superiority to "brute animals" because humans are "rational creatures."[20] And Thomas Aquinas in his synthesis of Christian knowledge, said that animals are "without intellect" and thus they were "not made in God's image."[21]

The lack of reason, an intelligent "soul," caused animals to have other defining characteristics. For medieval thinkers, animals would not participate in the resurrection; there would be no animals in heaven. Thomas Aquinas wrote "in that renewal of the world [paradise] no mixed body will remain except the human body." [22] For want of divinely sparked intellect, animals would not participate in the central Christian promise of an afterlife.

Animals' perceived lack of reason also served as the measure for much of medieval understanding of animal behavior. Since animals lacked the power to make rational decisions, medieval philosophers attributed animal action to instinct,[23] and animals (unlike humans) were incapable of acting apart from instinctive behavior. As Aquinas said, an animal's instinctive reaction "is as inevitable as the upward motion of fire."[24] This simile shows how Aquinas believed the processes of animals' minds were very simple, as irrational (or rather arrational) as the action of inanimate objects.

When medieval philosophers observed complex behavior in animals, they stretched for explanations that did not involve attributing rational thought to the creatures. For example, a much-discussed instance was why a sheep ran from a wolf. There was nothing obviously hazardous in the appearance of the wolf (that is, in its color, furriness, four-leggedness, etc.), yet a sheep ran in its presence. Such complex behavior as running from anticipated danger caused medieval thinkers some consternation. The behavior was complex, yet they would not accept that an animal could have enough intellect to interpret danger from sensory data that was not obviously dangerous. They solved this dilemma by positing a sixth sense, *estimativa*, that could perceive intentionality.[25] Thus, the sixth sense of the sheep could detect the wolf's malice, and the sheep simply responded to this sense by running, in the same way that it might instinctively recoil from the heat of a fire. Both were simple actions requiring no higher thought processes. This example shows the lengths to which medieval philosophers would go to keep the definition of animals as nonrational. It was easier to assume the existence of a sixth sense than to assume logical thinking.[26]

Some philosophers added several other internal "senses." Avicenna, for example, argued for an additional five to explain the vagaries of behavior.[27] Any real study of animal psychology would have to wait until after the end of the Middle Ages, when people left the Christian paradigm of animal-human separation behind.[28]

The medieval philosophers' conviction that animals lacked reason and an immortal soul formed the basis for their belief in the "natural" dominion of humans over animals, which supplemented the biblical verse and indeed determined interpretations of it. According to Aquinas, animals lack the "property to command," since "command is an act of reason."[29] One of the more popular depictions of animals in early Christian art is the portrayal of Adam naming the animals. One such example is shown in Figure 1. This scene was the moment when God gave Adam dominion over animals, for by naming them he showed that he understood their true nature and had the right and ability to control and use them.[30] Isidore of Seville developed his influential seventh-century catalogue of animals on the principle of dominion bestowed by Adam's naming of the animals. He opens his work by explaining, "Adam was the first to name the animals giving each a name according to its appearance and consistent with

Figure 1: *Adam Naming the Animals*
By Courtesy of the Dean and Chapter of Westminster

its natural condition."[31]

Isidore devotes the rest of his work to explaining the rationale for each name, that is, how each name reveals the character of the animal. For example, Isidore wrote that a cat received its name (musio) because it was the enemy of the mouse (mus), and the dog (canis) was named from the word sound (canor) because dogs bark.[32] Both animal names relate to the service the animals provide for humans. Isidore's text that served to define animals for the medieval world based that definition on the presumed dominion bestowed by Adam's naming of the animals. Adam, as a human, had the ability to command by virtue of his reason, where animals did not. In other words, Adam had dominion not only because the Bible said so, but because of the actual differences between humans and animals created by God and observed by rational people. Therefore, any change in this relationship would require not only repudiating (or reinterpreting) the biblical command, but changing the perception of the intellect of the two species.

Environmentalists who have been quick to blame Christian thinkers for stressing human dominance over nature have often focused on the Genesis text as offering a carte blanche of environmental exploitation.[33] As we have seen, however, this text did not necessarily yield that intepretation.[34] Some environ-

7

mentalists presume a previous idyllic symbiosis between humans and nature
during the classical period. In fact, in spite of evidence that many classical
thinkers dignified animals with human qualities and regularly saw humans acting
as animals, there is no evidence that they treated animals any better than our
medieval predecessors did.[35] It is true that the classical world had a different
view of animals, and certainly if that view had prevailed through the millennia,
we would have a different relationship with the natural world. That is not to
say, however, that it would be more benign, and it certainly would not have
yielded the same kind of concern that grows from our post-Darwinian association between humans and animals. In any case, speculations on what might have
been if other philosophies had prevailed are not particularly enlightening.
Instead, I want to look more closely at the early Christian position to see how
it worked in practice and how it was transformed.

I organize this book thematically and roughly chronologically. In the first
half I consider early medieval perceptions of the animals that served humans.
In the first three chapters, I explore the real animals of the Middle Ages and
study the way Christians interacted with the animals that were so central to
their lives. Since Christians had defined animals functionally, as serving humans,
I have organized my discussion along those lines. I begin with the fundamental
function of domestic animals: they serve as property. As property, they offered
their owners labor, materials, and status, and the first chapter explores this
relationship. The second chapter deals with the next major accepted function
of animals—food. Animals serving as food and property in a Christian world
were sharply differentiated from their human proprietors. Even in these functional relationships, however, there were ambiguities that pulled the species
together in ways that seemed to undermine the Christian position of separation. In these chapters I look at these tensions between the philosophic position
of separateness and the actual interactions between people and their animals.

In Chapter 3, I explore informal (and largely forbidden) relationships
between humans and animals—sexual ones. This analysis provides some insights
into people's behavior with their animals and also demonstrates that attitudes
toward the practice of bestial intercourse serve as a measure of medieval people's view of themselves in relationship to the animal world. In these attitudes
we can see the early Christian paradigm of separation between humans and
animals breaking down by the twelfth century.

There are any number of reasons for a change in people's attitudes towards
animals to have occurred in the twelfth century. The idea of separateness prob-

ably was strained by the ambiguities built into the functional relationship between humans and their animals. In addition, twelfth-century thinkers seem to have discovered "nature" and the physical world as something worth studying, something yielding information about the divine.[36] This approach to abstract nature may have helped undermine the earlier paradigm of separateness. I believe, however, that animals of the imagination were more influential in breaking down the barriers between the species than animals of the manors and villages of the medieval world. The second half of the book studies these illusory animals.

In the twelfth century, we can see a new popularization of animal stories that had been developed in the classical world and shaped by the classical view of animals. Chapter 4 looks at texts that show animals as human exemplars and examines the way animals as metaphors for human behavior may have led to changing the way people looked at themselves in relationship to the animal world. It probably did not change the way they looked at the many real animals that were serving them, however; that attitude change would have to wait until the modern period. But metaphors used in the twelfth century began to cause people to see the animal within themselves. This theme emerges strongly in late medieval literature, and Chapter 5 looks at the increasing blurring of the lines between humans and animals. In considering "Humans as Animals," I explore the late medieval preoccupation with half-human monsters and shape-shifting between humans and animals. Finally, werewolves serve as a metaphor for the rediscovery of the animal that is within us. It is this discovery of the animal inside that eventually led to the discovery of the human within animals. But that final step toward our modern perception is out of the medieval scope of this work.

The sources I use reflect the thematic structure of the book. I use predominately historical sources in the first half when dealing with real animals and predominately literary ones in the second when dealing with animals of the imagination. It is always a problem deciding which of the editions of the sources to cite in the notes. In most cases I have tried to cite the most readily available translation or edition of the texts, assuming that all but the scholars in the field would prefer the accessible text. Scholars who want to be led to the best edition in the original language can find that through the quoted edition or translation. The art work throughout reveals visually how people saw animals in life and in their minds.

I must offer a bit of caution here for those readers expecting a conventional work of history. This one is somewhat untraditional. I want to get at a cultural generalization of an idea. What did people in medieval Western Europe think of animals? Such a broad question raises immediate methodological considerations: what people? where? And, of course, it would be possible to find exceptions to any of my assertions. Just as it is possible to say that environmental issues shape an important segment of American thought in the 1990s, yet at the same time find plenty of exceptions to that assertion. Nevertheless, after all the cautions and exceptions, it is possible and useful to take a bird's-eye view of a subject to see the broad shapes, to understand the general outline. The details, the subtle differences between regions can be left for hawk-eyed looks at individual locations. Both views of the past are, of course, necessary. I have chosen the former.

In spite of differences between regions, it is possible to speak of a Western European culture. All the major sources I use are those that were widely distributed. This was true for diverse sources ranging from the major ecclesiastical writers to the fables and bestiaries. Other sources that I use that were more regional (such as individual law codes) present more of a problem. The comparison of many of them shows parallels that support the idea that there was a common concept that served as a basis for all of them. Closer regional studies will have to be done, however, to test and perhaps refine my thesis that there were two ways of looking at animals in the Middle Ages, the early Christian notion of separation and the blurring of the lines between the species that emerged in the twelfth century.

The medieval themes and preoccupations I explore in this book are not simply remnants of a world that is temporally and mentally far from our own. We still own animals, and questions of property and of our proprietorship still shape our laws and customs.[37] Our animal property can still bestow status if we own exotic breeds, and we wear animal parts comfortably in leather, if less comfortably in the more bestial fur. Meat remains a major (if increasingly controversial) part of our diet. People still have sexual relations with animals,[38] and we continue many of the prohibitions against the act. In cartoons and stories, animals still serve as human exemplars, and in fact, we raise our children surrounded by cute animal images, which reinforce the notion that there is little separation between the species.

In spite of all these similarities, there are striking differences between medieval views and our own. The blurring of lines that began in the twelfth century has increased into modern times. The clearest expression of that change is our attitude toward pets. We treat animals with the affection we accord children. That was not medieval practice. Medieval sources do not mention affection for their animals, and Thomas Aquinas again can serve to summarize medieval thinking on this subject. He says people cannot show animals charity (love) or even friendship, because animals are not rational creatures and fellowship is based on reason. Aquinas goes on to say that people can only feel "friendly" to animals metaphorically, not actually.[39] The keeping of animals for mutual affection would have to wait until modern times.[40] The environmental questions and animal rights questions of today are also new. The mentality that permitted the raising of these questions began in the twelfth century, however.

I began this book wondering what people in the Middle Ages thought about animals. In this Introduction, we see Christian thinkers confidently defining animals, focusing on their differences from humans. I ended up discovering with medieval thinkers that this question is inseparable from the question, "what do people think about themselves?" [41] It is likely that this is the underlying source of our continuing preoccupation with animals. We define ourselves as much by what we are not as by what we are. Our attitudes towards animals, our treatment of animals reveal our attitudes towards ourselves. In the Conclusion I return to the question of defining species, but with the ambiguities that late medieval society brought to it, and with the recognition that the underlying question of such discussions is the nature of humanity. I conclude this book hoping to offer insights into the animal that is within all of us, the animal that was discovered in the twelfth century.

Animals as Property

ANIMALS BELONG TO PEOPLE. THIS
was one of the earliest principles governing the relationship between humans
and animals, certainly antedating the Middle Ages that form the focus of this
book. Human ownership of animals was established when people first domesticated and bred dogs to help them in their hunting. Then people enclosed and
bred food animals instead of simply hunting them or driving them away from
their fields. In Western Europe, the first animals that were so claimed were
the wild ox and pig. Sheep and goats were brought into Western Europe
through the Mediterranean and were well established as domesticated animals
by classical antiquity. Sheep and goats are easier to work with and were
domesticated a thousand years earlier in the Middle East, but the wild species
were not native to Western Europe, so they were not initially domesticated
there but had to be brought in from the Mediterranean world.[1] Finally, horses
were domesticated first for food, then for labor. Well before the beginnings of
the Middle Ages in Europe, all these animals we have long considered domesticated were important pieces of property.

Of course, domesticated animals were not the only animals that interacted at some level with human beings. People's perceptions of their relationship with animals were also shaped by the wild animals that inhabited the fringes of settlement, from the mice that threatened their grain to the wolves that threatened their domestic animals. Therefore, animals could be both property and property destroyers.

Theologians of the early Christian church recognized such divisions in the animal world. Saint Ambrose of Milan explained the difference between the two kinds of animals by claiming that God himself controlled wild animals but man held power over the tame and domesticated animals.[2] Isidore of Seville in the seventh century compiled a book explaining the origin of the names of all the animals, a work that also served to define the animal kingdom throughout the Middle Ages. The two main categories in Isidore's organization were "cattle" (domestic animals) and "beasts" (wild animals). He further included a series of miscellaneous small animals, fish, and flying creatures,[3] but it is clear that his understanding of the animal world paralleled Ambrose's, expressing a clear distinction between wild and tame.

While Isidore's categories seem to organize the animal world in a way that was determined by the issue of human control, the animal world was never that simple. There were animals that existed on the border of the two realms of wild and domestic, so they do not fit his definitions in terms of human use. Cats are not properly domesticated animals. They are strongly territorial and share their territory with humans to their mutual benefit. Cats during the Middle Ages were seen as beneficial for catching rodents, so they were encouraged to share human space. I noted in the Introduction that Isidore of Seville wrote that a cat received its very name from its function as a mouser. Thus the cat was defined by its service to humans. A tenth-century Welsh law code succinctly describes the qualities looked for in a cat: "Her qualities are to see, to hear, to kill mice, to have her claws whole, to nurse and not devour her kittens."[4] These qualities were those one would expect of a wild cat, and more preciesely qualities of a wild animal that make it useful for human needs. They are the same qualities that simultaneously prohibit the animal's ever being "owned." Thus, it is useful as long as it possesses those characteristics, but as long as it does it remains incompletely domesticated. Cats were hardly more domesticated than the bees that were kept to make honey.[5] Figure 1 from the margin of a manuscript of St. Cyprian's letters shows a drawing of a cat carrying a rat.[6] The cat is drawn with all the attributes of a wild cat (fierce look, laid-back ears, and crouching posture) as it performs its function for humans, rodent control.

Figure 1: *Cat with Rat*
By permission of the Warden and Fellows, New College, Oxford

In the thirteenth century, Thomas Aquinas attempted to clarify the differences among animals by refining terminology. Following biblical precedent and Isidore, he called all domestic animals "cattle" and wild animals "beasts." Those animals that fell fully under neither category were called "quadrupeds." Two examples of the latter he claimed were goats and deer,[7] and cats would have fallen under the same category. These terms were rather vague and not universally used in this fashion, but they serve to indicate the reality of a world of many animals of varying degrees of wildness living more closely to humans than is the case in the twentieth century. I shall return to these wild and semiwild animals in the course of this book as they intrude on human perceptions. In this chapter, however, I shall consider primarily the "cattle," the domesticated animals that helped form the economic base of medieval society.

Once animals were transformed into property by being domesticated, the animals themselves were changed. The earliest effect of domestication was to reduce the size of the animals. The size of the brain also became smaller relative to the size of the body, and the fat content increased. Within a few generations of breeding in captivity, the bones of the face and the jaw became shortened.[8] These transformations occurred quite rapidly in the domestication

15

process and became archeologists' means of identifying the bones of domestic animals as distinguished from their wild counterparts. These transformations in size and bone shape show the retention of juvenile qualities in the full-grown animal[9] which is an organic equivalent to castration of male animals. A modern theory explaining domestication argues that humans and animals domesticated each other, both evolving in a way that juvenile qualities were retained into adulthood, and the juvenile qualities that were most important were inter-species cooperation and curiosity.[10] This theory of mutual domestication would have been completely foreign to the medieval mind. For them, domestic animals were subordinated to adult humans, remaining juvenile and tractable.

By turning animals into property, then, humans transformed the animals from wild co-inhabitors of the world to subordinates, essentially shaping the animals as if they were clay. This initial transformation seems built into the process of domestication, instead of being the result of long selective breeding. Such selective breeding did go on, and further transformed species, but the initial transformation was the result of an initial change in the relationship between humans and animals.[11] People's dominion over animals was expressed physically in this ownership relationship.

The medieval belief in human dominion was expressed in a complex of related ideas that included ownership, mastery, and control. These related ideas may be seen in an intriguing ecclesiastical law from the eleventh century. This law stated that since man had dominion over animals, it was forbidden for animals to have any advantage over humans. Therefore, people were to be feared by animals, not to fear them.[12] Such a law might raise interesting questions of how one would enforce feelings of fear on the part of animals, but clearly it should be understood as a statement of ideal relationship between owner and owned.

Finally, the relationship of dominion was perhaps best articulated by Thomas Aquinas, in his Christian summary of human knowledge. Thomas explained that Adam in paradise was given mastery over animals for three reasons: 1) nature has an observable hierarchy and man's position on the top of this hierarchy automatically gives him mastery of all that is below; 2) similarly, since the "order of Divine Providence" says that higher things govern lower, man as the image of God must govern; and 3) since man has reason ("universal prudence"), he must rule those beings that have only prudence in regard to particular acts.[13] This rather lengthy analysis can be summarized by Thomas's explanation of why it is all right to kill animals: the "life of animals...is preserved not for themselves, but for man."[14] Domestic animals of the early medieval villages were property, treated before the law like inanimate objects.[15]

Domestic animals were bred to serve specific functions. One obvious function was for food, which I will discuss in the next chapter. As property, domestic animals were valued for three things: materials (most important were wool and skins for leather and parchment), labor, and status. Thomas Aquinas mentioned some of these functions in passing. He wrote that in the Garden of Eden people would not have needed animals, for they would have needed no clothing since they would have remained innocently naked, nor food, since they would have been vegetarians, nor beasts of burden, "his body being strong enough for that purpose."[16] Aquinas here mentions clothing (materials), labor, and food, omitting only status as a function of animals, presumably too frivolous and vain for Christian mention. Throughout the Middle Ages, the use of domestic animals as property serving the three functions of materials, labor, and status served as a constant sub-text for people's perceptions of their animals and their relationship with these animals.

The earliest inhabitants of northern Europe built their economy on the ox. All modern breeds of cattle are descended from one breed, the *Bos primigenius*, the wild auruchs.[17] These were forest animals, browsing like deer. They gradually were pushed to the fringes of settlement and slowly became extinct while their domesticated descendents were sharing human territory. The wild aurochsen were probably extinct in Britain by the Bronze Age, but persisted in the forests of central Europe until 1627, when the last one was said to have been killed in Poland.[18] Other Germanic tribes, like the Anglo-Saxons, added pigs as a favored animal. Contact with the Roman world increasingly brought Mediterranean animals north. Goats, sheep, mules, and variant breeds of cattle expanded the northern domestic menagerie.

While the intermingling of northern domestic animals with Mediterranean ones diversified medieval farmyards, it also precipitated a confrontation of differing views. We have seen that church fathers strongly rejected Greco-Roman notions of animals, and the early medieval world tended to take its view of its animal property from the rural Germanic traditions. This derived as much from practical reasons as from anything more theoretical. After all, during classical antiquity Greece and Italy were based largely on a sheep economy. Oxen were used only as draft animals, but in Germanic Europe oxen remained central. Yet in time, the expansion of Rome spread different breeds of animals throughout Europe. Furthermore, the perception of animals as property seems to have always been central to the Germanic tradition and formed the foundation upon which other attitudes were built.

In order to look at animals as property, I shall first describe generally the actual interaction between people and their domesticated animals used for labor, materials, or status. Then I shall discuss how this interaction shaped people's perceptions of their relationship with the animal world.

Animal Use

Dogs were the first animals to be domesticated. Dogs and their wolf ancestors are highly social animals accustomed to hunting in communities with a dominant hierarchy. This allowed them to fit into human society easily and helped them accept humans as dominant. Humans must have seen fairly early the advantage of having dogs as hunting partners; thus they domesticated the animals and used them to help with the work of hunting. As human society diversified, the labor assigned to dogs also diversified. All domestic breeds of dogs descended from the wolf and served to labor for people in many capacities. By the historical period, this long domestication had led to the establishment of many breeds for specialized purposes. Some of the earliest written sources for the Germanic societies of the early Middle Ages, the law codes, mention many kinds of dogs. There were herd dogs (specialized for cattle, pigs, and sheep), watch dogs, and several kinds of hunting dogs. The laws refer to tracking dogs and hounds, hunting dogs, and running dogs. (These will be discussed more fully in the next chapter.) Some hunting dogs were identified by their prey, for example, deer dogs or rabbit dogs, further indicating the degree of specialization in domesticated dogs.[19] Of course, since dogs had been serving the same functions for millennia, they continued to do so throughout the Middle Ages. The twelfth-century "scientific" catalogue of animal knowledge, the *Bestiary*, described the functions of dogs:

> There are numberous breeds of dogs. Some track down the wild creatures of the woods to catch them. Others guard the flocks of sheep vigilantly against infestations of wolves. Others, the house-dogs, look after the palisade of their masters, lest it should be robbed in the night by thieves, and these will stand up for their owners to the death. They gladly dash out hunting with Master, and will even guard his body when dead, and not leave it. In sum, it is a part of their nature that they cannot live without men.[20]

The *Bestiary* not only lists the functions of the dogs, but shows how closely the species were linked in people's minds: animals cannot live without men.

In spite of the close relationship between humans and dogs, however, the most important animals to the medieval villagers were the large draft animals, who shared their biblical curse of having to labor on the land. From the earliest Middle Ages cattle were critical to people's labor. All the laws from the early Middle Ages refer to the all-important functions of plowing and pulling and specify penalties against those who would do anything to impede the animals' successfully fulfilling these functions. For example, the Visigothic laws penalized anyone who mutilated someone else's animal by cutting off its "lips, tail, or ears, or any other member" by requiring the offender to replace the animal with one of equal value. Similarly, the Alamans required payment from anyone who knocked out the eye or cut off the tail of a draft horse.[21] Such mutilations would have made the animals less effective, thus the owners deserved compensation for the lost labor. Animals' value as labor could be reduced by less drastic methods as well. For example, the Visigoths legislated that anyone who overworked a borrowed animal (either by making it pull too far or walk too long on the threshing floor treading grain) had to pay the owner a penalty, presumably for the reduced labor the owner would be able to exact from his own animal.[22] The Franks were perhaps most direct in recognizing the importance of the animals' labor, because in all the compensation laws, they include the requirement of "a payment for the time its use was lost" over and above the expected payment for theft or destruction of an animal.[23] This idea that the potential labor of an animal must be protected persisted throughout the Middle Ages. Walter of Henley in his thirteenth-century husbandry manual recommended that ploughmen and waggoners should be held accountable for the animals in their charge, making sure they were not "overloaded or overworked, or overdriven, or hurt."[24]

As Walter of Henley's advice suggests, in order to exploit an animal's labor, one has to care for it. Therefore, much thought was given to the appropriate care of animals. Cattle in northern Europe were kept either in enclosed fields or in cowsheds made of wood and thatched. It is impossible to determine whether cattle were housed at night against wolves all year around or only in the winter.[25] Walter of Henley's advice on husbandry suggests that during the high Middle Ages cattle were only housed during part of the year. He says: "And every night the cowherd shall put the cows and other beasts in the fold during the season, ...and he himself shall lie each night with his cows."[26] Cowsheds of the wealthy might hold up to a hundred cows, but more common was the situation of the smallholder who stalled a single animal in a section attached to the family home.

In Spain, cattle raising developed in a different (and highly influential) pattern. By the eleventh and twelfth centuries, the newly reconquered lands provided space for cattle ranching. This kind of ranching featuring range cattle driven for long distances by cowboys before slaughter developed in Spain and then was transplanted to the new world (including the American west).[27]

In the northern countries, cattle were given salt[28] but seldom fed anything besides hay and straw in the winter. Walter of Henley recommended that oxen, while stalled in winter or at work, should have about three pounds of oats with the oat straw and chaff each night. The medieval oat plant probably had a large proportion of straw to grain, so the animals were not overfed.[29] There is no reason to suppose that animals in the early Middle Ages were fed any more abundantly. Grain was too dear a commodity to share it generously with work animals.

Cattle were mainly supported in woodland and upland pastures until at least the twelfth century,[30] leaving the lower meadows for sheep. This browsing pattern recalls the animals' wild state when they were woodland animals. As the numbers of animals supported by the woods increased, the woods began to disappear. Even in the early Middle Ages, laws were passed to limit animal browsing in the forests in an attempt to preserve them.[31] The great medieval forests for the most part were unable to support the animals and humans that depended upon them. Cattle by the late Middle Ages changed into the pasture animals with which we are familiar. Browsing in the woods left the animal more vulnerable to attacks from forest predators. The old Norwegian laws held a herdsman accountable if animals in his care fell prey to a bear or a wolf.[32] Sometimes herdsmen were helped in their labors by cattle dogs,[33] and cattle wore bells to help keep them from being lost. Germanic law codes that repeatedly set penalties against stealing these bells, [34] testify to the importance of being able to keep track of one's property.

Most oxen were yoked when they were about four years old and usually worked for about four years. Some oxen could work six to eight years, but four was average.[35] Most oxen pulled with a yoke,[36] and some of the sources allow us to glimpse hazards of animal labor. The Norwegian codes accused someone of negligence if a "beast...is choked by a wooden collar." If, however, the collar were properly constructed, "if there is a swivel in the halter or a pole for the halter [to slide upon]," the person was held innocent of negligence.[37] This reference suggests that sometimes people tried to yoke an animal with a makeshift collar to bad effect. Walter of Henley also described other hazards. He said a draft animal might "be drowned by falling into ditches or water...; or the loaded cart may overturn and hurt the horse, or the driver may put out its eye or break its leg or thigh."[38] When an ox could no longer work, it would be stalled and fed to be slaughtered or sold for food and hide, often returning as much as it cost to its owner.[39]

From the early Middle Ages, horses joined cattle as work animals. Horses were used to pull carts[40] as well as for transportation. Excavations of horse bones from the eighth and ninth centuries in Anglo-Saxon England show bone outgrowths and bone fusions that are evidence of the animals being subjected to heavy strain.[41] Like cattle, horses were sometimes belled to keep them from getting lost. They were also hobbled and sometimes branded.[42] There has been much written about the advantage of the horse as a plow animal for its ability to work faster and longer than oxen.[43] These advantages were in part outweighed by the fact that horses were more expensive to maintain because they needed grain to supplement hay as feed.

The mixed benefits of using horses for plowing led to slow and varied spread of the practice. On large estates, the most effective plowing remained the task of large teams of eight oxen, but sometimes these teams were speeded up by the addition of some horses yoked to the team. Such a mixing of horses and oxen for plowing was only practiced in England towards the end of the twelfth century.[44] Only in northeast France did the horse largely replace the ox by the twelfth century. Italy and Germany continued with the ox throughout the Middle Ages; Spain shifted to mules by the late Middle Ages.[45] For most of the Middle Ages and throughout most of Europe, then, the ox remained the principle plow animal. On small holdings, however, peasants found the versatility of the horse a great advantage. Not only could the horse's greater stamina be used to plow with smaller teams, but the plow-horse could also be used for harrowing, carting, or riding.[46]

Even where oxen were used for plowing, horses were usually used to pull the harrow to break up clods and cover seeds. The horse's speed gave it a great advantage in finishing the harrowing quickly and effectively.[47] Horses' speed also made them particularly useful for hauling goods in carts. With all but the heaviest loads, hauling speed for horses was about twice that for oxen.[48] This was significant enough to make cart horses very desirable even though they had to be fed more than oxen. An additional cost in using horses was that an old horse that was no longer able to work did not bring as much return as an ox that could be stalled and sold for food. As Walter of Henley said, when a horse is old, "then there is nothing but the skin."[49] Modern analysts agree with Walter's analysis: calculations show that in the thirteenth century 16 oxen too old to work could be sold for enough money to buy 14 new oxen. The sale of 16 old horses, however, would yield only enough money to buy seven replacements.[50] In spite of this economic disadvantage, the advantages of horses for speed and stamina changed the picture of many late medieval villages. The large estates may have continued to be dominated by teams of oxen, but on small holdings many of the family oxen had been replaced by the family work horses.

Cattle and horses were valued for their skins as well as for their labor, so even inedible dead animals were valuable. Medieval laws dealt with questions of ownership of dead animals in order to regulate proprietorship of the valuable hide. Anglo-Saxon laws of King Ethelred (circa 1000) required that someone keep the hide of a slain ox for three nights until witnesses could ascertain that the dead ox was in fact the property of the man in possession of it.[51] The Frankish law code recognized the value of horse hide by including a section of penalties for people who skin dead horses without the consent of the owner.[52] The Lombard laws placed a high penalty against anyone who stole the skin of someone's animal that had been killed by a wolf.[53] Norwegian laws required that a man wait to skin a borrowed domestic animal that died until witnesses could ascertain the cause of death and any attendant liability before the valued skin was tanned.[54] The concern for holding people responsible for the hide of dead animals was repeated throughout the Middle Ages.[55] These references suggest that animals were skinned quickly and that the important principle of ownership continued after an animal's death, allowing the owner to profit from the hide.

Ox hides from mature animals are thick and compact, making excellent material for shoe leather.[56] Horsehide also was tanned for many uses. Hides from mature animals made excellent leather for shoes, clothing, and furnishings. In fact, animals that worked hard, laboring animals like the ubiquitous ox, had less fat under their skin than stall-fed animals, and thus the leather was smoother.[57]

Juvenile animals were often used to produce an even more valuable material in the Middle Ages, parchment. Parchment was made from hides that had been soaked and then stretched and dried, but usually not tanned like leather.

This process yielded a product that was stiffer than leather and perfect for writing. Medieval manuscripts from the earliest centuries preserve recipes for making parchment, showing how valuable these animal materials were.[58] The best parchment was made from calfskin, and this was called vellum (from the Latin *vitulus*, calf). This strong and thin skin was highly valued, so calves were slaughtered in late spring (April through July) while they were still milk-fed so their hides could be turned into fine vellum.[59] Even some of the earliest literary sources refer to using the skins of calves. For example, the early Irish story of the "Exile of the Sons of Uisliu" mentions a man who flayed a weaned calf for his daughter-in-law.[60] The finest vellum of all was uterine vellum. This vellum made from the skin of fetal calves was used to make the most valuable books (for example, Bibles). The importance of animals for parchment was significant. To get an idea of the extent of the demand, one need only consider the Gutenberg Bible, printed in the fifteenth century. One copy of the Bible required 170 calfskins, so the initial 35 vellum copies required the skins of nearly 6000 calves.[61]

It is difficult to approximate the number of draft animals that shared the medieval villages. Of course, there is a great range from the early Middle Ages to the late, and there would be a great variation from one country to another or even from one region to another. The statistics we can determine cannot do much more than give a sense of the number of beasts we are talking about. The sixth-century Frankish law code refers to herds of over twenty-five cattle.[62] The law also suggests a very low ratio of bulls, for one bull could "service cows of a three-village common." People must have gelded as many animals as possible to permit them to be tractable laborers. The same law refers to horses kept in a herd of seven to twelve mares and one stallion.[63] By the ninth century, the Saxons were able to pay annual tribute of 500 cows to the Frankish king, Clothair I, and later 300 horses to Pepin the Short,[64] suggesting a large draft animal population in Saxony. In the early tenth century in northern Scandinavia, a farmer was considered wealthy if he had 20 cows, 20 swine, 20 sheep, and 600 reindeer.[65] In this case, of course, the wealth was more likely to be counted by the number of reindeer he could claim in his territory. Italy did not have enough pasture land to feed large animals year round. The price of cattle was high, and in the thirteenth century, special pastures had to be set aside to graze plow oxen, which were usually rented.[66] English historians have studied these questions in detail, which allows us a more precise look at the numbers of animals in the countryside. In the thirteenth century, in South

Wiltshire (considered sheep country), there were 1,859 horses and oxen, 2,645 cows and calves to a total of 960 taxpayers. In the Blackbourne Hundred of South Suffolk (considered a more arable area), there were 1,432 horses and oxen, 4,298 cows and calves to a total of 1,339 taxpayers.[67] Such figures are important to keep in mind when we consider the ideas people had of animals, because the ratios of humans to animals show domestic animals to have been a significant presence in people's lives. In England in the fourteenth and fifteenth centuries, the numbers of animals increased after the Black Death reduced the human population. Thus the ratio of animals to people was even higher at the end of the Middle Ages. [68]

Cattle and horses served the property functions of both labor and materials, making them the most highly valued animals in the villages. The smaller animals, sheep, goats, and pigs, were kept for food and materials. In the early Middle Ages, sheep, not cows, were most valuable for dairy products.[69] Goats, too, were used for milk. The great value of sheep, however, was their wool. If the labor of the large draft animals defined in large part the medieval way of life on manors devoted to arable farming, the wool of the sheep defined the transition to commercial life that marks the modern world.

Sheep raising began modestly enough in the early Middle Ages, for the Frankish laws mention herds of about 40-60 sheep,[70] or about twice as many animals as in a herd of cattle. Excavations indicate that in Britain from the fifth through the seventh centuries sheep and goats represented just under 50% of domestic animal bones, with sheep outnumbering goats in a ratio of 40:1. Archeological evidence indicates that during this time sheep were butchered while they were young, showing they were probably used for meat rather than wool.[71] Eighth- and ninth-century excavations in England show that the sheep bones were mostly from mature animals. Thus by then, animals were likely to be kept for wool and milk rather than meat.[72] By the eleventh century the value of wool caused the numbers of sheep to begin to rise dramatically. For example, in England in Norfolk in the eleventh century, there were over twenty times as many sheep as oxen (about 92,000 sheep).[73] An impetus was given the European sheep industry in the twelfth century by the introduction of the merino sheep into Spain from Africa.[74] These sheep with their high grade wool spread north. Through the twelfth century in England, for example, the Pipe Rolls record the restocking of royal manors with large numbers of sheep.[75] By the thirteenth century in Spain, the huge herds of hundreds of thousands of sheep moving across great distances seeking pasture created administrative and environmental problems.[76] By the end of the Middle Ages in 1447, there were over 2.5 million migratory sheep traveling across Spain[77] and over half a million traveling through Italy.[78]

Sheep were even more vulnerable to loss to wolves than were the larger animals. Small sheep-holders brought their animals into the house at night to protect them, partitioning off half the house to accommodate the animals. Large holders built thatched sheephouses of stone or wood, some quite large. The Rothley sheepcote of the Templars, for example, was built to hold 342 sheep and 123 lambs.[79] During the day, shepherds led their herds to pastures, walking in front with a mastiff or wolfhound to protect the flocks that followed behind, herded by sheepdogs. [80] Like the other domesticated animals, sheep wore bells, and at least by the thirteenth-century, sheep were marked with riddle (an ochre dye) and their ears were clipped to show ownership.[81]

From the prehistoric period of their domestication, sheep seem to have been valued for their wool and were selectively bred for it. Domestication caused sheep to lose the hair outercoat that had protected their wild cousins, leaving only the valuable wool undercoat. Furthermore, they lost the capacity to shed the wool every summer as wild animals do. This was convenient for those wanting to use the wool without losing any of it. Women in medieval villages who were responsible for spinning and carding the wool were also responsible for washing and shearing the sheep. A detailed charter of the twelfth-century Templars set forth the requirement that each householder of five acres had to send one woman every day to milk, wash, and shear the landholder's sheep.[82]

The colors of sheep also changed during domestication. Breeds of sheep commonly appear in four basic colors, white, black, grey, and brown. The wild sheep from which most European sheep were descended were brown, grey, and black. The Romans had a preference for white wool and selectively bred for white-wooled sheep. The Roman preference spread white-wooled sheep throughout Europe and resulted in a predominance of white sheep for the wool trade.[83] Colored breeds of sheep remained on the manors of medieval Europe, however, offering colors of wool that were more varied than the overwhelmingly popular white. Brown soay sheep were common in Britain, black sheep were common in Scandinavia and Ireland, and the black Welsh mountain sheep offered highly prized wool in the Middle Ages.[84]

At least by the early thirteenth century, wool provided a good income. For example in England, the wool clip of Leicester abbey in 1297 represented one-third of the abbey's total receipts, and the wool of an individual sheep was worth half the total value of the live animal.[85] The wealth available to wool producers prompted large landholders to keep extensive flocks at the same time population pressures were forcing some holders to convert pastures to arable land.[86] Wool became so important that it diminished the other traditional uses of sheep: meat, dairy, and manure. The merino sheep in Spain were seldom used for mutton, and by the fourteenth century in England, mutton was virtually ignored as a food supply.[87] Profits to be made by the wool trade dominated shepherds' consciousness.

The valuable wool trade has been thoroughly studied for its impact in England. From the twelfth century, English wool was of such a high quality that it was much sought after by textile producers. The enterprising merchants of Flanders quickly became involved in the lucrative trade in wool, and in the twelfth and thirteenth centuries, the towns of Flanders were centers of the cloth industry.[88] The wool trade was immensely profitable for England from the late twelfth century through the Middle Ages. As testimony to the centrality of sheep to the English economy, the English barons in 1297 claimed that nearly half their country's wealth was derived from wool.[89] Even if the barons' statement is not strictly accurate, it does reveal a perception of the importance of wool, and the wool trade shaped English political decisions for centuries and British colonialism in Australia, New Zealand, and elsewhere.

Another example of the overwhelming profit of the wool trade was the large-scale transhumance in Spain. As early as the seventh century in Spain, there is evidence that passageway was reserved for the movement of sheep seeking seasonal pastures.[90] From the beginning of such movement, towns passed legislation against large flocks of sheep to reserve scarce pastureland for their oxen.[91] But by the thirteenth century, the struggle between those who valued the labor animals and those who valued wool was largely won by the shepherds in Spain. Shepherds organized together and in about 1273 founded the *mesta*, an association for the transhumance of sheep.[92] The mesta remained a strong political as well as economic force until the end of the Middle Ages, showing how valuable the trade in wool had become.

Compared to the valuable sheep, goats always remained poor second cousins. Always few in number in any holding, they served to supply milk and some meat. The laws of the Salian Franks that referred to herds of forty to sixty sheep mentioned only three or four goats in a herd.[93] Ironically, the qualities that made sheep's wool valuable made the skin less valuable for leather or parchment. Goat's skin, particularly kidskin, is much better.[94] Small holders keeping goats could expect a reasonable return on the hides. Goats have an advantage of being very hardy, able to browse on the most meagre growth. Thus, they may complement a herd of sheep without competing for the same grass.

The last but certainly not the least of the major medieval domestic animals was the pig. The European domestic pig was descended from the wild boar that inhabited the forests. Domesticated pigs can be kept in two ways: either allowing large herds to range in the forests guarded by a swineherd or keeping them in a sty. The Romans did both, and these patterns were available to medieval villagers. Although sty pigs grew much larger than the pigs that ranged in the forests, they presented the disadvantage of having to be fed. By the late Middle Ages, Walter of Henley recommended keeping pigs in a sty only when the ground was frozen.[95]

We can get some sense of how the Germanic people valued their pigs by the extensive references to them in the law codes. In the laws of the Franks, for example, there are more laws governing the care of pigs than of any other kind of animal. Laws refer to herds of pigs of up to fifty head that were tended by a swineherd. At least one pig in such a herd wore a bell, and it was designated as the "lead sow," more valuable than the rest. Sometimes they were in pasture, and sometimes locked in an enclosure. (The penalty was greater if someone stole a pig from a locked enclosure than from an open field.)[96] The Visigoths and Saxons also favored pigs, and pig husbandry in England may have reached its quantitative peak just prior to the Norman conquest.[97] For one example, in a ninth-century Anglo-Saxon will, a man bequeathed 2,000 pigs to his wife.[98]

The last function animals as property performed was to enhance the status of their owners. The desire for high status animals led to some selective breeding of all domestic animals from prehistoric times. For example, traits with no particular practical advantage, like distinctive coloring, long hair or ears, or even a tightly curled tail (as in pigs and some dogs), were bred for status.[99] Similarly, animals with a poor appearance could reduce the status of their owners and thus reduce their own value. This status function of pets can be seen today, with breeds that have distinctive features favored (and more expensive) than their more ordinary-looking counterparts. Such distinctive features are cultivated even at the expense of the animal's intelligence (as in collies) or function (as in large dogs like German shepherds with bad hips).

For the early Germanic tribes, status from owning animals came not only from some particularly distinctive animals, but from ownership of large numbers of animals. The Celts based their economy on their cattle and measured their wealth and prestige in these terms.[100] One of the most important of the early Irish tales is "The Cattle-Raid of Cooley." This work, written about the eighth century, reflects many of the values of the ancient Irish and expresses the strong association between cattle and wealth and status. The story centers on a dispute between Queen Mebd and her husband, King Ailill, over which of them is the wealthiest. The king wins the accounting of wealth because he owns a great bull, known as the white-horned one. (Note the distinctive characteristic that brought special status.) The queen wants to even the score by the acquisition of a bull that is considered to be equal to the king's.[101] It is this struggle for status given by ownership of an animal that precipitates the cattle raid that is the subject of the epic.

Other Germanic tribes also used animals as a chief source of wealth, and therefore status. In eleventh-century England after the Norman conquest, the Domesday surveyors considered pigs "poor man's animals" and were thus not scrupulous about counting them.[102] The defeated Saxons had favored pigs; the victorious Normans disdained them.

As the tribal societies from the early Middle Ages became more complex, specialized, and hierarchic, the status of animals also became more complicated. In the "Cattle Raid of Cooley," the basis of the economy was cattle; almost everyone had some. The status of the animal was enhanced by size and the distinctive feature of the white horn. In the more stratified societies, some kinds of animals had higher status that others. Animals like horses and hawks that did the same work as their noble counterparts, that is, war and hunting, were of a higher status than animals that did agricultural labor like their lower-class owners. The animal world mirrored that of the human, and as it did so the ability of some animals to enhance the status of their owners was even more important than in the earlier tribal society.

Throughout most of the Middle Ages, horses were considered the highest status animals. Jordanus Rufus wrote in thirteenth-century Italy: "No animal is more noble than the horse, since it is by horses that princes, magnates and knights are separated from lesser people and because a lord cannot fittingly be seen among private citizens except through the mediation of a horse."[103] Jordanus expressed what many surely felt. A nobleman was set apart and above commoners by the horse beneath him.

In the earliest centuries of the Middle Ages, after the fall of Rome, the horses available in northern Europe were small. Excavations of the bones of the horses of Anglo-Saxon England reveal horses we would consider pony-sized.[104] By the eighth century, the Franks realized the advantage in warfare to specially bred larger horses. Professor R.H.C. Davis has written one of the best analyses

Figure 2: *Dappled Horses* Add. ms. 11695, f. 102v.
By permission of the British Library

of the development of horsebreeding in the Middle Ages, and he shows convincingly that the horsebreeding that took place beginning in the eighth century led to increasingly larger and stronger warhorses, culminating in the *equus magnus* of the fourteenth century, which was as tall as 17 or 18 hands.[105] It may have taken until the fourteenth century for warhorses to reach a size that we associate with effective warhorses, but size was not the only factor that determined a horse's value in war. Isidore's description of horses, repeated in twelfth-century bestiaries, shows that the defining element of a horse was its warlike spirit:

> The spiritedness of horses is great. They exult in battlefields; they sniff the combat; they are excited to the fight by the sound of a trumpet....They are miserable when conquered and delighted when they have won. They recognize their enemies in battle to such an extent that they go for their adversaries with a bite.[106]

Of course, only the best horses were *destriers* (*dextrarius* in Latin), the spirited warhorses described by Isidore.

Selective horse breeding did not produce only warhorses, but a large diversity of types of horses. Palfreys were the finest riding horses (although not warhorses), thus appropriate mounts for highborn ladies in romances. Destriers and palfreys represented the highest status horses, but breeds ranged all the way down to the *affer*, the cheapest farm horse.[107] Most medieval horses were cart or plow horses working unspectacularly in the fields and villages. In the medieval imagination, however, the noble horse was associated with the noble occupation of warfare.

Like other status animals, horses were bred not only for functional reasons (size and strength), but for distinctive appearance. For example, horses were bred to have long tails and manes, purely decorative items that paralleled medieval people's value of high status attributed to long hair. Prehistoric wild horses had only short manes (like zebras). Throughout the Middle Ages, horses that had other distinctive traits were particularly valued. Figure 2 shows dappled horses that derived from the best Spanish breed, and the portrayal of the dappling in the art suggested the high status of the rider.

Then, as today, distinctive traits raised the price of an animal. For example, in twelfth-century England, a palfrey cost between 20 and 30 shillings, but a special white palfrey was reserved for the papal legate and cost 33 shillings.[108]

Literary evidence parallels these examples from art and economics to show the increased preoccupation with a horse's appearance as a sign of status. *Beowulf*, probably composed in the eighth century before much selective horse breeding could have taken place, describes warhorses. The poet says

The king then ordered eight war-horses
with glancing bridles to be brought within walls
and onto the floor. Fretted with gold
and studded with stones was one saddle there![109]

The significant thing about these horses was their trappings, not the horses themselves. One can contrast this with the descriptions of the horses in *Song of Roland*, written about 1100, well after specialized breeding had begun to produce a recognizable warhorse. The poet in this case related the names of the horses. Of the five heroes' horses named, three were named for their distinctive colors: Count Gerin's horse "Sorel," Ganelon's horse "Brown Spot," and Charlemagne's horse "Ash-Grey." (The other two horses were named "overtake the deer" and "valiant".) Archbishop Turpin's horse was not named, but it, too, had distinctive coloring: "a pure white tail he bore, a golden mane."[110] Thus, as horses were bred for their noble function of warfare, they also were bred for distinctive characteristics that brought high status to their owners.

A final example from the Scandinavian countries that shows the prevalence of the perception of the high status of horses is *Hrafnkel's Saga*, a short saga written in the thirteenth century. At the center of the story was Hrafnkel's "one treasured possession which he held dearer than anything else he owned. It was a pale-dun stallion, with a black mane and a black stripe down the back. He called the horse Freyfaxi....Hrafnkel loved this horse so passionately that he swore a solemn oath to kill anyone who rode the stallion without his permission."[111] Of course, someone rode the prized stallion, precipitating the action of the saga. Notice again the description of the stallion, showing distinctive markings that are traditionally a sign of a domestic animal that would bring status to its owner.

The importance of animals that confer status to their owners was pervasive through the literature and other texts of the Middle Ages. The examples here could be multiplied, but perhaps enough has been said at this point to demonstrate that status was the third motive for people to keep animals as property. I shall return to the relative value of these status animals below.

This discussion so far has established the physical relationship between humans and their animals that served as property. These animals were important for labor, materials and status, and lived closely with the humans who owned them. It is relatively easy to look to the sources for these functions of animals. It is more difficult to establish what people thought of the animals that were so central to their economies. Yet that is crucial if we are to understand people's perceptions of their animals and of themselves.

Animal Values

One of the ways to understand what people thought about their animal property is to study the laws that were written to regulate this ownership. Obviously, the most basic legal principle concerning property animals is that it is a crime to take someone else's animal. The eleventh-century Norwegian laws stated the principle succinctly: "If a man takes a hawk..., he is a thief."[112] But the laws against theft show there were subtle differences in the nature of the property. For example, there was a larger penalty if someone stole an animal that was locked up rather than ranging free.[113] It seems demonstrable that possession increased the property tie, and thus the penalty, for theft. But even when an animal wandered away from its owner, the property tie was not broken. All the codes were unambiguous about stating that people also could not steal animals that strayed from their owners' control. For example, the Ostrogothic legislation said, "If you find a stray cow or horse and hide it, you shall pay four times its value."[114] The church was in complete agreement with treating the theft of animals as a crime, and church laws echoed secular legislation on the subject. The earliest penitentials dating from the sixth century added religious sanction to secular prohibition by claiming that anyone (clergy or laity) who steals "any beast of his neighbor" must do penance as well as make restitution.[115]

The laws also protected from theft animals that were on the border of human control. Deer of many varieties, whether or not they were shackled as proof of ownership, were considered property and covered under theft laws.[116] Bees in marked hives were protected by the same kinds of laws.[117] There were even circumstances when wild animals were considered property and protected from theft. For example, if a hunter wounded an animal and was trailing it, no one else could intervene and claim it for twenty-four hours. Similarly, if a wild animal were trapped, the owner of the trap could claim ownership over the animal caught.[118] By the thirteenth century, the law on the subject was articulated a bit more fully. Bracton said, "Wild beasts, birds and fish are owned by no one until they are captured. Then they are the property of the captor. If they escape, they again belong to no one and become the property of the next taker."[119] Animals on the borders of human life offered some ambiguities in being considered property; their position depended on the exact circumstances of the interaction between human and animal. The legal discussions of the problem, however, show that ownership remained a central component of the relationship even between humans and animals on the fringes of human control.

The laws, then, reaffirm what we have already seen—that people viewed animals as significant pieces of property. In addition, the early codes can offer more subtle information on people's perceptions of their animals. The Germanic laws were based on the concept of wergeld, or the value of an individual to the community. This concept extended to the animals of the community; the penalty for injuring or stealing a highly valued animal was greater than that for a less valued animal. By establishing the hierarchy of value articulated within the laws, we can begin to understand another aspect of people's perceptions of their animals in the early Middle Ages.

Before I proceed to some conclusions on this subject, I want to offer a few cautions. First, the laws were written by the nobility and express predominantly a noble perception of valued animals. Whatever the laws may say, it is not likely that an individual villager would value a hunting hawk more highly than his own plow ox. This noble perspective parallels the social hierarchy, however, and as such is a fair indicator of what society in the broadest terms valued. There are, of course, a number of differences between the law codes that come from such a large geographic area. For example, there are differences in the amount of money in circulation, which would yield differing penalties for animals. Beneath these differences, however, the Germanic tribes had a remarkably similar valuative hierarchy of animals.

The monetary system from the third to the eighth centuries was based on the Roman gold coin, the solidus, and the smaller denomination coin, the tremissis. There were three tremisses to each solidus. The French sou, the Spanish sueldo and the English shilling were all varients of the solidus. (See the Appendix for a discussion of the relative value of the coinage, along with a chart that summarizes the values of the animals.)

In all the codes, the value of an animal was based on the function it served for the community rather than some other standard (size or scarcity, for example). In the hierarchic society of the early Middle Ages, warfare was the highest-valued function, and animals shared in the prestige accorded this job. As we have seen, these animals were also the ones most able to increase the status of their owners, so it is not surprising that these were the most valuable. In most of the codes, animals that participated in warfare and the related activity of hunting were given the highest monetary value. Warhorses, hawks, hunting dogs, and semidomesticated deer that assisted in hunting carried the highest penalties for their theft.[120] One illustration of the degree to which function influenced the value of an animal is horses. War horses in general were valued four times as much as draft horses,[121] but in this early period it is not likely that the breeds of horses used for these two purposes were sufficiently different to warrant such a dramatic difference in value.

The earliest law codes, those of the Salian Franks and the Visigoths, were the only ones that did not ascribe such a high status to hunting animals. This may be because the Visigoths and Franks did not restrict hunting to the nobility. When hunting was thus stripped of its prestige, the animals participating in the activity were valued in terms of utility rather than prestige. For example, in the sixth-century laws of the Salian Franks, the compensation owed for stealing a nobleman's stallion was the same as that for stealing a cart horse.[122]

After animals for war or hunting, the most valued were animals that were used for labor. Oxen and mares did much of the hard work of plowing, harrowing, threshing, and pulling carts, and all the codes ranked them highly,[123] though not as highly as the hunting animals. The laws of the Alamans are typical in valuing a draft mare at about half the worth of a hunting animal.[124]

The last animal function that the laws address is that of food. Animals serving primarily as food were valued less than laboring animals. For example, in the Alaman laws, a cow (primarily a food animal) was valued at one third the amount of a draft horse, and the Burgundians valued cows, sheep, and pigs equally at about half the rate of a draft animal.[125] While food animals were the least valuable in all the Germanic codes, there was no real consistency about which food animals they valued more. For example, the Franks seem not to have distinguished among the food animals: they established the same penalty (3 solidi) for stealing a young pig, a nursing calf, or a hen.[126] Size or scarcity seem not to have been value-adding considerations. The Burgundians valued cows, sheep, and pigs equally, but goats, which were about the size of sheep, were worth only one third as much as the other food animals.[127] Simple size, or food quantity, seems not to have been the predominant factor determining value.

The Anglo-Saxons, too, used criteria other than simply size for assessing their food animals. The Laws of Aethelstan indicate that pigs were worth about twice as much as sheep,[128] even though sheep could also provide wool and milk products. The other Anglo-Saxon codes express this same hierarchy.[129] Throughout the Anglo Saxon period, pigs provided the favorite meat (replacing the previous Celtic preference for beef). So taste at times could add value to a food animal.

In addition to the direct penalty assessed for stealing or injuring a draft animal, we can get a sense of the value of the animal by penalties assessed for stealing the bell of certain animals. Presumably, if the bell were stolen, the animal was at greater risk of being lost, so a higher value was placed on the bell of a valuable animal. The bell theft penalties reaffirm the hierarchy of labor over food animals. For example, in the Visigothic code, a thief was assessed a penalty of two tremisses for stealing a bell from a cow and 1 solidus for stealing the bell from a mare or an ox.[130] These animals are approximately the same size (and would wear approximately the same size bell), but they were unequal in function, the latter two being predominantly labor animals and the former predominantly a food animal.

It may seem inconsistent that hunting animals (that helped provide game for the table) were valued so highly, while food animals (a certain dietary supply) were devalued. The likely explanation is that hunting animals were valued for something other than their ability to produce food. In fact, they were valued because hunting is similar to war, a noble pursuit. They were valued for being on top of the functional hierarchy, not for providing food.

By the eleventh century, the laws were not based so strictly on wergeld figures, so they no longer offer such a clear statement of hierarchy of animal values. The prices of animals, however, offer a similar scale that allows us to see if people changed their minds about what animals were most important to them.

Not surprisingly, throughout the Middle Ages high status animals remained the most expensive. In the eleventh century, Norman price listings show the range of prices for horses was large. This shows the successful selective breeding that by then had created a variety of horses. As R.H.C. Davis has noted, "When the most expensive horse is valued fourteen times higher than the cheapest, we can be sure the demand for quality is supreme."[131] The demand for quality in many ways paralleled the demand for status. This trend continued, and by the twelfth century there were four main classes of horses: military, hunting, riding, and agricultural. The prices paid for such horses indicate the range: "a cheapish riding horse would cost 24 times as much as a peasant workhorse, a good palfrey 400 times as much, and a good warhorse 800 times as much."[132]

Among the farm animals, draft animals, particularly oxen, remained by far the most valued. To show this continued preference, we can look at the ratio of ox to sheep prices. By looking at a ratio, we can avoid considering the fluctuations in actual prices and consider what animals were most valued relative to other animals. In the Germanic laws, the ratio ranged from about 2:1 (the ox about twice as valuable as a sheep) to about 5:1.[133] The twelfth century in England was a period of agricultural prosperity, and prices for farm animals rose. In the 1190s, attempts were made to freeze prices, and the figures set the ratio of ox to sheep at about 3:1 or 4:1.[134] By the late thirteenth century in England, the average value of bovines was about three times that of sheep,[135] and that relative popularity of oxen continued into the fourteenth century.

What all these figures indicate is that in the minds of the people, patterns of value established early in the Middle Ages did not change very much. People continued to value the animals that engaged in "noble" pursuits just as society valued the estate that fought over that which labored. Similarly, people continued to value animals that eased their labor over and above any others. This remained true even though the medieval economy had undergone changes. In his fine study of English livestock prices in the thirteenth century, D. L. Farmer has pointed out that in the midst of rapid price rises, the price of sheep did not rise as much as that of oxen. He notes, "in view of the development of the wool industry in the thirteenth-century, this is rather surprising."[136] The economy changed more rapidly than the attitudes of the people driving it.

So far, I have been looking at how people valued their animals and how they preserved the hierarchy of animals of status, labor, then materials throughout the Middle Ages. To understand how people looked at their animals really tells only half the story, however. People's attitudes toward their animals are shaped as much by their attitudes toward themselves vis a vis the animal world. So we have to put people into the equation.

Attitudes and Ambiguities

One can begin to assess the early medieval view of the relative value of people and animals by comparing the wergeld values of people and their animals. Such comparisons reveal that people continued the Christian formulation of a dramatic difference between themselves and their bestial property. The Visigoths ranked a nobleman 500 times more valuable than the noblest animal.[137] The Franks valued a man's nose or ear at twice the value of a stallion.[138] The Burgundians valued one tooth of a nobleman at more than twice the value of the most prized falcon. One tooth of someone from the lowest class equaled a valuable hunting dog.[139] For the Alamans, the thumb of a man was almost twice as valuable as the best stallion.[140] These laws ranking value confidently claimed people's position as far above the animal kingdom. This assessment echoes Christian writers who articulated a theoretical position of unbreachable difference between humans and the animals over which they had been given dominion.

As humans perceived animals as property, they confidently placed themselves in a position not only superior to, but distinctly separate and different from, their animals. A property relationship is not unambiguously one-sided, however. Property ties link the owned and the owner in ways that are subtle, yet binding. A close look at even the earliest medieval sources suggests that the repeatedly stated highly privileged human position was not as secure as might first appear.

One of the basic links derived from the property relationship between the two species was that human owners were held liable for the behavior of their animals, and animals sometimes shared the penalties given to human misbehavior. Presumptions of liability had ample biblical precedent since they appear in Old Testament scripture, so Christian notions could blend easily with Germanic assumptions. All the early laws held owners responsible for damage done by their animals. The Visigothic laws stated that if an animal inadvertently damaged crops, the owner had to replace the loss.[141] If someone owned an animal he or she knew to be vicious, the owner took on an additional responsibility, for if such an animal killed anyone, the owner had to pay the price of a homicide.[142] The Franks said that if someone's animal killed someone, the animal's owner would have to pay half the wergeld of the slain individual and give the murderous animal to the family to compensate for the other half of the wergeld.[143] Such legislation made an animal's owner as responsible for the "crime" as if the owner had committed it. The Franks and Burgundians, too, stressed the responsibility of owners to pay reparations for property damaged by their animals.[144] The later Norwegian laws specifically said that if someone's animal commits an injury and the owner does not give proper recompense (including turning the animal over to the injured party), "it is as if he had done the injury."[145]

The laws of the Alamans introduced the possibility for owners to take on different levels of responsibility, depending upon the type of animal involved. For example, the laws provided that if a horse, pig, or ox killed a man, the owner had to pay the entire wergeld.[146] But, if a man's dog killed a man, the owner needed only to pay half the wergeld.[147] This legislation may suggest that people perceived dogs to have the capacity for more individual agency, beyond their owner's responsibility. This belief and the concomitant belief in a dog's agency was not fully agreed upon. The disagreement is revealed in a related law:

> And if the relatives of the deceased seek the entire wergeld, let all...doors [of the dog's owner] be closed, and let him always enter and leave through one door; and let the dog be hung nine feet above that entrance until it becomes completely putrefied, and drops decayed matter, and its bones lie there. And he cannot enter or leave through any other door. And if he removes the dog from the entrance or enters the house through another door, let him return the other half of the wergeld.[148]

This grotesque test sorely tried an owner's capacity to let his dog follow its own course without interference even in death. It also provided some punishment for owning a murderous dog, but punishment was not as important in the Germanic codes as responsibility, and responsibility was determined by the amount of wergeld owed. If the owner intervened in the natural decay of the dog, then the owner took full responsibility for his dog and had to pay full wergeld just as he might for his horse, pig, or ox.

The Lombard laws continued the recitation of liability for damage done by animals, but added a caution. An owner was liable for damages done by his animal, but there could be no feud begun by an animal's actions, because "the thing was done by a dumb animal without any intent on the part of its owner."[149] While humans and animals were joined in responsibility, there was still a separation preserved. Animals lacked reason and intentionality, thus the character of their action was somewhat different from that of people.

No matter how vigorously people defended the idea that they were different and separate from their animals, they were in fact joined in responsibility for appropriate social behavior. Many of the laws noted an increased liability when people brought their animals even closer to them with ties of food. The Norwegian laws noted that an owner had to pay additional compensation for damage done by a vicious animal if the owner gave it food after judgement is brought against the animal.[150] Similarly, the laws of Alfred doubled the penalty an owner had to pay for a vicious dog if the owner gave it food after it had been shown to be dangerous.[151] These laws establish two important points in the perceived relationship between humans and their animals: 1) Food was a defining point of the relationship between humans and animals, and taking on responsibility for providing food for an animal joined the two together more closely. (I will look at this food tie in more detail in the next chapter.) 2) There were degrees of taking on responsibility for one's animal. Just as the man who took down a decomposing dog took on more responsibility for the animal's actions, someone who joined the animal more closely to himself by feeding it took on more responsibility.

In all these instances, we can see that humans were held responsible for the actions of their property. This is consistent with the early Christian position that animals are not rational, thus not fully responsible. The ties of liability offer a paradox. On the one hand, they grow from the vision of animals as qualitatively different from humans, yet they join humans and animals together in ties of responsibility. This is characteristic of the early medieval view of animal property. By contrast, at the end of the Middle Ages, when there was much more ambiguity between the species, as we shall see, some animals were held solely liable before the law for their own behavior. We know of 93 cases of criminal proceedings against animals, and the earliest is in 1266.[152] Penalties against animals were varied. A vicious dog was imprisoned for six months, a run-away ass had its ears cut off, and a murderous bull was hung.[153] These trials of animals assume that animals are "rational" enough to be held accountable for their actions. This attitude is very different from that of the early Middle Ages.

In the early Middle Ages, domestic animals and their owners were linked in mutual responsibility, but wild animals were exempt from such ties. The Norwegian laws said, "Bears and wolves are outlawed everywhere for no man wants to be answerable for their doings."[154] By outlawing these animals, the Norwegians placed them outside the human community, exempt from its bonds of mutual obligation.

The mental images that caused people on the one hand to claim superiority over the animal world and on the other to note the reality that they were joined to their animals in liability for their animals' behavior was expressed in some laws that punished people by reducing them to a bestial level, an ultimate humiliation. The Burgundian laws have dramatic examples of this reduction. If someone stole a valuable hunting or tracking dog, the laws stated, "he shall be compelled to kiss the posterior of that dog publicly in the presence of all the people."[155] The guilty human in this case was publicly reduced to bestial behavior. In another such example, if someone tried to steal another's falcon, the laws prescribed, "let the falcon eat six ounces of meat from his breast or head."[156] Falcons grip with their talons to eat, so the guilty party would have been damaged during this process. In fact, the individual would have been reduced to animal food, both symbolically by the falcon eating from his/her body, and actually, because of the probability that the falcon would include some of the human flesh in its meal. This reduction of human to animal food was probably a humiliation lower than the reduction to bestial behavior experienced by the thief kissing the dog's posterior.

Figure 3: *William the Conqueror's Horse* Bayeux Tapestry
Reproduced with special permission from the Bayeux Tapestry, City of Bayeux

Just as humans were liable for their animals' actions, sometimes animals shared in the shame of their felonious owners. Bracton preserved a law that claimed if a nobleman was found guilty of rape, "his horse shall to his ignominy be put to shame upon its scrotum and its tail, which shall be cut off as close as possible to the buttocks. If he has a dog with him, ...it shall be put to shame in the same way; if a hawk, let it lose its beak, its claws and its tail."[157] This law points to the degree that the image of the nobility was linked to their noble animals. The humiliation of the most valuable noble animals was certainly seen as additional punishment for the owner. Furthermore, by removing the powerful elements of these animals, their weapons and their potency, the nobleman himself was rendered symbolically less powerful.

This association between the power of the nobleman and the power of his horse can be seen in the figure of William the Conqueror's horse in the Bayeux Tapestry (shown here in Figure 3). The horse is shown with an erection, demonstrating that it is a stallion. Mares or geldings were never used in warfare during the Middle Ages.[158] While this may have had some practical purpose (stallions were more aggressive and presumably more inclined to join in the battle), the purpose was probably more symbolic than actual, since mares and geldings were used in battle during the Renaissance. In fact, the man and his stallion were linked in a complex tie that metaphorically associated sexuality with power.[159] In the tapestry, William's power was expressed by his horse's erection. The lines separating horse from man were very thin indeed.

The interactions between people and animals described in the earliest medieval texts was complex. In the earliest centuries, the primary relationship between the two was the property relationship. This relationship joined with Christian theology to lead to an expression of separation that was extreme. The difference in monetary value between animals and humans reiterated the dramatic difference between humans and animals that the Christian tradition articulated. The actual relationships and perceptions of the relationships were more complicated than a simple, and repeated, statement of separation. Ties of property bound the owners as surely as the owned. These links tied the species together in ways hardly articulated and created a relationship between humans and animals that introduced the possibility of uncertainty in considering the place of humans in the natural order of the world. This uncertainty was almost imperceptible in the early medieval laws, but it grew slowly over the centuries as we shall see as this book traces other forms of relationships between humans and animals.

2

Animals as Food

OUTSIDE THE GARDEN OF EDEN, the oldest interaction between humans and animals is that of predator and prey (both humans and animals at times fulfilling each role). In the Middle Ages, wild, semiwild, and domestic animals were consumed for food. Indeed, Thomas Aquinas identified animals' central purpose as serving as human food. To him, animals' lives were preserved "not for themselves, but for man," so there was no crime in killing animals.[1] In this, as in so many other things, Aquinas's theology summed up medieval thought. Animals were killed without concern for the animals themselves. The only restriction on killing an animal was if the animal were the property of another. Beyond that, animals existed for human use. Thus wild animals were hunted for food, domestic animals were raised for food, and predators that threatened these animals (or their owners) were hunted remorselessly. Bears and wolves became extinct in areas of human habitation, and such removals were considered unambiguous benefits to human dominion.

At first glance, the relationship between predator and prey, consumer and food expresses the same extreme distancing as the relationship between owner and owned discussed in the first chapter. But just as the ties of property linked humans and animals together in unforseen ways, ties of food joined humans and animals despite attempts to define them as qualitatively different. As Mikhail Bakhtin so eloquently explained this relationship: "The encounter of man with the world, which takes place inside the open, biting, rending, chewing mouth is one of the most ancient, and most important objects of human thought and imagery....The limits between man and the world are erased."[2] It is not only modern thinkers who recognize the joining of humans and the world through food. Aquinas explained that human bodies grew because food was converted into "the true human nature."[3] Aquinas was expressing the ideal Christian position on digestion: animal flesh is converted to human flesh. Yet the very statement of conversion reveals the blending of human and animal that is implied in consumption. In fact, the medieval texts much more often reveal a preoccupation with the notion that one becomes what one eats, rather than one transforms what one eats. This fixation led to a number of rather strange medieval speculations and regulations. As early as the third century, a church father wanted to forbid people from eating hares or hyenas because it was believed that both these animals had unusual and promiscuous sexual habits and that if people ate their flesh they would take on the same sexual attributes as the animals.[4] In this case, people believed that one could even take on character traits through one's food.

In reflecting upon becoming what one eats, Aquinas and the thirteenth-century scholastics wrestled with the question of to what degree one's very flesh became the animal flesh that was consumed. This preoccupation led Aquinas to address a question that sounds most peculiar to modern ears: if semen were made from excess food, that is, the "flesh of cows, pigs and such-like" why was not the "man begotten of such semen...more akin to the cow and the pig, than to his father or other relative?" His answer, that the human form imposes its likeness on the animal matter,[5] is perhaps less interesting than the original question, which recognizes a disconcerting ambiguity in the strict lines that were supposed to separate humans from the animals they ate.

In this chapter, then, I shall first look at the wild and domesticated animals that formed an important part of the medieval diet. Then I shall explore medieval perceptions of their relationship between themselves and their animal food and look at their many attempts to legislate a separation that blurred within the open mouth of human appetite.

Wild Animals

From time well beyond record, people hunted animals for food. The varieties of animals bred as hunting partners for humans testifies to the age of this practice. In the Middle Ages, the most important of these were dogs and raptorial birds.[6] Medieval hunting practices are varied and woven through many aspects of medieval life. Here I shall just describe the major animals involved and the way food remained central to an activity that began as survival and then became sport.

There were two main methods of hunting large forest game in the Middle Ages, and both required a close partnership between humans and dogs. One (the oldest) depended upon hounds finding the scent and working with mounted hunters to drive the game toward hidden archers. The dogs then would track wounded game. Some of the most vivid descriptions of the medieval hunt appear in literature, in which the poet's skill brings the chase to life. One example is in the fourteenth-century poem *Sir Gawain and the Green Knight*. The poet describes a deer hunt in which a large group of hunters, "a hundred wonderful hunters," drove deer to archers:

> They drove does deeper
> Into valleys, and arrows slanted down,
> Great broad arrows flying at every
> Turn, cutting deep in brown hides.
> Hah! They screamed, and bled, and high
> On slopes they died, hounds hurrying
> After them, and hunters with horns, blowing
> So hard that the echo seemed to crack
> Cliffs. And deer that escaped arrows
> Were caught by keepers, cut down and killed.[7]

This kind of hunting provided for a large amount of game; the king in the hunt described by the *Gawain* poet "killed so many no one could count them. Huntsmen and keepers came together, proud, and quickly collected the bodies in a pile."[8] Sometimes, however, the goal was not so much a large amount of meat, but a more complex hunt, more sport than food.

This second form of hunting was a highly ritualized hunt that depended upon a specially trained hound leading a hunter to an animal suitable for the hunt. Then many dogs would be released to chase the animal while their handlers followed, guiding and encouraging the hounds with calls and horns. Once the dogs had brought the animal to a standstill, they held it at bay while one of the hunters killed it with a sword or spear.[9] A hunt of this kind required more skill from the dogs and provided more sport rather than the larger quantities of meat obtained from the first kind of hunt. This sport hunt for the best hart is described in Gottfried von Strassburg's, *Tristan*, a thirteenth-century romance. The hounds King Mark of Cornwall had "chased a hart of ten [points] to a spot not far from the road. It let them overtake it, and there it stood at bay. Hard running had robbed it of all its strength. And now the huntsmen, too, were there with a great clamour, blowing for the kill."[10] This is the kind of hunt favored in the romances since it more closely approximated single combat between a hero and a perfect animal.

Even these brief descriptions of hunting styles show that the success of the hunt depended as much on the skill of dogs as of humans. From the earliest Middle Ages, people had bred a variety of dogs for specific hunting tasks. The early Germanic law codes mentioned a bewildering array of dog breeds, many of which we cannot precisely identify with modern breeds. Some dogs were designated as "tracking hounds," presumably tracking by scent ahead of the hunters as modern hounds do. The Bavarian laws distinguished between these tracking hounds and those "which follow footprints while being led by a leash." Such tracking dogs were carefully trained to seek out and select the game in silence before the actual hunt began. During the hunt, hounds would chase down the prey while braying and responding to commands from human hunters. These hounds were sometimes designated as running dogs; for example, the Burgundian code described them as having "heavy pads on their feet to run over stones." Greyhounds were mentioned specifically, but not exclusively, as running breeds, and the *Gawain* poet praised the skill of greyhounds "so huge that leaping on a deer from behind they tore him down, right there, as fast as the telling."[11] Figure 1 shows a strong and finely formed running dog chasing a hare through the initial letter of a twelfth-century German manuscript. One of the eleventh-century Norwegian laws testified to the importance of the running breeds, for it said that during a hunt, a deer belongs to whatever man starts the running of the dog, no matter who kills it. When men were hunting in a group, the deer was divided up, but the valuable hide belonged to the owner of the running dog.[12]

Some dogs were trained to help kill the prey, instead of just leading their human partners to it. The Germanic laws mention rabbit dogs and dogs that hunted larger animals like bears and buffaloes. From many of the illustrations in manuscripts, it seems that these larger hunting dogs resembled our mastiffs.

Figure 1: *Hound Chasing Hare* Metro Colon Codex xcv.
Courtesy of Dombibliothek Cologne and Hill Monastic Library, St. Johns, Minnesota

Wolfhounds, too, were highly valued as partners in the struggle against predators. Perhaps the highest degree of specialized hunting dog might be the smaller
dogs that the Bavarian laws described as "dogs which hunt game under the
ground"; they probably resembled the modern dachshund or some breeds of
small terrier.[13]

The goal of the hunt was always to provide game for the table. Hunting
customs (which became highly ritualized in the late Middle Ages) served con-
stantly to remind all participants of that fact. Perhaps the most involved
literary description of butchering animals after the kill may be found in *Tristan*,
in which Tristan demonstrates his courtly manners by butchering a deer in a
ritual fashion. The butchering (or "excoriation" as the text calls it) is described
in great detail, taking up a full chapter in the romance. The following short

47

passage will give an example of the kind of minutia that interested the medieval audience:

> He [Tristan] addressed himself next to severing the breast from the chine [backbone] and from the flanks, including three ribs on either side. (That is the way to break up a hart. Those who know how to take out the breast are sure to leave these ribs on it.) Then he quickly turned and removed the hind-quarters most expertly, both together, not one by one.[14]

The emphasis on converting the game to food returns even highly ritualized sport hunting to its initial purpose of providing meat for the table. The highly ritual butchering converts the wild hart, a worthy opponent, into food worthy of human consumption. It also expresses and imposes human domination of the wild animals that inhabit the world.

Even the dogs as hunting partners participated in a ritual celebration of the game as primarily food. According to medieval hunting manuals, hunting hounds were fed only on bread when they were in the kennels; their only meat was given to them at the site of a kill after a successful hunt. Thus the animals would never forget the close association between the hunt and meat.[15] At the end of the hunt, when the animal was butchered, the choicest bits were hung up and set aside for the lord. These included the testicles, tongue, and certain of the other internal organs. The hounds also received their share in a ritual manner. The curée (ritual rewarding of the hounds) involved urging the hounds to bay and allowing them to eat portions from the hide or body cavity of the slain animal. Figure 2 shows two greyhounds receiving their *curée* from the body cavity of a deer. In *Sir Gawain and the Green Knight*, the poet describes how the hounds are rewarded for their successful hunt of a deer:

> They set out liver and lungs and tripe
> On a fresh-flayed skin, mixed with bread
> Soaked in blood, and fed their hounds.

The hounds also received their share of a wild boar, when the huntsman carved "Out the intestines (broiled on coals, Dressed with bread, they were fed to the dogs).[16] Tristan, too, did not neglect the dogs in his ritual excoriation of the hart:

> He chopped the milt [spleen] and the lungs, and then the paunch and the

great gut (and what other dogs' fare there was) into suitably small pieces, and spread it all out on the hide. This done, he summoned the hounds with a loud 'Ça, ça, ça!' They were all there in a trice, standing over their reward.[17]

Figure 2: *The Hounds' Reward* Devonshire Hunting Tapestries
Courtesy of Victoria and Albert Museum, London

The ritual surrounding the rewarding of the hounds goes beyond the practical need to reinforce the hounds' desire to hunt. If that were the only motivation, the hunters could casually toss the hounds odd scraps of the butchered animals. Instead, the curée took the form of a ritual feast, and medieval feasting always served to reinforce the sense of community and communion of the participants. In this case, then, humans and animals were joined in celebrating the victorious hunt by sharing the meat.

Helped by these hunting partners, medieval people took a great array of game, and it always remained an important part of the medieval diet. The hounds were used mostly in the hunt of wild forest game, particularly deer and boar. The early Germanic laws that I described in Chapter 1 legislated values of several kinds of deer, black deer, red deer, and roebucks,[18] thus indicating some of the diversity of the early medieval game. Each kind of deer had its own attractions for the medieval hunters. The hart was the most highly prized, for it was noble in appearance with fine antlers, and it gave the hounds a challenging run. The fallow deer offered a less exciting hunt but a better meal at the end. It was smaller than the hart but had proportionately more meat.[19] The roebuck was smaller still and provided good and relatively tender venison for the table.

The hunting treatises of the late Middle Ages recommended that only a large buck (with antlers of at least ten points) be selected for a full hunt; the ten-point hart killed in *Tristan* met this criterion. This may have been the ideal for a literary or sport hunt, but bone excavations in eighth- and ninth-century England show that most deer were killed while they were young, less than one year old. This could represent hunters either taking the easiest prey or selecting the tenderest meat.[20] It could be that in the early Middle Ages people depended more on game for a large portion of their diet but later depended more on domesticated animals, thus emphasizing the sport of the hunt. In any case, one can see a perennial conflict in the hunt: was it for sport or for food? Obviously, it filled both functions; while the treatises would write of the thrill of the hunt, hunters were equally concerned with filling their larder.

The impulse toward concentrating on venison rather than on sport must have led to deer farming or semidomestication of deer. In the late Middle Ages we have many references to deer parks as special preserves for hunting. Forest areas enclosed with fences served to simplify the hunt by restricting the range of the deer. There are clear references to such parks in Charlemagne's France and in the Domesday Book in England,[21] and they persist throughout the Middle Ages.

The evidence from the early medieval laws indicates even more intense domestication, however, than simply a restriction of the range. The laws referred to "domesticated" stags and stags that were shackled and branded.[22] The Salian Laws even referred to strong penalties against anyone who stole a domesticated stag "which has been trained for hunting, and it can be proved by a witness that its owner has had it on the hunt and has killed two or three animals with it."[23] While one cannot be absolutely certain of the uses to which a hunter might put a "trained" deer, the likeliest explanation is that it was used as a decoy, luring its wild counterparts to the kill. There are even literary sources that refer to does that were sufficiently tamed to provide milk. Gerald of Wales said "I saw cheese made from deer's milk...The Countess of Chester...kept tame deer. From their milk she made three small cheeses."[24] St. Kevin was said to have fed an infant on doe's milk.[25] Clearly the practice of milking does was considered remarkable, but not impossible. The presence of deer even tame enough to be milked means that although hunting offered sport, medieval people valued venison enough to ensure a supply even at the expense of the best hunting. In the late Middle Ages, deer in the parks were fed on hay or oats in the winter, and domestic cows were brought in to suckle deer calves.[26] Many deer lived on the border between wild and domesticated.

Boar was the second most popular game animal. Boar hunting offered dangerous sport, for the animals were five feet long and three feet high and could grow tusks up to twelve inches long.[27] Size alone did not make this animal dangerous; when enraged, it charged without regard for its own safety. The *Gawain* poet described a boar hunt with characteristic vividness. After the dogs had cornered the animal, "his hooves pawed at the ground, foam grimaced on his snout; and he sharpened his tusks, waiting." The hunters were reluctant to approach,

> So many had been gored
> By those tusks, that fear
> Of being torn
> Held them: he seemed wild, he seemed weird.

Finally, the lord confronted the animal alone with his sword:

> And man and boar blended in steaming
> White water; but the boar had the worst, for the lord
> Had measured his charge, and aimed his sword
> Into his throat, and planted it deep."[28]

The charge of a 250-pound enraged boar must have been impressive, and it would have taken strong nerves and an equally strong arm to place the sword in exactly the right spot. A hunter would not get a second chance against such a prey.

The hunter who succeeded in bringing down a wild boar alone was credited with great bravery and honor, and the honor was first noted by food ritual. In France, if a man were able to kill a boar with a sword without help from his dog (like the lord in *Gawain*), he was rewarded with the kidneys and the fat of the back. The dogs that hunted the difficult boar were the bravest and strongest available, and they, too, were rewarded with ritual food offerings. Most of the internal organs were reserved for the dogs. These were broiled on a fire and mixed with boar's blood and bread and fed to the dogs as a reward.[29] The boar remained a powerful figure in medieval imagination, feared and respected. It represented power, invincibility, fearlessness and appeared in literature marking these qualities.[30] It also represented male sexuality, which I will discuss in the next chapter. Beyond bearing a heavy metaphoric weight, however, wild swine also remained a favored food. The *Gawain* poet culminates his description of the boar hunt with the festive meal at which the boar was served.[31] The hunt is incomplete without the meat as a victory feast.

Other small game supplemented the medieval diet, even if the hunting was less spectacular than that of the larger animals. Of the smaller game, hare offered the best hunting, and hounds could be kept in shape for hunting deer by following the fast and wily hare. Medieval hunters would have recognized that the hound shown in Figure 1 was in for a long run, for the hare is shown with his ears forward. According to medieval hunting tracts, this indicated that he was strong and confident of escape. Only when he held his ears back was he tiring.[32] While the hare offered good sport, its value for food was ambiguous. As I noted above, some churchmen warned of the dietary implications of the hare's suspect sexuality. Some medical tracts warn of hare meat causing sleeplessness and producing melancholy humours.[33] But for all the warnings, cookbooks offered recipes for hare meat, and it seems most likely that hare always formed a part of the medieval diet.

Hares were native to most of Europe, but rabbits were native only to Spain. The Romans brought them out of Spain as a food source, and they spread throughout Europe. Unlike hares, rabbits live below ground, so different techniques were used to hunt them. Most successful was the use of ferrets. Hunters put nets over as many of the warren holes as they could find. Then they released a muzzled ferret into the hole and caught the emerging rabbits. (The muzzle prevented the ferret from staying underground for dinner.) Small hounds that were bred to go underground were also used to hunt rabbits. They were more reliable than ferrets, but also more expensive. The most convenient way to obtain rabbit meat, of course, was to breed the animals domestically. Medieval monks particularly engaged in such production, breeding rabbits in walled, paved courtyards to keep them from going underground. Monks favored eating newly born or unborn rabbits, for they were not considered meat and thus could be eaten on fast days.[34] (I must confess the subtlety of this distinction escapes me, so I'll have to leave it with no further explanation.)

The human/hound partnership, supplemented by nets and traps, yielded a diverse diet of large and small game. But dogs were not the only hunting partners. Raptorial birds offered a way for their owners to catch large and small game birds, always popular at table. Raptorial birds were not fully domestic animals like dogs. They fell into Aquinas's category of semidomestic, or what we would consider "tamed." Thus, the hunting birds people used were those found in the wild, not specially bred animals like breeds of dogs. Frederick II in the thirteenth century wrote a comprehensive treatise on falconry, his favorite sport, and Frederick's defining element of the raptorial birds was their diet. He said, "Raptorial species do not eat grain or similar food cultivated by man.... As a result they do not associate with men and do not easily become domesticated."[35] Frederick's description is telling because it reaffirms the degree to which medieval people identified an individual (human or animal) by its diet, and furthermore it shows that they believed this identification by diet permanently kept raptorial birds outside the realm of the domestic. Since hawks remained wild, Frederick was adamant that a good hunting hawk must be caught (preferably netted) after it had received its early hunting lessons from its parents. The necessity of capturing wild hawks led to a brisk and lucrative trade in hawks.[36]

It took a good deal of time and patience to train a wild hawk to turn it into a hunting partner. The wild bird was calmed by sealing its eyelids: a stitch was placed in the lower lid, which was threaded with linen thread. The thread was then tied over the bird's head, keeping the lid closed. (Sometimes the upper eyelid was threaded and pulled down, but the effect was the same.) The temporarily blinded bird could then become accustomed to human voice, touch, and most importantly to depending upon humans for food. Once tamed, the bird's sight was slowly restored by adjusting the thread. Then the bird began training for the hunt. It was taught not only to respond to the lure, but always to look to humans for food. The best birds were trained to hunt prey not normal to their wild state. Hawks could be taught to hunt large birds like ducks, geese, and even cranes and herons. Such hawks were, of course, the most valuable.[37]

For a hawk to hunt a crane required the kind of interaction between human, hound, and hawk that warmed medieval hearts. As cranes rose, two falcons attacked one crane and brought it to the ground. Then greyhounds ran to the prey to kill the crane before its thrashing could damage the more delicate hawks. Finally, the hunter claimed the crane which would likely become his dinner, but first he rewarded his hunting partners. The hawks received the crane's heart and some bone marrow, perhaps served ritually on a white gauntlet.[38] In his detailed treatise on falconry, Frederick II wrote of the care the hunter should take in allowing the hawk to eat the heart of its prey. He dismissed the practice of adding bone marrow to the hawk's reward.[39] The hound received its customary reward, and the three were ritually bound together in eating the fruits of the hunt.

A successful hunt like this was elegant in its demand for cooperation, but it was the ideal rather than the norm. Frederick II described many of the things that could go wrong in such a hunt: sometimes the captured crane or heron (or other birds in the flock) injured the falcon; sometimes an inexperienced hound could hurt the falcon. Any of these events could make a falcon understandably unwilling to try again for such large game. Frederick II offered considerable advice about curing such birds rendered "cowardly" by hunting accidents.[40]

Even if the hunt itself were successful, there were other hazards to depending on falcons as hunting partners. Raptorial birds, like cats, existed on the borders between wild and domesticated animals. The birds continued to do what they had done in the wild, but they did it in the service of their human partners, and only as long as the bird perceived that its food supply was linked to humans. A constant hazard of falconry was the inclination of the bird to soar and not return. A peasant who was lucky enough to find and catch a hawk wearing jesses on its legs marking it as trained could count on a good reward for returning it to the local nobleman. Ownership of such a wild creature was always a problem. If the hawk wore jesses, ownership was easy to prove, if not, the issue became murky. Bracton in thirteenth-century England attempted to sort out the legal status of tamed animals: if wild animals are tamed and "customarily go and come back, or fly away and return,… then they belong to the owner as long as they have the intention of returning."[41] Surely this law did not solve the problem of straying hawks, since the legal problem of proving an animal's "intentions" in court must have been almost insurmountable. Instead, the law simply highlights the difficulties of working with tamed wild animals. The rewards of the excitement of the hunt and the accessibility of game birds seem to have been well worth the difficulties of working with raptorial birds.

Domestic Animals as Food

Consuming meat from domestic animals was more convenient than hunting, but also more expensive. As Fernand Braudel explained in his large work *Civilization and Capitalism*, if one considers only caloric intake, agriculture on a given surface area can feed ten to twenty times as many people as stock grazing on the same area. Therefore, there is a direct correlation between size of population and reliance on vegetable foods at the expense of meat.[42] This economic analysis presupposes that given the choice (that is, when subsistence is no longer a problem), people will eat meat despite its being less cost-effective. Nick Fiddes offers a different explanation in a study of the symbolism of meat-eating. His work suggests that meat-eating "represents human control of the natural world. Consuming the muscle flesh of other highly evolved animals is a potent statement of our supreme power."[43] In this case, the choice of a largely carnivorous diet expresses the value of a strong dominion over nature. During the early Middle Ages until the turn of the millennium, people in most of Europe satisfied both explanations for meat-favoring societies: Europe was sparsely populated enough for people to indulge a taste for meat, and people valued expressing their power over nature.

In the early Middle Ages, most people ate a diverse diet that included a good deal of meat. People, rich and poor, looked to large and small game, fish, small birds, acorns, whatever they could gather to supplement the production of their fields and barnyards.[44] From the fifth to the seventh centuries in northern Europe, sheep, goats, and pigs were slaughtered for food. In some areas (especially the continent) the animals were butchered when they were over two years old, in other areas (Anglo-Saxon England particularly), the animals were butchered much younger.[45] It is difficult to explain exactly what caused such differing habits. It may have been scarcity of pasturage that lead to butchering younger animals; it may have been acquired tastes for more tender meat. Or, the evidence available may simply mean that we have not excavated a sufficiently broad number of sites to form clear conclusions about the age of butchered animals. In Italy, young sheep and goats were seldom butchered for meat. They were used for milk products, while fowl, pork, game, and fish made up the protein in the Italian diet.[46] All archeological excavations, however, confirm a diversity of meat in the early medieval diet.

This diversity included an early medieval taste for horsemeat. A Scandinavian folktale describes what would certainly have been a typical pattern: a fat and aged draught horse died while being worked. He was immediately skinned to be eaten "according to heathen custom," as the Christian author explained.[47] Christians very soon identified eating horsemeat with heathenism, probably in recollection of ritual eating patterns that had little to do with the practical consuming of a dead work horse. Nevertheless, the church was vigorous in prohibiting the practice, and the results of such prohibitions show up in the excavations of Anglo-Saxon England. From the fifth through the seventh centuries, there was a trend toward increased consumption of pork at the expense of horseflesh.[48] By the eighth century, the Christian penitential writer Theodore of Canterbury proclaimed confidently (if unduly optimistically) that "It is not custom to eat horses."[49] In fact, excavations of eighth- and ninth-century England show that small horses that died when they were from 15-20 years old (a good old age for a horse) were butchered and the bones chewed.[50] In some areas of Europe, (for example, Russia), people never gave up the practice of eating their horses.[51] In other areas, there are references to people eating horsemeat during times of famine, for example, in Italy and England in the fourteenth century.[52] It is inconceivable that during times of famine everywhere people would refrain from eating horsemeat due to church prohibition. More likely, through the late Middle Ages, the church could proclaim that it was no longer *custom* to eat horsemeat, even if the practice continued in exceptional circumstances.

In most areas during the early Middle Ages, people's love of horsemeat gave way to a taste for pork. Pigs were an excellent source of meat because they were not bred primarily for anything else. Oxen were most important for labor, so by the time they reached the stew-pot the meat was tough and less flavorful. In most regions, sheep became too important a source of wool and milk to be slaughtered young for meat. Pork, on the other hand, was readily available, and pigs could be slaughtered young for flavorful meat. Some of the meat was eaten fresh after the slaughter, but most was boned and salted as bacon to be eaten later.[53] The natural environment in the early Middle Ages was conducive for keeping large numbers of semiwild pigs. They were kept in herds to browse in the rich oak forests and provided a regular and popular element of the diet. By the late Middle Ages, however, there was an increase of arable land at the expense of woodlands and pastures. In the fourteenth and fifteenth centuries, pig rearing increasingly tended to be limited to pigsty farming, in which fewer numbers of pigs could be raised. Consequently, from about the eleventh century onwards (and with varying speed in different regions), pork no longer was a central portion of the diet of the peasants.

The nobility, of course, could always enjoy the fruits of even the more limited pig raising. Even when the population declined after the Black Death of the fourteenth century and when arable land was taken out of cultivation, that did not mean the return of large-scale wild pig raising. As the land stayed fallow, the natural pastures that grew up offered more suitable forage land for sheep than for pigs.[54] As I described in the last chapter, however, sheep were more often raised for wool, milk, and cheese, not meat. Thus, the increase of pastures for sheep in the fourteenth century did not necessarily mean an increase in poor people's meat consumption.

As we can see, during the early Middle Ages, the main difference between the diet of the social classes was volume; the rich ate more than the poor. As time passed, population pressures caused meat to become more expensive and the cost-effective quality of a more vegetarian diet led to more separation between the menus of the rich and the poor. As is usually the case, the rich were able to continue to indulge their luxury, but meat left the bowls of the poor. By the late twelfth and thirteenth centuries, domestic animals as food had become a mark of status as surely as game animals. A nobleman was perceived as noble in part because of the noble food (meat) he ate. A diet of meat expressed both economic advantage (one could afford meat) and power over nature, and as society became increasingly hierarchic, power over lower classes. By the late Middle Ages, it was only the nobility that satisfied both explanations for meat-favoring societies.

Through the high Middle Ages, food took on social stratification, and by the fourteenth century, social classes were defined in part by their diets. The agricultural revolution of the eleventh century brought more land into cultivation and brought more varied grains and legumes into the medieval menu. The European trend toward increasing arable land led to a reduced consumption of meat on the part of the poor. Slowly the rural diet was simplified, reduced to a predominance of grain and vegetables, supplemented by milk products and some meat.[55] In the thirteenth century, an average peasant family of 4.68 persons consumed annually six quarters five bushels of grain (wheat, oats, and barley), two flitches of bacon, milk and cheese from a cow (before the thirteenth century, the milk products would more than likely have come from sheep or goats), garden produce, and some ale brewed from barley.[56] This peasant diet relied heavily on milk products for complete protein, but households that had only one or two cows would not have much milk available. In the thirteenth century, a cow yielded between 120 and 150 gallons a year. (A modern American cow produces an average of 1600 gallons a year.) Medieval yields were low because cows continued to be valued primarily for labor, and only incidentally as a source of milk products. Therefore, they were not fed in ways to increase their milk production. Peasant families that relied on sheep for milk products fared little better. Even though these animals were raised primarily for milk, they still yielded only between seven and twelve gallons a year.[57] Therefore, a family would need at least ten sheep to equal the production of their working milk cow. This equivalency ratio was recognized in the Middle Ages as well. A husbandry manual written by Walter of Henley states, "twenty ewes which are fed in pasture of salt marsh ought to and can yield cheese and butter as…two cows."[58] Thus, Walter recognized the formula that ten sheep were needed to produce as much milk as one cow. While peasant families were unwilling to spare scarce grain to add to cows' diets to increase milk production, at least the early Irish recognized, as modern farmers do, that production could be increased if cows listened to music while being milked.[59]

The diets of the wealthy relied more on meat and game. The nobility often scorned milk products and fresh vegetables as peasant fare. Meat consumption among the aristocracy continued to expand from the thirteenth to the fifteenth centuries. Such tastes did not come cheaply. Food for noble households could take from one-third to as much as two-thirds of the annual income, and average per capita consumption of meat or fish in noble households was two or three pounds per person per day.[60] In most areas, paralleling modern tastes, beef was the most popular form of meat, followed by pork, then mutton. Fowl was much less popular.[61] This diet was abundant in volume; noblemen consumed about 4,000 to 5,000 calories per day.[62] The imbalance created by social distinctions that relegated vegetables to the peasant diet brought with it its own health problems to the nobility, but those are out of the scope of this study.

In the fourteenth and fifteenth centuries, the peasant diet changed a little. The population had been reduced from the Black Death, so peasants were able to mimic aristocratic meals a bit more. They ate more food, drank more ale, and included more meat in their menus.[63] This change was only a relative one, however. Peasants even in the fourteenth century never brought their meat consumption up to that of the nobility, or even up to that of peasants in the early Middle Ages.

A thirteenth-century German poem, *Meier Helmbrecht*, reveals how deep-seated these dietary distinctions had become. The poem tells of a fairly well-to-do peasant youth who aspired to upward mobility and left the farm to join a band of robber-knights. In the course of the poem, the poet contrasts the way of life between peasant and nobility. He lists food "the like a peasant never knew," including roast goose, boiled and roasted hens, two kinds of meat, and wine. The youth also enjoys fish, which he says was absent from peasant households. Finally, young Helmbrecht cuts short his visit to the family home, longing again for the noble diet provided by his ill-gotten gains. He says, "Because of this extended fast, / My belt is three holes smaller now. / Beef I must have from some toothsome cow."[64] Young Helmbrecht's taste for aristocratic fare was as shocking in its breach of the established order as was his life of crime. Both were ended by the hanging of the young man; the social order was restored.

By the late Middle Ages, social distinctions were preserved in the methods used to cook meat as well as in the kind of meat people ate. In spite of the hardships of cooking on open fires or tending erratic ovens, people prepared meat in all the ways with which we are familiar. They baked, roasted, grilled, fried, or boiled their meat depending on the cut, the cook, and the consumers. Stews with boiled meat were staples of all social groups. Peasants might have their stew-pot full of legumes and vegetables flavored with a little meat. The nobility in the late Middle Ages had more elaborate meat stews flavored with onions, spices, and vinegar in broth thickened with bread crumbs.[65]

More elaborate were the roasts that were prepared on spits and brought to the noble board. These were often stuffed with suet and bread crumbs and flavored with salt, pepper, and saffron.[66] Roasts were probably higher status foods in part because the animals that were slaughtered for roasts had to be more tender than those that were boiled for a long time in stews. Early slaughter was more expensive. This noble love of roasts was expressed by Charlemagne's ninth-century biographer, who wrote of the emperor: "He came positively to dislike [his doctors] after they advised him to stop eating the roast meat to which he was accustomed and to live on stewed dishes."[67]

The recipe books of the late Middle Ages show increasingly complex recipes involving the use of expensive ingredients that appealed to the palates of the nobility. These dishes also appealed to their desire to be set apart from the common people by the foods they ate. This trend toward luxurious eating continued into the modern period.[68]

Attitudes Toward Food

As I noted at the beginning of this chapter, one of the prevailing attitudes toward food may be summarized by the statement "you are what you eat." This organizing principle applied not only to individuals at the biological level, but also to communities. One of the ways communities defined themselves was by what they ate.

In traditional societies one of the main ways communities celebrated and preserved their cohesiveness was through feasting. Eating together served to reinforce the fact that the community was a cohesive body of people.[69] In fact, not only communal eating, but the foods people eat and the way they eat them serve to define the identity of a group. This remains true today, as we define ethnic groups by the food they eat and recoil from groups that eat things (sheep's eyes, horse meat) that we do not. In the Middle Ages, people's diets, too, served to define their group identity.[70] As I discussed above, in the late Middle Ages, diet defined social structure, but even in the early Middle Ages, Christian culture defined itself in part by food.

The Christians inherited and confronted a strong tradition of dietary regulation from Judaic scriptures. The dietary laws, particularly in Leviticus, expressed and preserved a view of the world in which things were clean or unclean, or more precisely holy or unholy. One of the elements that defines holiness in many religions is "separating that which should be separated."[71] Humans seem to like clear categories of things, or rather, we like things in clear categories. We are uncomfortable with things that are ambiguous, on the borders. (I shall return to this important border region in Chapter 5.) Mary Douglas proposes in a convincing argument that Jewish dietary prohibitions derive from the desire to order the world by only eating animals that conform to expected categories. For example, on earth four-legged animals walk; crawling things violate this category and are forbidden. In the water, scaly fish swim with fins; other water creatures are forbidden.[72] The world was ordered in an clear (and thus ritually holy) way by acceptable and forbidden foods.

Dietary laws not only separated clean and unclean animals, but they separated peoples into categories. The prohibitions in Leviticus say to the ancient Hebrews such foods are "unclean for you."[73] The foods are not defined as unclean in an abstract way; they are unclean for the people addressed. This phrasing points to the way eating habits forge a cohesiveness and definition within a group. The people who abstain from these forbidden foods form one identity. By observing these laws, Jews at every meal ritually acknowledged and recreated an ordered world by separating those things that should remain separate. Furthermore, they identified themselves as a group that should remain separate from others, and in their separateness, preserve a holiness. The food we eat and the way we eat it have cosmic significance.

Early Christians identified themselves as "not Jews" in part by rejecting the dietary prohibitions that united Jews as a separate group. Christians, too, defined themselves by their eating habits, but they had to develop a different pattern from that which had defined ancient Hebrews. In addition, Christian thinkers were defining themselves as "not pagans," so they rejected some eating patterns that were associated with paganism. The Irish penitentials that date from approximately the sixth century (and later) were influential in articulating and forwarding church law in many subjects, including that of dietary prohibitions. As such, they form an important source of information about how Christians defined themselves through their food. Within the penitentials, there are a number of regulations that address Christian identity in opposition to Jews or pagans. I was somewhat surprised to see that neither of these categories of prohibition were given much space or emphasis in the earliest church codes. The pagan ritual that received most mention was the prohibition against eating horseflesh[74] discussed above. It seems that by the sixth century defining oneself as "not pagan" was not a significant preoccupation, at least not with regard to diet.

The incorporation of Old Testament dietary prohibitions was more problematic. In this case, people were dealing with requirements established in scripture, so Christians were confronted with a conflict. If they followed scriptural rules precisely, how would Christians define themselves as "not Jews?" The most obvious conflict between Christian taste and scriptural instruction had to do with eating pork. The pig was Biblically unclean, but was a favorite among the Germanic tribes. However, there was also Biblical precedent in ignoring such prohibitions in the letters of St. Paul. In this tradition, Ambrose said, "One thing... seems to me ridiculous, that anyone should vow to abstain from the flesh of swine....For no creature of God taken with Thanksgiving is to be rejected."[75] Paul's and Ambrose's position prevailed, and the preoccupation with certain animals as unclean for food disappeared from church legislation. By focusing on New Testament rejection of Old Testament prohibitions, Christian communities could define themselves as different from Jews and thus identify their community in part by diet. Medieval writers did view some animals as more suitable than others for human consumption, but these choices seem to have had more to do with the animals' diet than with Old Testament tradition. I shall discuss this food hierarchy more fully below.

A second kind of Jewish dietary law involved correct slaughtering of the animal to be sure, among other things, that the animal had been bled properly. Christians in general, however, tended to reject ritual slaughter because it was too similar to pagan rituals in which portions of the animal were sacrificed to the gods.[76] The penitentials did continue, however, the tradition that rejected blood as polluting. Churchmen defined animals that drank blood as polluted, and therefore unfit for human consumption. They considered it an even worse pollution if humans were to eat flesh that was saturated with blood. In the Canons of Adamnan, one can find a full explanation of the rejection of blood-laden meat. The author explains that animals that died while trapped by their extremities (for example, having their legs broken) were unsuitable for food because the blood that flowed from the wound was only extremity blood: "[T]he thicker and denser blood in which life had its seat remains clotted within the flesh. Thus, unless the infliction of a wound disturbs the seat of life, there is not shedding of blood but merely injury to an extreme part; and therefore he who eats such flesh shall know that he has eaten flesh with blood."[77] Since blood was associated with the essence of life, blood was to be avoided when that which was alive was changed into food. While Christian thinkers rejected the kind of ritual slaughter that had traditionally rendered Jewish food kosher, they kept what they considered to be the essence of Old Testament prohibitions: the blood that bestowed life had to be removed.

These regulations designed to separate Christians from Jews and pagans form a small part of the penitential literature. Much more voluminous was a third category of Christian dietary prohibition: rules designed to separate human from animal by diet. Not only are these last kinds of regulations most numerous, but they are most significant to this work, since they reveal people's attitudes towards the animals they ate.

The first level of prohibitions designed to reaffirm the difference between people and animals involved an exploration of bestial eating. Churchmen in particular attempted to define bestial ways of eating, then tried to urge people to avoid such habits. Bestial eating could be defined in several ways: the manner of eating, the manner of obtaining food and the menu. Ambrose defined a bestial manner of eating in the fourth century. He said that the structure of animals, their inability to stand erect, led to their eating with their stomachs horizontal to the ground. "They therefore seek their sustenance in the earth, solely pursuing the pleasures of the stomach toward which they incline."[78] Beyond this general definition, Ambrose noted that animals had different physical characteristics based on their diet: carnivores have short necks to "bend to the earth in the act of feeding," herbivores need longer necks to reach their food, and elephants have trunks to obtain food.[79] Ambrose's descriptions show that he was defining animals largely through their appetite. A fifteenth-century author confirmed this definition, saying, "Every creature by nature is most readily caught with food."[80] If animals were defined by their preoccupation with food, then humans could descend to the bestial by succombing to a similar preoccupation.

Under ordinary circumstances, it would be fairly easy to avoid such bestial behavior. Ambrose warned people to eat in an upright position: "Leave to animals the sole privilege of feeding in a prone position."[81] This prohibition also surely served as a renunciation of the pagan Roman practice of eating reclined on couches, but the words Ambrose chose reveal his additional concern of defining humanity as distinct from animals. For Ambrose, to eat as a Roman was to descend to the bestial. The Scandinavian laws, too, seem to try to define and preserve humanness by eating habits. The laws established a penalty against one who "lies down under another man's cow to suck her."[82] This may simply show a concern about someone stealing another person's milk, but the way the law was phrased suggests the penalty was in part for a man succumbing to his bestial appetite and eating like an animal.

Aspiring holy men faced extraordinary circumstances in their struggles against the appetites of the flesh. Peter Brown has described the consequences for men whose attempts to overcome the animal urge of hunger failed: "the ascetic felt driven to wander as free and as mindless as a wild beast, gnawing at the scattered herbs, mercifully oblivious, at last, to the terrible ache of a belly tied to morsels of human bread."[83] In the desert, people saw perhaps more clearly than others in society how easily one's humanity could be lost.

To avoid descending to bestial appetites, however, it was not enough simply to avoid grazing in the manner of an animal. People also reflected upon what might be a bestial menu. When they did so, they tended to focus on the diet of carnivores. Biblical passages argued for vegetarianism as a more holy state than that existing in the fallen carnivorous world. In Genesis, humans and animals eat only vegetables in the Garden of Eden.[84] In this spirit, some aspiring holy people avoided meat to avoid taking on an animal-like, carnivorous nature.[85]

Of course, we have seen that medieval Europeans favored meat as a high status diet, so they could never fully equate meat eating with bestial. However, people did define a vegetarian diet as the preferred one for the animals fit for human consumption. We do not eat carnivores. The reasons for this are complex and probably still not fully understood. It is likely that most people assume that it is a question of taste. The meat of carnivores is too strong. In Nick Fiddes's analysis of attitudes toward meat, he suggests that carnivores exist in the same power relationship over other animals as we do. Therefore, carnivores are too much like humans in their function as hunters and thus to eat them would be too much like cannibalism.[86] Medieval sources repeated the injunction against eating carnivores, without explaining their reasoning. We are left only to speculate on the motives.

Frederick II defined birds that were good to eat specifically on the basis of their diet. Birds that ate grain alone were best, those that ate flesh and grain were inferior, and those that ate purely flesh (even fish) were unsuitable to eat.[87] In this way Frederick II continued the belief that carnivores are unsuitable as human food.

Our consumption of land animals parallels Frederick II's observation about birds as food. All the food animals favored by humans are herbivores, except pigs, which are omnivorous. The penitential writers noted this distinction based on diet, saying that cattle were more "clean" than swine because cows "feed only on grass and the leaves of trees." The penitential legislators did, however, make provision for salvaging for the dinner table pigs that had eaten carrion. The pig had to be kept until "it has been reduced and returned to its original thinness." Then the offensive carrion was no longer part of the pig flesh, so the pig was once again suitable for human consumption.[88]

Thus, while it was possible to define a manner of eating bestially, it was difficult to define a strictly bestial diet. For one thing, it seems that bestial eating lay in excess. For example, the carnivorous eating of a carnivorous animal would have been excessive. Another kind of excess may be found in the twelfth-century chronicler Gerald of Wales's account of the Irish. Among his many criticisms was one of the Irish diet. He said the Irish did not grow much food; they lived primarily on the meat and milk products of their pastoral animals. "They live on beasts only, and live like beasts."[89] Gerald apparently believed that the diet of the Irish made them closer to animals than others who might eat a more refined menu.

In addition to the ratio of meat to grain, the way meat was eaten determined its appropriateness for human consumption. In the most extreme case, eating one's meat raw was considered bestial. The penitential authors said that meat, even the most "clean" kind of meat, that of vegetarian cattle, had to be cooked before it could be "accepted by men."[90] In the romance *Yvain, or the Knight and the Lion*, the author shows that Yvain in his madness descended to the level of a beast, for the man lived in the woods, killed animals, and "ate their flesh uncooked, completely raw." The author of the romance contrasted this behavior with that of the lion, for whom such eating was "what Nature meant for him."[91] Here again, medieval writers reflected upon the differences between humans and animals, in this case the difference between Yvain and his lion. The natural behavior for the lion was unnatural for the man—humans and animals were qualitatively different, and their eating habits were to reflect that fact.

As much as churchmen tried to distinguish humans from animals by the food they ate, it was obviously difficult to do so. Even if one were to choose a more "spiritual" menu, that of the vegetarian, one still shared this diet with many herbivores in the animal kingdom. Much church legislation, then, focused on the one food that was to be definitively human, the spiritual food of holy communion. The influential Celtic penitentials began as early as the sixth century to insist that the host be rigorously guarded from animals that might eat it. The Welsh penitential of Gildas insisted on three forty-day penances for anyone who "loses a host, leaving it for beats and birds to devour." This penance was repeated by the widely circulated seventh-century penitential of Cummean. This penitential added other clauses to include various possible instances of animals that might eat a host. For example, it prescribes penances for someone who fails to guard a host so that a mouse eats it. Even more vividly, the penitential insists upon a penance for forty days for anyone who vomits up the host after mass. If, however, a dog "laps up this vomit" (thus consuming the regurgitated host) the individual's penance was increased to a hundred days.[92] One cannot help but wonder whether this last instance was a regularly occurring problem. It seems that the combination of circumstances that would place a vomiting individual in the same location as a dog after mass would not occur often enough to call forth legislation against it. It does, however, express the very real desire to preserve the one purely human food, spiritual food, away from animals.

Figure 3 shows a small section of the famous Chi-Rho page of the Book of Kells. This manuscript was a product of the same Celtic Christianity that produced the detailed penitentials that showed a preoccupation with keeping the spiritual host away from animals. This figure shows two cats who have caught by the tails two mice who seem to be nibbling on a round object marked with a cruciform, probably a communion host. Scholars have not come to any consensus about the meaning of these animals; they simply all agree that the figures have some symbolic meaning.[93] It may be that the illuminator was indicating the important principle that sacred food must be guarded from animals. The cats in this case represent the quintessential guardians fulfilling their one expected role of keeping the mouse population under control.

The penitential writings that expressed so vigorously the importance of keeping human spiritual food away from animals also introduced a great many

Figure 3: *Cats and Mice* **Book of Kells**, TCD MS 58, f. 34r.
With permission of The Board of Trinity College, Dublin

other food-related prohibitions. These are particularly important for under-standing the influential early medieval view of animals because they represent a large body of strictly ecclesiastical legislation. Since it was the church that was most interested in promulgating the view that people were significantly different from animals, this legislation represents an effort to keep animal and human apart, particularly with regard to food, an area in which it was especially difficult to keep the separation clear.

Since Old Testament law insisted on correct slaughtering techniques before food could be eaten by humans, it is not surprising that the Bible prohibited people eating animals that had been killed by other animals. Exodus states, "you shall not eat any flesh that is torn by beasts in the field; you shall cast it to the dogs." Leviticus continued this kind of prohibition, saying, "the fat of an animal that is torn by beasts may be put to any other use, but on no account shall you eat it."[94] The penitential writers also continued this prohibition, but expanded it and dwelled on it to such an extent that it seems to reveal con-cerns deeper than an attempt to avoid violating Old Testament law. (After all, we have seen that the penitential writers were willing to dismiss most of the Levitical prohibitions without much discussion.) In fact, one penitential writer specifically dismissed the presumably biblical reasons for avoiding animals killed by other animals. He writes that the problem with such animals is not that they may have been improperly bled, but that their blood "has been shed by beasts."[95] The reason for the penitential preoccupation with avoiding food partially eaten by animals must lay elsewhere than in the Hebrew concern for ritual cleanliness.

For early medieval churchmen, the main problem with eating food that had been partially eaten by animals seems to have lay in the defining quality of the food. If an animal had begun to eat it, it was animal food. If a person then ate the same food, did that define the person as an animal? If so, then the lines between human and animal that were being strictly drawn in the early Middle Ages would have been disconcertingly blurred. As the Canons of Adamnan repeatedly said, only bestial men eat food that has been partially eaten by beasts. Only "human beasts eat the flesh that has been served to beasts."[96]

All the penitentials repeated such prohibitions. If someone found an animal that had been killed and partially eaten by wolves or dogs, they were forbidden to consume the remainder of the meat[97] or even eat the marrow of the bones once the wolves had abandoned the carcass.[98] Some regulations attempted to address questions that surely arose because people were reluctant to waste good meat. For example, Theodore of Canterbury raised the question of whether it was permissible to eat "meat wounded by a beast." He said yes, if the man made the kill. If the animal had made the kill, the meat was forbidden.[99] In this case, the hunter created the food: an animal hunter made its kill animal food, a human hunter made his kill into human food, and the boundaries between them were to be preserved.

In addition to prohibiting food that was killed by an animal, church laws also defined as unclean food or drink that had been partially eaten, or "contaminated," by an animal. Once again, the act of eating, not the food itself, seems to have defined the appropriateness of the food for human consumption. For example, the penitentials prescribed varying penances for eating food that had been eaten or contaminated by animals: the Bigontian Penitential assigned one day's penance for eating something contaminated by a mouse, five days' for a cat, forty days' for "flesh torn by beasts," and one year's penance for drinking what a dog had contaminated. The actual length of each penance changed a bit with varying penitentials, but they all kept both the preoccupation with avoiding "animal" food, and the hierarchy of seriousness of the pollution depending upon the animal involved.[100]

The differential penalties that were established to distinguish among animals offer some insight into people's perceptions of their animals and into the concerns that lay behind many of these prohibitions. There was a striking difference between the penance of one day for pollution by a mouse and that of one year for contamination by a dog. To give some idea of the seriousness of the sin of eating that which was contaminated by a dog, the one year's penance was the same as for someone who committed incest or patricide,[101] so it was looked on as a serious violation. The penitential writers did not explain why the penances were so different, so we can only speculate on their motives. It seems that we can at least partially eliminate size of the animal as a consideration, because to eat an animal partially eaten by a wild beast called for a penance of only forty days. Presumably, such wild beasts would be at least as large as a wolf or bear or wild cat, all larger than the average domesticated dog. The most likely explanation is that the greatest penance was assigned to the animal that lived closest to humans, and was thus most threatening to the boundaries that separated the two. As I noted above, dogs were the first animals to be domesticated, and their early domestication was due to the many parallels in the social organization of humans and wolves. If one's concern is to keep humans and animals separate, one would tend to focus most intensely on the animals that lived most closely to humans. One can continue to see this inclination in the insults we choose today. The level of insult increases with the degree to which the animal is associated with humans. It is worse to be called a dog than a cat or a lion. Thus, the varying penances imposed for the sin of eating food that had been made animal food by contact yields further insight into the early church's preoccupation with defining human and animal worlds as separate.

The secular Norwegian law code was highly influenced by church law and continued this prohibition of "unclean" food. This code dates from about the eleventh century, however, so it is considerably later than the penitentials. With the passage of time, it seems that some of the vigor of the early codes had faded a bit, and some ameliorating clauses were added that permitted more food to be accessible. This was probably particularly important for hunting societies. If one's hunting dog took a bite of the kill before the hunter arrived on the scene, it would be counterproductive to waste the whole carcass. The Norwegian laws permitted meat killed by a dog (or a tame wolf) with some cautions. First, the hunter had to be the owner of the animal, and then the hunter had to cut away those portions of the carcass that had been bitten and sprinkle the area with holy water.[102] The holy water essentially performed a magical transformation, converting the carcass from animal food back to human food, and permitting the hunter to use his dog's kill.

If food that had been partially eaten by animals was forbidden because it inappropriately blurred the lines between humans and animals, then animals that had reversed the order of God's world by eating people were even more strenuously forbidden. When the food became the diner, it was impossible to right the order by converting the animal back to food. The penitentials declare, "Swine that taste the flesh or blood of men are always forbidden....Hens that taste the flesh of a man or his blood are in a high degree unclean, and their eggs are unclean."[103] This legislation could attempt to keep the right order in a food relationship between humans and animals, but legislation could not alleviate the deep fear that has shaped people's concern with becoming food.

The fear of being eaten largely shaped people's relationship with the wolf. Wolves were a threat to the medieval economy because of their diet of domestic animals. They were, however, a greater threat to the medieval psyche from their perceived capacity to acquire a taste for human flesh. Medieval armies always knew they were followed by packs of wolves. The wolves feasted on the dead horses that fell on the battlefield, but they also fed on dead men. Edward the Duke of York wrote:

> When they feed in a country of war...they eat of dead men...and man's flesh is so savory and so pleasant that when they have taken to man's flesh they would never eat flesh of other beast, even though they should die for hunger; for many men have seen when they have lost the sheep they have taken and eaten the shepherd.[104]

Scandinavian sagas offer more vivid description of wolves eating the fallen in battle. One such example comes from *King Harald's Saga* and describes Thord's dream of the upcoming battle for Britain in which Harald fell. In the dream, in front of the defending army, Thord saw "a huge ogress riding a wolf, and the wolf was carrying a human carcass in its mouth, with blood streaming down its jaws; and as soon as the wolf had eaten the first corpse, she hurled another into its mouth, and then another and another, and the wolf gulped them all down."[105] This dream combines medieval realities of wolves following armies with medieval fears of being eaten. Wolves were perceived as dangerous, threatening predators feeding on humans and feeding their fears.

Wolves were hunted everywhere. In France they were hunted for sport, but in most regions they were hunted to be exterminated. Therefore, people used traps of all kinds: pits, nets, and bows set to go off when triggered. The Burgundian law code particularly warned trappers to be careful of the latter so a human would not be inadvertently shot by a trap set for a wolf.[106]

Wolves were considered useless. The meat was inedible, even hunting hounds had to be rewarded for their wolf hunt by placing chopped mutton in the cavity of the slain wolf, for even hounds would not eat wolf meat. The hide was considered too difficult to tan in a way that would remove the wolf odor. The hunt for the wolf was for one purpose only, to remove a perceived threat that humans would become food for an animal. The hunts were successful; by the end of the Middle Ages wolves were extinct from all but the fringes of Europe. The fear of the wolf remained in folklore and in human imagination as a fear of being consumed. Just as food is associated with life, it is equally linked with death. Human life is sustained by eating dead flesh of animals; human death is completed by the body's consumption by worms and the very earth itself. The greatest scholars of folklore and traditional imagery see this image as one of the central components to people's vision of themselves. Mikhail Bakhtin wrote, "The gaping mouth is related to the image of swallowing, the most ancient symbol of death and destruction."[107] The food people eat is transformed first into their own flesh, but then ultimately into feces and dirt. In death, a similar corruption occurs with the human body.

In the twentieth century, we have been remarkably successful at distancing ourselves from the physical reality that our bodies are food for parasites. In the Middle Ages, that reality was ever-present. Augustine wrote, "All men born of the flesh, are they not also worms?"[108] Piero Camporesi in his vivid analysis of early modern views of death describes the intimate association between humans and the worms that inhabited them and consumed them in life as well as in death. Death was only the final victory of the small creatures who had lived in and on the body of the human host.[109]

Literature that spans the whole of the Middle Ages reveals the medieval preoccupation with being eaten by worms. The early Anglo-Saxon poem "The Soul's Address to the Body" powerfully articulates a *memento mori* theme through the image of the gluttonous worm:

> The worm is called glutton [Gifer], whose jaws are
> sharper than a needle; it ventures to
> the grave first of all,
> so that it tears the tongue, and pierces the teeth,
> and from above eats through the eyes into the head,

and opens the way for other
worms to food, to high feasting, when the weary
body grows cold which erstwhile for long
he guarded with garments. Then it is the food and sustenance of
worms in the earth. To every wise man that may be a warning![110]

The late medieval thirteenth-century travelogue *Mandeville's Travels* demonstrat-ed this continuing preoccupation by describing societies that avoided this digestion. Mandeville in one instance describes ritual cannibalism where family and friends eat a dead friend: "They say that they eat the flesh of their friend because that worms should not eat him in the earth, and for to deliver him of the great pain that his soul should suffer if worms gnawed him in the earth."[111] In another case, the author describes a people who hung the dead in trees, for "they say that it is better they be eaten with fowles, which are angels of God, than foully to be eaten in the earth with worms."[112] In both these examples, by offering alternatives to being eaten by worms, the author reveals his own and his audience's preoccupation with the voracious small creatures. Through medieval times, people believed in the spontaneous generation of worms out of rotting flesh; thus the presence of worms in a living body was a constant reminder of people's present and forthcoming bodily decay. We are food for worms now and in the future.

The recognition that human bodies were in the last analysis food for animals did not make people complacent about that idea. Pre-Christian societies demanded proper burials so that the flesh would not become carrion for scav-enging birds and beast. The ancient Greek audience watching Sophocles' play joined Antigone in recoiling with horror at her brother's body being left unburied to be eaten by animals.[113] Pagan Romans attempted the ultimate degradation of Christians by feeding them live to wild animals or by scattering their dead bodies for animals to eat. The impressive victories of the Christian martyrs as preserved in their passions frequently revealed a victory over the deep-seated fear of becoming food. The inquisitor of the Iberian martyr St. Vincent scattered his bones to be consumed by beasts. The bones were mirac-ulously saved for the veneration of the faithful.[114]

One of the most remarkable accounts of a martyr's victory over digestion is that of Ignatius of Antioch. Ignatius asks proudly to become the food of beasts, "by the teeth of the beasts I shall be ground." In this request, Ignatius is not asking to become animal food, but instead, he says that the teeth of the beasts will convert him into *Christ's* food.[115] Ignatius's interpretation of his upcoming martyrdom shows more than a victory over fear; his example shows the Christian promise of a miraculous overturning of the natural order of the world in which human bodies are consumed in death. Ignatius through his martyrdom is ground by the beasts' teeth to become Christ's food, and thus part of Christ's body (as the food gets incorporated into the flesh of the consumer). Then, by becoming part of the body of Christ, the saint achieves a victory over death, decay, and becoming food for (and transformed into) the hungry beast that ground his flesh. Miraculous accounts like these of martyrs' victories over the jaws of beasts were tales of victory over death. The stories reinforce the deeply held fears of being eaten, which is, after all, the human fear of death.

The restatement of the fear of being eaten by beasts appears in the texts throughout the Middle Ages in incidents large and small. The early Christian second-century *Physiologus* warns that the devil will lure a Christian into sin and "make you food for the beasts."[116] In the sixth century, Gregory of Tours writes with horror of the Thuringi, who not only killed hostages, but "having broken their bones they gave them to dogs and birds for food."[117] Thomas Aquinas characterizes savage animals as those that "attack a man that they may feed on his body."[118]

Christian thinkers from the earliest centuries of Christianity were products of their times, sharing the same fears that haunted their pagan counterparts. The fear of being eaten by beasts entered into Christian thought and became centered on damnation, or the eternal death that was contrasted with the eternal life of salvation. For example, the Book of Revelation in the Bible describes birds eating human flesh.[119] But this was not the only biblical passage that lent itself to the articulation of fear of becoming animal food. When Augustine explained the passage in Genesis where the serpent is condemned to eat earth, the church father linked this to the concept that sinners are earth and will be converted into earth. Thus, "the sinner has been handed over as food for the Devil."[120]

The associations between damnation and being eaten can perhaps be seen most vividly in visionary accounts by people who had been granted a glimpse of hell in their lifetimes. A number of such visions span the Middle Ages, and these express horrifying visions that reveal the deep fear of becoming animal food. St. Peter's Apocalypse that dates from the mid–second century describes how "a worm that does not sleep will devour their entrails."[121] The fourth-century Apocalypse of St. Paul also describes souls consumed by worms but adds other souls "on a spit of fire, and beasts were tearing them."[122] The same theme continues with all the variations offered by human imagination. In the ninth century, the monk Wetti saw a prince whose punishment was to have his genitals mangled by animal bites, and in the twelfth century, an Irish knight described his fearful vision in some detail:

> Fiery dragons were sitting on some of them and were gnawing them with iron teeth, to their inexpressible anguish. Others were the victims of fiery serpents, which, coiling round their necks, arms, and bodies, fixed iron fangs into their hearts. Toads, immense and terrible, also sat on the breasts of some of them and tried to tear out their hearts with their ugly beaks. [123]

An Irish monk in the twelfth century wrote another description that was immensely popular throughout the Middle Ages and was translated into many languages. The monk Tundale's image expresses the horror of repeated digestion in an endless punishment:

> This beast sat in a swamp of frozen ice. It devoured whatever souls he was able to find. While they were in his stomach they were reduced to nothing through this punishment. He vomited them into the frozen swamp of ice, and there they renewed their journey to torment. [124]

These images continue through the visionary literature of the Middle Ages until the best-known image portrayed in Dante's *Inferno*, where Lucifer in the pit of hell eternally eats the souls of those who betrayed their masters. [125]

These images in literature are echoed in illustrations. Hell is repeatedly shown as a mouth consuming the tortured souls. See Figure 4 for one such example.

In other iconography, the whale is shown as the devil, opening his large mouth and luring the lost into the bowels of hell. [126] Crocodile's jaws, too, represented the gates of hell. [127] Christian thinkers, then, preserved the images that had haunted pagan thinkers so much so that feeding Christian martyrs to beasts had been perceived as an ultimate humiliation. Christian thought offered more than a continuation of these images, however. It offered a victory over bestial appetite and bestial death.

Christianity offered salvation for those who could cultivate that within themselves that was human (rather than bestial). We have seen that Christian legislation tried to urge people to avoid bestial eating as part of the cultivation of a humanity that was separate from animal. Of course, it was impossible to

Figure 4: *Fall of Angels into the Jaws of Death* Ms. Junius 11, f. 3.
Courtesy of The Bodleian Library, Oxford

legislate that humans should not become food. The church could, and did, express its horror at humans being eaten by animals or even being eaten by bestial humans, cannibals.[128] The outrage against cannibalism was part of an outrage against the reversal of the natural order of the world that would make humans food.

Christian legislation established dietary rules that defined Christian behavior, and indeed, Christian identity. In return for compliance with these church laws and in return for sustaining oneself with the spiritual food of holy communion, the church offered no less than victory over digestion itself. As we have seen in the examples of Ignatius, Vincent, and other martyrs, the first victory the Church promised was over digestion by wild animals. In the fourth century, Ambrose directly addressed pagan concerns that it would be impossible for flesh that had been eaten by animals to be resurrected. He claimed that it would not be difficult for God to reassemble that which had been consumed.[129] Augustine, too, reassured believers that bodies consumed by animals would be resurrected and the flesh restored to its original owner.[130]

The promised resurrection of the body offered victory not only over the appetites of wild beasts that were able to get their teeth into human flesh, but it offered freedom from death itself. Christ's resurrection had conquered the worms, the dragons, the devils, all the animals that inhabited people's imaginations and waited to consume their flesh after death. Augustine promised that although the devil "goes about seeking someone to devour," Christ "took food, as it were, from a trap."[131] Thus bodies were saved from the appetites of death itself. (See Figure 5). But what about the human appetites that linked people so uncomfortably close to the animals they ate? The resurrection promised freedom from that appetite as well.

Figure 5: *Christ Leading Souls from the Mouth of Hell*
Ms. lat. 11907. f. 231r.
Courtesy of the Bibliothèque Nationale, Paris

The scholastics of the thirteenth century brought the theology of the resurrected body to its highest development. They wrestled with the question of whether the risen body was made up of animal flesh converted into human flesh. If this were so, was the resurrected flesh human or that of *boves et oves*, "cows and sheep"?[132] It will surely come as no surprise that the schoolmen decided that the risen flesh was indeed fully human, not animal. But such reflections on the nature of the risen flesh led to a particular view of the humanity that would exist in paradise. Theologians determined that resurrected bodies would need no food because risen bodies would undergo no further change in paradise. Since people would no longer need food, Aquinas determined that there would be no animals in paradise.[133]

This medieval notion of paradise without animals and without food is not the only possible vision of an afterlife. Some religions that believe in reincarnation can include members of the animal kingdom among the reincarnated. The second-century Christian apologist Tertullian rejected this notion of transmutation of souls, however, and in his rejection, he focused on the Christian preoccupation with the relationship between humans and their diets. Tertullian said it would be impossible for a human soul to become a bear or lion, for the soul could not forget its previous existence as a human and eat carrion or human flesh. Furthermore, Tertullian said that there would be no justice in punishing a sinner by reincarnating him as a cow, for example. As a cow, the individual would be eaten by humans, and thus "find his tomb in a human body," which would not be punishment.[134] Some twentieth-century theologians, shaped by modern acceptance of people as animals, argue for a paradise that includes salvation for all living things.[135]

The medieval image of paradise articulated most fully by the scholastic theologians reveals a consuming preoccupation with separating people from an animal-like appetite. It represents a logical expression of ecclesiastical desires to separate people from animals. Paradise would contain only that which people praised as their humanity. The victory over death was also a victory over hunger and a bestial appetite for food.

3

Animal Sexuality

IF PEOPLE COULD DESCEND TO A
bestial level through their appetite for food, they were even more vulnerable
through their sexual appetites. As we saw in the last chapter, early Christian
thinkers defined appropriate human (Christian) behavior with regard to eating.
They also attempted to do so with regard to sexual expression.[1] They tried to
identify what was animal sexuality, that is, how and why animals copulated,
and at times how animals felt when they copulated. After that, they attempted
to urge humans to have intercourse in ways that differentiated them from animals. In this way, early medieval church thinkers continued to try to preserve
the distinct difference between the human and animal worlds. Of course, such
an idealized difference was impossible to maintain even in the property relationship or the food relationship. It was even more difficult to define oneself
as "not-animal" with regard to sexuality.

In this chapter, I shall look at the nature of sexuality, exploring first what
were considered defining elements of animal sexuality. Then I shall look at the
even more difficult problem of intercourse between humans and animals.

Medieval attitudes towards bestial intercourse changed from the beginning to the end of the Middle Ages, and this changing attitude shows an increasing recognition that it was very difficult to preserve the ideal distinction between humans and animals. The animal within each human became insistently visible as people considered bestial intercourse.

Sexual Characteristics of Animals

From the earliest centuries of Christianity, theologians speculated on the nature of sexuality to address the issue of Christian sexual expression (to be distinguished from pagan sexual expression). As part of this analysis, Christians articulated the nature of *animal* sexuality too. For Christian thinkers, considerations of sexuality began with the Fall. One tradition of biblical study said that the serpent taught Eve to have intercourse, that is, to behave as animals do.[2] Augustine cautioned people against a too-literal interpretation of this belief by assuring his flock that the serpent "never physically defiled Eve."[3] Whether or not Eve had bestial intercourse with the serpent, sexual intercourse by this analysis is by definition bestial, and serpents frequently are metaphors for sexuality.[4]

The belief that all sexual intercourse was bestial continued to be widespread, but it was not the only possible interpretation. Clement of Alexandria, for example, claimed that humans could not have copied animals in intercourse because that would have shown human nature to have been weaker than animal nature, and such a reversal of the order of things was impossible.[5] Clement's approach to sexuality defined the act as human, not bestial, following one Jewish Midrash, which explained that Adam and Eve had taught the animals to have intercourse: intercourse, then, represented animals acting in a human fashion.[6] Such a positive view of sexuality did not predominate in the Middle Ages, in part because it seemed to violate the notion that humans acted rationally, and sexual intercourse seemed to have more to do with passions than with reason.

The earliest and most persistent Christian distinction between humans and animals was that humans had reason and animals did not. This definition seemed to influence Christian thinkers' peception of sexuality and extended into their analysis of human versus animal intercourse. Augustine as early as the late fourth century established the notion that during sexual intercourse "there is an almost total extinction of mental alertness; the intellectual sentries...are overwhelmed."[7] If sexual intercourse banished reason, and if reason were the defining quality of humans, then sexual intercourse was bestial and threatened one's humanity. Even Clement, the apologist for moderate Christian sexuality, said that Adam and Eve had rushed into intercourse "like irrational animals."[8] The irrational passion implicit in the act of intercourse led Thomas Aquinas to say that "in sexual intercourse man becomes like a brute animal" and that insofar as people cannot "moderate concupiscence" with reason, they are like beasts.[9]

Augustine and Aquinas can serve to define medieval perceptions of sexuality that maintained that sexual intercourse since the Fall was a bestial activity. It was a carnal pasttime that had nothing to do with intellectual enterprise. This general position served as a backdrop to more detailed discussions of sexual intercourse. One presumption was that humans set themselves apart from the animal world by having intercourse in as human a way as possible. Thus there was considerable attention to the different degrees of bestial intercourse—that is, how do animals do it?

Medieval thinkers believed that animals by and large exhibited more lust than humans did. This idea, of course, derives from the belief that lust is the opposite of reason, so as animals lacked reason, they expressed more lust. In general, they characterized lust as that which was uncontrolled (including other manifestations of lack of control like noise, lack of moderation, etc.). Augustine accepted animals as inherently lustful, so much so that he believed lust was not evil in an animal because it was "natural."[10] His point was that reason was "natural" for people, and thus lust was "unnatural"; in animals the reverse was true. Augustine's association of lust with animal passion might be best seen in his discussions of human erections. He believed human lust was expressed most readily and visibly in men's erections, which he called "bestial movements," because erections were not controlled by the human mind and thus had more in common with animal passions.[11] It is not surprising, then, that from this perspective medieval writers emphasized excessive lust in their descriptions of animal sexuality. Albert the Great, for example, characterized animal intercourse as "loud and noisy," as opposed to human intercourse, which was quiet. He explained this by saying that humans were "discrete, rational, prudent, and bashful."[12] Albert thus emphasized the rational in humans and identified the particularly lustful activities of animals with excess noise.

We can see medieval identification of lust with animals in descriptions of specific animals as well. For example, the classical author Oppian, whose work survives in an eleventh-century manuscript, reported that female bears were forced to lick their cubs into shape at birth because they were born half-formed due to the female's insatiable desire to have excessive intercourse during pregnancy.[13] More commonly, bears were representatives of male sexuality and a symbol of lust.[14] In another example, people believed foals were born with an extra piece of flesh on their forehead, loin, or genitals. The mare quickly ate this bit of flesh, knowing it to be an aphrodisiac much desired by humans.[15] In both these instances, animals were linked with excessive lust, and their behavior is understandable only in terms of such lust.[16]

A final example of the lust of animals, and specifically male lust, occurs in Oppian's description of the boar:

> Unceasingly he roams in pursuit of the female and is greatly excited by the frenzy of desire....He drops foam upon the ground and gnashes the white hedge of his teeth, panting hotly; and there is much more rage about his mating than modesty. If the female abides his advances, she quenches all his rage and lulls to rest his passion. But if she refuses intercourse and flees, straightway stirred by the hot and fiery goad of desire he either overcomes her and mates with her by force or he attacks her with his jaws and lays her dead in the dust.[17]

From the early Middle Ages, male sexuality had been linked to power and an active expression of desire. This description of the boar's behavior (with its implied motivations) demonstrates in an extreme way this medieval view of male sexuality, with its emphasis on power and dominance. The boar depicted in Figure 1 taken from a fourteenth-century calendar shows the elements that were associated with the boar and its sexuality: the tusks, tail, and testicles are treated prominently in an otherwise almost stylized animal. This is a typical way of portraying boars in medieval illustrations. The boar's sexuality, framed in its excess in description and illustration, was condemned as too bestial and lustful. But hunters valued a boar's testicles as a dish that might endow the hunter with some of the boar's sexual power.[18] The popularity of this symbolically charged delicacy indicates the complexity of considerations of sexuality, both human and animal. While church writers were condemning the raw animal passion of the boar, hunters were trying to take on that same potency. In spite of such ambiguities, however, churchmen carried on with their attempts to identify bestial kinds of sexual intercourse.

In addition to excess lust, bestial intercourse was identified by position. Penitential writers forbad dorsal intercourse because it was too animal-like.[19] Similarly, Alexander of Hales in the thirteenth century continued the prohibition,

Figure 1: *Wild Boar* Ms. Rwl. d. 939, part 3.
By permission of The Bodleian Library, Oxford

condemning "knowing your spouse in a way of the beasts which is against human nature."[20] Dorsal intercourse was not only seen as being too much like animal behavior to be appropriate for Christian intercourse, but it also was thought to generate increased lust, which was also bestial. Thus, it was doubly dangerous. With few exceptions (to allow for obesity, for example), the only appropriate position for human intercourse was reclining face to face (the "missionary position").

The analysis in Jewish commentaries is perhaps most explicit in explaining the preferred status of the missionary position for intercourse. The Midrash states that all animals "copulate face to back, save three who copulate face to face—humans, serpents, and fish, and they copulate face to face because at some point God spoke directly to them."[21] Humans may seem to be in rather peculiar company in this analysis, but the significant element is that face to face intercourse was seen to mirror a conversation with God. Serpents and fish, then, were engaging in human-style, indeed almost sanctified, intercourse by face to face copulation. The rest of the animals in this tradition were left with purely bestial positions.

A final characteristic of bestial intercouse in the minds of many medieval thinkers was that some animals were frankly considered perverse, and thus deviant sexual practices were seen as bestial. There is a peculiar inconsistency

81

in considering this characteristic of animal intercourse, because people defined "perverse" animal intercourse as that which deviated most from human intercourse. If we use their own logic, such intercourse would have been appropriate for animals which were by definition different from humans. Medieval thinkers, however, by and large accepted such tautological arguments without too much discomfort. Thus hyenas were considered sexually strange because people believed with classical authors that hyenas changed their gender, showing a disconcerting blurring of gender lines.[22] This gender confusion caused some Christian thinkers to believe that hyenas had a special oriface for homosexual encounters.[23]

Other animals, too, received the reputation for unusual, and therefore particularly bestial, intercourse. *Physiologus* explained that female weasels were impregnated through oral intercourse and gave birth through their ears.[24] Hares were seen as exceedingly promiscuous, but were also associated with anal intercourse. As early as circa 100, Barnabas wrote against eating hares because one might then become a "corrupter of young boys."[25] Throughout the Middle Ages, people recounted the story that due to their peculiar sexual inclinations, hares grew a new anus each year, so that, according to Clement and others, "he has the same number of openings as the number of years he has lived."[26] Goats, too, were considered particularly promiscuous and hermaphroditic.[27] Even some birds were not exempt from attribution of "bestial" sexuality. Isidore of Seville said partridges had homosexual inclinations, "for male mounts male and blind desire forgets gender," and his attribution was repeated often throughout the Middle Ages.[28] Thus, another characteristic readily attributed to animal sexuality was readiness to engage in sexual variations considered perverse according to the standards of "normal" human sexual expression. Consistent with medieval thought processes that sought clear categorizing, as some animals were associated with certain sexual practices, these practices were considered bestial when practiced by humans.

Medieval thinkers did not, however, have a clear and consistent understanding of what they thought was bestial or "unnatural" intercourse. After the twelfth century, there was considerable inconsistency about what sort of intercourse was "against nature," and this inconsistency was primarily expressed with regard to homosexual intercourse. Beliefs about hyenas and hares notwithstanding, some thinkers, including the influential Thomas Aquinas, argued that homosexual intercourse was unnatural because animals did not practice it. Gilles de Corbeil, physician to the king of France in the late twelfth century, wrote: "The most

ferocious beasts are better than man because they have intercourse and reproduce according to what is their natural function."[29] Aquinas continued this
argument, saying that humans who engaged in homosexual practices were
"unnatural" because heterosexual union was the "natural" practice among animals.[30] A twelfth-century poem perhaps best shows the peculiar inconsistency
that permeated the discussion of homosexual expression:

> A perverse custom it is to prefer boys to girls,
> Since this type of love rebels against nature.
> The wildness of beasts despises and flees this passion.
> No male animal submits to another.
> Animals curse and avoid evil caresses,
> While man, more bestial than they, approves and pursues
> such things.
> The irrational obeys reason's law;
> The rational strays far from reason.[31]

The poet virtually ignores medieval beliefs about the "perversity" of animal sexuality that was dominated by such passion that it was completely irrational,
yielding such activities as practiced by weasels and hares. At the same time,
he acknowleges that "perversity" was the province of animals by calling homosexual men bestial and irrational. This suggests that the notion that humans should
engage in "rational" sex lay at the heart of all these discussions. Inconsistencies
in the use of animals to exemplify either "natural" or "perverse" sexual practices
was a function of late medieval thinkers' willingness to use animal metaphors to
try to prove their point, even at the risk of inconsistencies.

In spite of many of these seeming ambiguities in attitudes towards animal
sexuality, thinkers actually did establish criteria by which to assess sexual activity. Both humans and animals could be judged by how bestial their copulation
was. During intercourse, some animals could seem more human than others.
For example, elephants were thought to mate "free from wicked desire." In the
place of lust, they ate a mandrake root together to generate desire.[32] Since they
lacked lust, their intercourse approached the ideal described by Augustine for
humans: intercourse totally without passion. The thirteenth-century Count of
Foix described bears as copulating face to face,[33] which he considered remarkable because it was not bestial. Vincent of Beauvais also remarked on bears'
human-style lovemaking: "Bears do not make love like the other quadrupeds,
but can embrace each other mutually, like human beings." Some medieval
thinkers believed that bear semen was compatible with that of humans', so that

bears could impregnate women.[34]

While people were interested in animals that seemed to emulate human intercourse, they were more interested in humans that descended to the animal level by their sexual activities. People who were motivated by lust resembled animals. Clement of Alexandria was one of many who expressed this notion. He said adulterers were like stallions "because they have become like the most unreasoning of animals....For he who sins agains reason is no longer rational, but is an irrational animal wholly given up to lust."[35]

It was bad enough for people to descend to the bestial by expressing sexuality that seemed to resemble that identified with animals, for that violated the notion that people were a category apart from animals. Not surprisingly, medieval churchmen were even more disapproving of people who had intercourse with animals, a final blurring of lines between humans and animals. The attitudes toward bestiality changed over the thousand years of the Middle Ages. And in these changing attitudes, one can see a shift in people's perception of themselves in relation to animals.

Bestiality

It is likely that intercourse with animals had been one expression of human sexuality for as long as people lived closely with their animals. It is, of course, impossible to get any kind of data about frequency of such sexual contacts before the modern period, but we may perhaps make some general suppositions based on evidence from other periods. Jonas Liliequist has made a study of seventeenth-century trial records for bestiality in Sweden. The testimony of those charged offers some fascinating insights into the practice. It seems that young boys who spent a good deal of time herding animals (particularly cattle in this case) treated bestial intercourse as a game. They taught each other the techniques; they performed the activity in groups as well as individually. As Liliequist notes, "It was the definite opinion of the authorities that bestiality was a boy's game sometimes growing into a man's habit."[36] In studying twentieth-century American life, Alfred Kinsey calculated that 40 to 50 percent of all farm boys experienced some sort of sexual animal contact.[37] These two examples may serve to suggest the range of the activity, and to indicate the probability that such activity exists where there are adolescent boys, animals, and an absence of strong sanctions to prevent their union. (Girls and women were not exempt from the practice, but their activities seem to have been less frequent and more associated with household pets than barnyard animals.) The main purpose of this discussion, however, is not to demonstrate the extent of the activity, but to look at people's changing attitude toward sexual contact with animals. The attitudes reveal people's perceptions of themselves and their animals regardless of exactly how many people were engaging in the practice.

Early Christian thinkers inherited two main traditions that had something to say about bestiality, the Germanic myths and the classical Greco-Roman litera-ture. In the mythology of both, humans and animals had intercourse. In the Germanic myths, heroes were described as having qualities of strength or fierceness because of an animal ancestor. For example, the founder of the Danish royal house was said to have been the result of a marriage between a bear and a woman.[38] Many of the early Irish myths refer to such heroic liaisons, many favoring references to intercourse with horse gods.[39]

The classical tradition was probably more significant to medieval Christian thinkers, because they were reconciling the whole corpus of classical works to Christian thinking. In this tradition, gods appeared regularly as animals to have intercourse with humans. If gods were indulging in the pastime, one assumes that such relationships were not completely forbidden to humans. This view is reaffirmed in the "scientific" treatises on animals. Aelian's *On the Characteristics of Animals*, written about A.D. 170, was a popular, influential compendium of ani-mal lore. Within his treatise, Aelian included more than a dozen examples of bestiality. He tells of a groom who falls in love with a mare, consummates the "strange union," and continues the relationship until he is killed by the mare's jealous foal.[40] A goatherd "under an erotic impulse lay with the prettiest of his goats" and is so pleased with the relationship that he brings the goat gifts and sweet herbs to make "her mouth fragrant for him if he should want to kiss her." In this case, too, jealousy is his downfall, for he is killed by an angry male goat. The neighbors of the goatherd do not object to the relationship, but instead build the young man a fine tomb and deify the issue of the union, a goat with the face of a man. Aelian's moral in this tale was not to avoid such intercourse, but to recall that animals can be jealous just as humans can.[41]

Curiously, most of Aelian's anecdotes of bestiality identify the animals as the initiators of the relationships, and his catalogue includes a wide variety of ani-mals. According to Aelian, "baboons and goats are lecherous, and...have intercourse with women....And even hounds have assaulted women....One woman in Rome was accused of adultery and the adulterer was a hound. Baboons are wanton and have fallen madly in love with girls and have even raped them."[42] In another instance, a snake falls in love with a girl and consummates the union repeatedly. The girl tries to escape his amorous overtures by leaving for a month, but upon her return, she discovers the snake was constant in his affections and angry at "being despised."[43] A ram and a goose fall in love with a beautiful woman musician.[44]

Men and boys were also objects of animal affection, but Aelian usually left the gender of the animal ambiguous, allowing for the possibility that he imagined some of these love affairs were homosexual. Aelian again showed the diversity of animals subject to such passion. "I am told that a dog fell in love with Glauce the harpist. Some however assert that it was not a dog but a ram, while others say it was a goose. And at Soli in Cilicia a dog loved a boy of the name of Xenophon; at Sparta another boy in the prime of life by reason of his beauty caused a jackdaw to fall sick of love."[45] In other instances, a goose falls in love with a handsome boy,[46] and a female snake succumbs to passion with a gooseherd and protects her beloved from the jealousy of the male snake.[47] Aelian continued his inventory, describing the affections of a horse[48] a dolphin [49] and a seal, who was remarkable because its love object was an ugly diver. In the moral of this story, Aelian tells us not to be surprised at such an event, for even people sometimes fall in love with ugly people.[50]

All these examples from Aelian yield some significant insights into Aelian's (and the classical) view of animals. Animals were not very different from people. They suffered the same emotions of love, anger, and jealousy; they had the same aesthetic appreciation for beauty and were able at times to set aside that aesthetic to appreciate someone from the highest motives of love. According to Aelian, the god of love "does not overlook even brute beasts."[51] And as he summarizes, "So it seems that it is in fact a characteristic of animals to fall in love not only with their companions…but even with those who bear no relation to them at all.[52] There was so little distinction between humans and animals that half-human/half-animal births were unremarkable, and the gods could appear as animals without diminishing their power and stature. It seems to have been no threat to people's humanity to appear at times indistinguishable from animals.

As the early church fathers wrestled with the classical heritage and selected those elements suitable for Christians, they rejected this intimate relationship between humans and animals. The Bible was clear on maintaining appropriate distance between species: "You shall not let your cattle breed with a different kind; you shall not sow your field with two kinds of seed."[53] This prohibition also applied to bestiality: "You shall not lie with any beast and defile yourself with it, neither shall any woman give herself to a beast to lie with it: it is perversion."[54] With this clear directive, Augustine wrote with scorn of pagans who worshipped gods who behaved so scandalously: "Jupiter himself is changed into a bull or a swan to enjoy the favors of some woman or other."[55] This rejection of such intimacy affected the selection of the classical heritage. Aelian's work was influential during the Middle Ages. It inspired works of natural history and animal lore culminating in the bestiaries of the twelfth century.[56] Yet, while copyists drew many of the interesting animal anecdotes from Aelian, including many sexual ones such as that of the transsexual hyenas,[57] they did not reproduce the tales of bestial intercourse. The Middle Ages had its own tradition on the subject that drew more from the Christian texts than from the classical. And Christian texts were shaped by the Christian ideal that humans and animals were, and should remain, separate, and humans should not "brutalize" their immortal souls by intercourse with beasts. For Christian thinkers Aelian's anecdotes were neither amusing nor remarkable; they were degrading and dehumanizing. They were omitted whenever possible.

The early medieval desire to prohibit bestiality came from Christian impulses that began with the patristic reflections on human nature. The pagan Germanic tradition seemed to have lacked this concern, as we might expect in a tradition that preserved tales of human/animal intercourse. In spite of offering detailed information and regulation about daily life (described in the first chapter), none of the early Germanic secular law codes prohibited bestiality. It seems that this omission could derive from two sources: either people were not having intercourse with animals or no one cared whether they did or not. I suggest the latter explanation for two reasons. First, it seems unlikely in rural society that such animal contacts did not occur, and second, as soon as Christian legislation appeared, prohibitions against bestiality appeared, suggesting the activity was going on. The evidence from the early laws indicates that for the pagan Germans animals were important as property and as food, and it was in these areas that they legislated. Christians added legislation to restrict sexual contact between the species.

Of course, in the absence of specific explanations, it is difficult to identify the precise motivation behind such Christian legislation. One motivation might have been to abolish anything that was "pagan" in order to define more clearly that which was Christian. This motive certainly operated on much legislation, like the prohibition against eating horsemeat, and it likely in part operated here. Just as Christian legislation defined appropriate Christian sexuality,[58] as distinct from pagan, this legislation against bestiality further defined Christian sexual expression. However, in the formulation of these laws, Christians also furthered their notions that humans were qualitatively different from animals. This second motive was consistent with Christian (as opposed to pagan) definitions of humanity. Christian legislation against intercourse with beasts was significant in defining boundaries: boundaries between Christian and pagan and boundaries between human and animal.

In Western Europe, early Christian legislation on sexual behavior developed from two main sources. The first was formal conciliar decrees originating mostly in the Byzantine Empire and the Holy Land. Among its sexual regulations, the Council of Ancyra in 314 prescribed strict penalties against bestiality: fifteen years of penance for youths under twenty, twenty-five years for married people over twenty, and for a married person over fifty, he or she had to wait until the end of life to receive communion.[59] This strict penalty seems to derive from patristic concern for maintaining the strict distinction between human and animal, rational and irrational, for the council introduces its prohibition by writing "Of those who have acted or who act irrationally."[60] Humans were not to descend to the level of irrational beasts in their sexual lives. Basil of Caesarea continued Eastern prohibitions in a letter written in 375, which acquired the weight of conciliar decree in the Greek East by the sixth century;[61] this letter called for fifteen years of penance.[62]

Evidence for the Eastern tradition on the subject was not limited to conciliar decrees. John Climacus, the seventh-century monastic writer in the Holy Land, addressed the question of bestiality with a realism and even compassion that the formal conciliar legislation lacked. He recognized the difficulties facing the celibate in their battles against lust. He joined patristic thinkers in stressing the distance between humans and animals, saying, "the height of lechery is that one raves even over animals and over inanimate things" and told of the dangers of lust to men who were able to avoid temptation by women.[63] He described a man who had been in charge of the monastery's donkeys and who "wretchedly fell under the sway of wild donkeys and was deluded." The moral warning for Climacus was that "the sin of fornication does not require the availability of another body."[64] Yet the sin was not unredeemable, for he described a bursar of the monastery who had fallen into sin with the monastery's animals in his youth, confessed his sin, and was let go with a simple reprimand.[65] This simple reprimand indicates that in spite of strict Eastern conciliar legislation, the Greek church never feared bestial intercourse as much as the West. It seemed no

more disruptive to society and the marriage bond than other sexual alternatives, so in the East churchmen repeatedly lowered the strict penances that
remained on the books from conciliar legislation.[66] In the West, however, over
time churchmen looked at the act with increasing concern.

The West combined Eastern legislation with its own penitential tradition.
The penitentials began in Ireland as a way to offer churchmen manuals for heal-
ing the souls of their sinful parishioners. These handbooks spread to
Anglo-Saxon England and then to the continent, influencing the important
canonical collections of the eleventh century and later. As Pierre Payer has
explained: "For 500 years the penitential literature continued to be the principal
agent in the formation and transmission of a code of sexual morality."[67]

A review of the whole body of penitential legislation reveals that the history of attitudes toward bestiality was more complicated than the clear-cut
Eastern prohibitions suggested. For example, the Eastern father Basil seems to
have considered sexual sins to be largely one category, linking bestiality,
homosexuality, and adultery together by assigning all three the same
penance.[68] Most Western churchmen, however, including the authors of the
penitentials, thought sexual sins carried different weights, and that opinion
shaped the future of sexual legislation. Churchmen faced a number of decisions
about the mitigating and aggravating conditions of the act, and in making these
decisions, they shaped perceptions of both the sin of bestiality and of animals.

All the secular Germanic law codes recognized age as a mitigating factor in
determining penalties for all kinds of crimes,[69] and the penitentials continued
this practice with regard to bestiality legislation. This is consistent with the
evidence we have from the early modern period that saw bestiality as a boys'
game, with more serious consequences if a boy did not outgrow it. The age of
maturity varied in the secular codes from ten to fifteen years,[70] and the ecclesiastical legislation also varied from an unspecified age of maturity to accepting
the age of twenty as defined by the Council of Ancyra. The Vinnian Penitential
gave a light penance of a hundred days for a "boy" who sinned with a beast
before taking the sacrament,[71] and the Cummean Penitential confirmed this
penance and added that a boy of fifteen years would do penance for forty
days.[72]

Age was linked to maturity and responsibility, and the codes further tie
these to matrimony. As the Council of Ancyra stipulated a longer penance for
anyone over twenty-five and married, so did the penitentials believe the sin was
greater if an individual violated the marital bond by having intercourse with an

animal. For example, even the mild Penitential of Columbanus required six months' penance for bestiality for a single man and double that for a married man.[73] Churchmen might have shown some understanding for the sexual sins of a youth (whether they be homosexual or bestial play), but once a man had taken up the responsibilities of age and marriage, his sexual energies were to be channeled only through the marital bond.

Ecclesiastical rank brought additional responsibilities, the violation of which brought concomitantly greater penalties in ecclesiastical law. Churchmen were supposed to be even more spiritual than the laity, and thus even further from beasts. Therefore, in their case the sin of bestiality represented a crossing of even greater boundaries. In the sixth-century Welsh Grove of Victory Penitential and the Penitential of Columbanus, clergy were to add one year to penalties for laity. In the case of bestiality, that would bring the penalty up to two and a half years or three years,[74] and these examples are representative of all the penitentials.

Factors of age, marital status, and ecclesiastical rank served to increase or decrease penances for all sexual sins. There were also other mitigating factors specifically for bestiality, beginning with ecclesiastical attempts to define the nature of the act of bestiality. The character of the penitentials themselves required the development of a hierarchical ranking of sins. For example, if adultery were worse than fornication, it received a greater penance. As churchmen determined bestiality's rank among the sexual sins, they began to reveal their view of the relation between humans and animals. The earliest penitentials ranked bestiality close to masturbation, making it a mild sexual sin. For example, the Penitential of Columbanus (circa 591) directly equated one who engages in "fornication with a beast" with one who "has defiled himself with his own hands." Both received a penalty of six months or a year, depending on marital status.[75] This penitential ranked other sexual sins more seriously: fornicating a single time received three years' penance and sodomy received ten.[76] The influential Cummean Penitential (circa 660) reveals a similar ranking. A fifteen year-old boy engaging in bestiality or mutual masturbation before communion would receive a forty day penance in either case. Again for comparison, this penitential prescribed seven years for sodomy.[77]

By treating bestiality like masturbation, churchmen were in fact showing that they perceived animals to be profoundly different from humans. They ranked almost as John Climacus's "inanimate things," hardly worthy of consideration. The mild penance may also show a certain security in the differences between humans and animals. When there was no threat of blurring the lines between species, there was no need to regulate strictly the distinctions. The early Germanic world viewed animals primarily as property and food, and this attitude was reflected in the view of the early Irish penitentials that sexual intercourse with animals was the same as sexual intercourse with nothing at all. This casual attitude toward animals and intercourse with them began to change as the conciliar legislation from the East began to influence the penitential compilers.

The Council of Ancyra equated bestiality with homosexuality: "Concerning those who...mix with cattle or who are polluted with males."[78] This association reached Visigothic Spain as early as the late sixth century with Martin of Braga, who included the prohibition in his canons appended to the Second Council of Braga.[79] This shaped the Spanish penitentials from the seventh or early eighth centuries, which gave a twenty-year penance for those who committed sodomy or bestiality.[80]

The later Irish penitentials slowly became influenced by the Council of Ancyra. As they were affected by the conciliar decrees, the insular penitentials shifted their perspective on the nature of bestiality. The ninth-century Carolingian capitularies directly quoted the Council of Ancyra, linking bestiality with homosexuality,[81] and the English Bigotian Penitential, compiled no earlier than the late eighth century and heavily influenced by the Continental material, completed the shift from treating bestiality like masturbation to treating it like homosexuality. It says, "One who often has intercourse with a male or with beasts, shall do penance for ten years."[82]

Equating homosexuality with bestiality not only escalated the penalty, but it expressed (and perhaps began to cause) a change in the way people looked at animals. Instead of being an inanimate, irrelevant object, the animal partner became just that, a partner in an "unnatural" act, just as homosexuality was an act between two partners. The notion of animals as essentially willing partners in the act points again to the profound differences between our view of the world and the medieval one. We require a willing partner to have enough intellect, or reason, to consent. In the medieval world, sex was ruled by lust, not will, and since lust was a "bestial" quality, animals certainly shared in that, so they could be partners in sexual activity. The shift of animals from object to partner raised the possibility of another mitigating or aggravating factor in the penalties for the act, the nature of the animal partner involved.

The eighth-century penitential of Egbert of York said the "Confessor ought to distinguish between the quality of the cattle [domestic animals] or of the men,"[83] but unfortunately offered no advice on what "qualities" domestic animals might have that would affect the nature of the act. The Spanish penitential increased the penalty for intercourse with "small animals,"[84] but did not explain why. Were small animals considered more "bestial" than large animals? Was the size differential considered more "unnatural?" Was this a practical consideration recognizing the damage likely to be done to a small animal? The sources do not yield satisfactory answers to these questions, but the inclusion of the qualifier demonstrates the changing view of animals that saw them as something other than obects for masturbatory use. In this same spirit, the St. Hubert Penitential of the mid–ninth century distinguished between sexual relations with "clean" or "unclean" animals, prescribing a penance of twelve years for the former and fifteen for the latter.[85] The eastern Slavic penitentials (influenced by the Council of Ancyra) also distinguished among animals, stipulating a greater penalty for intercourse with a mammal than with a fowl,[86] again without explaining the reasons for the differentiation. Perhaps mammals were seen as more similar to humans, and therefore, more of a threat to the blurring of boundaries between the species.

Once the animal was seen as a partner in the sin, the issue arose not only of varying the penalty depending on the animal, but of whether punishment was appropriate for the animal. The penitentials before the mid–eighth century, which dealt with bestiality as masturbation, thus effectively ignoring the animal, also ignored the prospect of penalty. After the animal became a participant in the equivalent of a homosexual encounter, churchmen turned to Leviticus and found the prescribed penalty for an animal involved in sexual contact: "If a man lies with a beast he shall be put to death; and you shall kill the beast."[87] The Canons of Theodore of Canterbury (circa 741) elaborated on the biblical requirement: "Animals polluted by coitus with men are to be killed the flesh thrown to dogs. But what they give birth to may be used and the hides taken."[88] This was reaffirmed in the ninth century by Hrabanus Maurus in his response to the moral question of what to do with animals involved in bestiality. He quoted the Levitical condemnation and reasserted the practical view expressed by Theodore that there was no reason to waste the offspring of the animal.[89]

By the turn of the millennium, church law on the subject of bestiality had developed enough to have demonstrated a change in perceptions of animals and of sin. As churchmen increased their fear of the sin of bestiality, the animal participants were given greater importance. From nonentities, they had become participants that had to receive greater punishment than the human participant. Church legislation then influenced secular laws. The later Norwegian codes included its prohibition of bestiality specifically as part of newly incorporated Christian legislation. The Norwegian laws of the eleventh century forbad men to have carnal dealings with animals, "which is forbidden to all Christians" and "which destroys his rights as a Christian," and prescribed the severe penalty of castration and outlawry.[90]

The growing body of legislation on the subject left a complexity of laws that were often contradictory. This is, of course, inevitable as ideas change, but as early as the late eighth century, Egbert of York expressed his confusion with the penitential tradition on the subject: "He who has sinned with cattle or a mule, ten years; some [say] seven; some, three; some, one; some a hundred days as for boys."[91] The early canonists of the eleventh century inherited and continued the discrepancies observed by Egbert. Burchard of Worms (circa 1020) and Ivo of Chartres (circa 1090) repeated the previous prohibitions, including the penalties ranging from forty days to twenty-five years penance.[92]

In repeating the Levitical requirement that the animal be killed, Ivo added an explanation absent from the penitential tradition. He said that the animal must be killed to erase any memory of the act.[93] This reasoning seems to provide a corrective to considering the animals as partners bearing some responsibility and thus deserving punishment for the act. Ivo's explanation made the killing important to affect the surviving humans, not to punish any animal guilt. This explanation was continued by the later scholastics, who insisted that the separation between humans and animals was so great that animals did not have enough will for one to "attribute praise or blame to acts of animals."[94] Ivo's explanation of the necessity to execute the animal was also reiterated in literary sources. For example, Gerald of Wales told of a lion that was executed for having intercourse with a woman. He said the lion was killed "not for its guilt, of which its nature as a brute exculpated it, but as a memorial." [95] Such explanations that seem to reach for a reason to kill an animal with which humans had been involved sexually appeared only when people had become more uncertain about the distance between human and animal natures. On the one hand, they believed animals to be sufficiently involved in the sexual act to deserve some punishment, but on the other hand to treat animals as equally blameworthy would be to violate the desired separation that was the point of much of this increasing legislation. In their uncertainty, they repeatedly asserted the differences in a way that had been unnecessary in the early Middle Ages when people took the differences for granted. By focusing on memory as the purpose for execution of "guilty" animals so they would not serve as reminders to people, medieval thinkers could have both punishment and distance.

In spite of Ivo's addition to the growing body of legislation on bestiality, the canonists by and large did not dwell on bestial intercourse. Burchard, Ivo, and the influential Gratian concentrated on legislation to solidify the marriage bond and increasingly to criminalize extramarital sexual offenses.[96] As Professor Brundage has summarized, in the eleventh century bestiality joined homosexuality and masturbation as "unnatural" offenses carrying "sanction of *infamia*" depriving the practitioners of respectable status in society.[97] However, in the eleventh and twelfth centuries outside the classrooms of the canon lawyers, people's views on the relationship between humans and animals were changing in a way that would cause the scholastics of the thirteenth century to rank bestiality as the worst of the sexual sins.

There is no reason to think that the act of bestiality was particularly curtailed during this period of growing sexual legislation against it. Some nonlegal sources report the activity in a fairly casual manner. For example, a tenth-century Spanish text describing famous physicians relates one anecdote from the career of Yahya' b. Ishaq, who practiced medicine in Cordoba. The author tells how a peasant comes to Cordoba crying out in pain. The peasant tells the physician he has been unable to urinate for several days. The physician orders him to place his swollen penis on a flat rock and quickly punches it with his fist. The patient faints in pain, but pus and urine flow, curing the peasant. The physician explains his diagnosis: "you have cohabited in the anus of an animal and therefore a grain of animal feed was stuck in your urethra and caused the inflamation." The moral of the story as told by the author was not to avoid the dangers of animal contacts; instead he said this anecdote showed the brilliance of the physician in making such an accurate diagnosis.[98]

Scandinavian society had a long tradition of using attributions of bestial intercourse as insults. This tradition appears in the literature of the thirteenth century, but it is not new to that century. The violence in *Njal's Saga* was forwarded when Skarp-Hedin accused Thorkel of sexual contact with a mare: "You would be better employed picking out of your teeth the bits of mare's arse you ate before you came here—your shepherd saw you at it, and was amazed at such disgusting behavior."[99] Even more graphic was the insult expressed in *Ale-Hood*:

> You didn't notice the fat stallion that Steingrim had till it was up your backside. That skinny mare you were on faltered under you...and I've never been able to make up my mind whether it was you or the mare that got it. Everybody could see how long you were stuck there, the stallion's legs had got such a grip on your cloak.[100]

These insults were in a tradition of sexual attacks (including being the passive partner in a homosexual encounter) that cast aspersions on one's masculinity.[101] The attribution of bestial intercourse, particularly of being the passive partner in the act, would have been especially insulting since it further degraded the masculinity (indeed the very humanity) of the participant.

Peter Damian, the eleventh-century churchman who was vigilant in exposing sexual sins, retold a tale that seems to have dated from about the eighth century in Islamic civilization. In his version, a countess plays wantonly with her husband's pet ape. The animal succumbs to her advances and the woman and ape become lovers. The ape becomes enraged when the count is lying with his wife and kills the husband.[102] This story is so reminiscent of the tales told by Aelian that it likely marks the return to Western Europe of a classical tradition that had been transmitted through the Islamic sources. Damian's retelling of the tale probably says more about his own interests in sexual diversity than in any particular resurgence of Aelian's bestiality tales.

Gerald of Wales, a twelfth-century chronicler who like Peter Damian could not resist fantastic tales, reported instances of bestiality in his work the *The History and Topography of Ireland*. Gerald claimed that the Irish were so rural, "living like beasts," that they were "particularly addicted to such abominations."[103] Gerald then proceeded to tell tales of men who had intercourse with cows and women who had intercourse with goats and a lion.[104] Gerald's anecdotes reveal a bit more than either his anti-Irish bias or popular belief of the prevalance of human/animal intercourse. Gerald recounts tales about half-human births generated from such intercourse. Men fathered half-human monsters on their cows or oxen, and Gerald stretches credulity to its limits by recounting an incident of a man who passed a calf from his bowels as "punishment attendant on some atrocious crime," presumably having been sodomized and impregnated by a bull.[105] These anecdotes caused Gerald to reflect upon exactly what it meant to be human rather than an animal,[106] and this question is the significant one here. If some people in the twelfth century could tell stories of such births, then the lines that separated human from animal were begining to blur. The penitential writers had seen no reason to kill the calves of animals that had been used for sexual intercourse, so great was the separation between the species. By the twelfth century, Gerald of Wales would wonder whether the killing of such an animal should be considered homicide since it was half human.[107]

Gerald's preoccupation with the products of human/animal intercourse point to a change in perceptions of the relations between humans and animals. The belief that human/animal unions were fertile undermines the doctrine of a fundamental divide between humans and animals. It so profoundly brings the species together that it makes a dramatic statement that in the twelfth century new ambiguities between the species were surfacing. I will talk more about this increasing uncertainty about the separation of species in the last two chapters, but here I will look at the effect of this uncertainty on the images of and legislation against bestial intercourse. As the lines between the species seemed to blur, legislation against bestiality increased in an attempt to create more clear boundaries between human and animal when popular imagination was losing track of such barriers.

Not surprisingly, the increasing concern with bestial intercourse was expressed in the later Middle Ages in religious works urging the faithful to preserve their humanity in the face of its possible loss. A thirteenth-century anecdote that was from a collection to be used by preachers to bring moral lessons to the people presents a charming image of how easily one might lose one's humanity through the appetites:

> A man who had sinned in a bestial manner wished to do penance in like manner and so ate grass frequently every day. After a time, he began to wonder to what order of angels one would belong who had done such penance. An angel answered him: "By such a life you do not deserve to belong to the order of the angels, but rather to the order of the asses."[108]

The protagonist of this little tale had made two mistakes; he not only had sex with animals, but ate like animals. Indeed, he could look forward to no human heaven.

The visions of hell that were written in the twelfth century offer more frightening visions of a damnation of being bestialized. These visions begin to show the fear of and preoccupation with bestial intercourse that increased after the twelfth century. Earlier visions revealed fear of being eaten (as I described in the last chapter). By the twelfth century, new fears were added. The Monk of Evesham in 1196 described punishment of people who had presumably engaged in bestial intercourse. He wrote with horror:

> The most loathsome and severe of all remains still to be told, because all who were punished there had been guilty of a wickedness in life that is unmentionable by a Christian....Those therefore were continually attacked by huge fiery monsters, horrible beyond description. Despite their opposition, these committed on them the same damnable crimes that they had been guilty of on earth....Until that time I had never heard or thought that both sexes could have been corrupted by such filthiness.[109]

Visions of bestial intercourse did not only plague those guilty of the act on earth, but became part of the general vision of the horror of hell. In 1149 Tundale's vision contains a description worthy of a science-fiction film:

> All of the men and the women who descended into the swamp were actually made pregnant by the beast...The offspring they conceived stung them in their entrails like vipers,...These beasts that were born had burning iron heads and the sharpest beaks, with which they tore the body to pieces wherever they came out.[110]

These twelfth-century visions of hell point to another preoccupation that seemed to grow in that century. People seemed to worry more about demons than they had earlier, and this contributed to increasing ecclesiastical concern with bestial intercourse. While the early medieval world had its share of demons, churchmen did not believe they could physically interfere with humans, particularly sexually. Demons made of air were not substantial enough to have sexual intercourse with humans; such experiences were illusions or dreams.[111] By the twelfth century, that changed. Incubi and succubi seemed everywhere to seduce women and men who did not guard themselves against such attacks.[112] Jeffrey Burton Russell has attributed this change to the development of scholastic theory,[113] but additionally, the belief in substantial incubi coincided with the growth of the idea of purgatory in the twelfth century.[114] This was not coincidental. Just as souls were seen to be substantial enough to punish, demons were substantial enough to have intercourse with humans. Not only could demons have intercourse, they could beget offspring upon human women. Scholastic thinkers explained the process by which such generation could take place between species. Aquinas is representative in his explanation that "for the purpose of generation, one and the same demon being succubus to a man and transferring the seed thus received by acting as incubus to a woman."[115]

The development of this idea (and this fear) was rapid. In the twelfth century, Guibert of Nogent told of demons who lusted after women,[116] and even claimed that his mother was attacked by a lustful demon.[117] Also in the twelfth century, Gerald of Wales told of a man who was begotten by a demon upon his mother.[118] Perhaps the most famous of the twelfth-century incubal impregnations was that of the magician Merlin. In the version written by Geoffrey of Monmouth, Merlin's mother is questioned by King Vortigern as to the circumstances of Merlin's conception. She says that she has had relations with no man, instead

> some one used to come to me in the form of a most handsome young man. He would often hold me tightly in his arms and kiss me....Many times, too, when I was sitting alone, he would talk with me, without becoming visible; and when he came to see me in this way he would often make love with me, as a man would do, and in that way he made me pregnant.

The king is astounded by this narration and calls his wise man to ask him if this is possible. The wise man explains that demons can assume mortal shape to have intercourse with humans.[119]

By the thirteenth century, the gossipy chronicler Caesarius of Heisterbach had so many stories of demons having intercourse with men and women that he could say, "there is nothing wonderful that demons should make love to women."[120] In the thirteenth century, the belief in such intercourse moved from literature to the courts. In 1275 at Toulouse, Angèle de la Barthe was convicted of having intercourse for several years with an incubus. She was burned at the stake.[121] Courts were also prepared to protect society against the issue of such a union. In 1308, Guichard, Bishop of Troyes, was tried for sorcery, and among the charges was the claim that he was the son of an incubus.[122]

In virtually all the incubal appearances recounted in the sources, demons appeared as handsome men or beautiful women. But in the popular imagination, the devil and his followers were pictured as half or wholly animal. The devil could appear as almost any animal, but most frequently as a serpent, goat, or dog.[123] Therefore, the word attached to the sin of demon intercourse was bestiality. The serious, heretical crime of intercourse with the devil was thus linked with the earlier seemingly innocuous act of intercourse with an irrelevant object. During the twelfth century, all "unnatural" intercourse began to be linked with heresy,[124] and bestiality became inexorably joined to the heresy of dealing with the devil.

By the thirteenth century, the animal world seemed much more threatening than it had in the early Middle Ages, when in spite of ambiguities in the property and food relationships, animals were separated from humans by a chasm of difference. Now animals were believed to be able to mingle with humanity and create offspring, and the fearful world of demons was linked to the earthly menagerie. These ideas shaped the composition of the *Summae* that represented the highest development of medieval thought.

Thomas of Chobham (circa 1158-1233) identified bestiality as a grave sin calling for extreme penalties. The human offender was required to do penance for fifteen years (twenty if married), and in addition, to go barefoot throughout his or her life, never enter church, and permanantly abstain from meat, fish, and intoxicants. The animal participant was to be killed, burned, and buried to prevent any memory of the crime to be renewed.[125] Alexander of Hales (d. 1245) continued Thomas's abhorrence, although in less detail. Alexander identified bestiality as the greatest sin against nature, for to sin with "another species" and with "things irrational" represents the furthest departure from human nature, and thus the most unnatural sin. The penalty for Alexander was simple and extreme: kill the human and the animal, and thus erase the memory of the act with the participants.[126]

The greatest of the schoolmen, Thomas Aquinas (1224-1274) continued this view of bestiality but elaborated it into a more complete system. He said that "unnatural vice" was "contrary to the natural order of the venereal act as becoming to the human race." The four kinds of unnatural vice were masturbation, homosexuality, "unnatural manner of copulation," and bestiality.[127] Within these unnatural vices, Aquinas ranked bestiality as the worst: "the most grievous is the sin of bestiality, because use of the due species is not observed."[128] In Thomas's ranking one can see that the guiding principle was to observe and preserve the differences between humans and animals. The most grievous sin was to forget one's humanity while engaging in the act that along with consent defined marriage.

Although the schoolmen ranked bestiality as the most "grievous of sins," in practice the courts were more preoccupied with prosecuting homosexuality.[129] Yet as these theorists increasingly legislated the exclusivity and the sanctity of the marital bond, they also solidified the idea of the evil of corrupting that bond by "unnatural" intercourse and the mingling of species. The ideas of the theorists slowly found expression in the secular law codes. For example, the late thirteenth-century Spanish law code, the *Siete Partidas*, expresses the increasingly repressive attitude toward homosexuality and bestiality. It calls for the death penalty for both sexual crimes.[130] Such repressive legislation brought with it the idea that the separation between humans and animals was a matter that could not be taken for granted and thus had to be actively preserved. This laid the groundwork for our attitudes toward the practice of bestiality, as well as future prosecution of the act. During the late Middle Ages and Renaissance, authorities began active prosecution of homosexuality and sodomy, and bestiality, too, became a matter for capital enforcement. In the fifteenth-century trial records of Majorca, several people were executed for the crime (no longer just sin) of bestiality,[131] and by 1534, bestiality had become a capital crime in England and Sweden.[132] Through the seventeenth century there were a number of executions of both humans and animals for the crime.[133] Keith Thomas has noted that these executions occurred because the early modern period was uncertain about the distinction between humans and animals: "the separateness of the human race was thought so precarious, so easily lost, that the boundary had been so tightly guarded."[134] Jonas Liliequist has observed the same fears in the trials in Sweden. He writes that the reason for the persecutions "can be found in the underlying cultural meaning of bestiality as a transgressional act— transgression of the culturally constructed boundaries between man and animal."[135]

In the two previous chapters, I have explored relationships between humans and animals that remained fairly constant throughout the Middle Ages. As property and food, animals could be defined as "other" than human, even though both relationships contained ambiguities that made the relationship less clear than it appeared on the surface. These relationships also remained constant because they were central and necessary to human life. When we turn to the subject of bestial intercourse, however, the situation is changed. Since sexual contact with animals was not necessary to human survival, there was more room for people's attitudes to influence legislation and literary discussion of the act. Therefore, bestiality references offer a barometer of changing views toward animals.

From this analysis, one can see that in the thousand years that we consider the medieval world, perceptions of animals changed. At the beginning,

Christian writers confidently proclaimed a significant difference between humans and animals, and it seems that the predominately rural population was fairly comfortable with its relationship with the animal world. By the late Middle Ages (certainly by the twelfth century), this comfortable certainty was disrupted. The separation no longer seemed so clear, and as I indicated above in bestiality legislation, it seemed to require more effort to maintain. In a way, this chapter marks the turning point in the medieval view of animals. The first two chapters express the early medieval world—separation with ambiguities. The last two chapters express the mentality of the late medieval world, in which it becomes increasingly difficult to tell the difference between humans and animals.

4

Animals as Human Exemplars

THE RELATIONSHIPS BETWEEN
humans and animals I have discussed so far have been concrete. Animals serving
as property, food, and even sexual partners belonged to the real world of
human experience. These animals were the ones featured in medieval literature
and were the ones medieval illustrators selected when they included animals in
the central illustrations of their manuscripts. By the twelfth and thirteenth centuries, however, different sorts of animals also appeared in the literary sources.
These were animals of the imagination, fable animals, fantastic animals. The
appearance of these animals marked a growing emphasis on a new relationship
with animals. Animals become important as metaphors, as guides to metaphysical truths, as human exemplars. These imaginary animals exerted an even more
important influence over the relationship between humans and animals than did
the ox pulling solidly before the plow or the sheep placidly providing milk or
even the farm animals leading their keepers into sin.

Metaphoric animals live in the borders of human imagination, where any
particular actual animal is almost irrelevant compared to its symbolic meaning.

Even our twentieth-century culture that prides itself on a scientific approach to the animal kingdom is not immune to this metaphoric view of animals. I think the best modern example is our perception of lemmings, the small rodents we picture charging suicidally over a cliff. Lemmings no more commit collective suicide than medieval beavers committed self-castration to avoid hunters, but our image of lemmings remains a powerful cultural symbol of reckless behavior as we persist in believing in that myth.

Medieval society inherited a number of classical writings with a view of animals that revealed them to be very humanlike and to serve as human exemplars. We saw this classical view of the intimate relationships between the species in the last chapter in Aelian's description of human and animal intercourse. Christian writers found his descriptions objectionable not only to their sense of sin, but to their perception of the relationship between humans and animals, so they edited out most of those stories. The classical world, however, produced other writings that expressed a comparable perception without the obvious sinful overtones. How would the medieval world deal with stories of animals that talked to humans and offered humans examples of how to live their lives? The most famous literary expressions of the similarities between humans and animals were found in fables. A comparably influential scientific/religious tract was the *Physiologus*, a collection of animal narratives that formed the basis for medieval bestiaries. In the growing medieval popularity of both these works, we can trace the transmission, modification, and partial acceptance of the classical idea that humans and animals were more similar than Christian thinkers had been willing to admit.

From these texts, we can see that animals can serve not only as property, food, and sexual objects, but as human exemplars. During bestial intercourse, the actual boundaries between humans and animals slip away, but when people use animals to give examples for human behavior, the divisions blur in an even more significant way in people's minds. By the thirteenth century, the metaphor of animals acting as human exemplars was accepted, and by popularizing and spreading this view, medieval thinkers probably inadvertently changed the way people looked at animals and, of course, how they looked at themselves. A scholar of the fourteenth century has written that during that time, "all saw animals as exhibiting human traits, as having conscious motives or even moral standards,"[1] and this trend continued into the Renaissance (and beyond into our own time). The lines that separated humans from animals were becoming very narrow indeed, and as I showed in the last chapter, this blurring led to increased fear of and repression of bestial intercourse, in an attempt to preserve a separation that had already been lost. From the twelfth century on, animals were no longer just property and food, but also human exemplars. Of course, this new symbolic emphasis of animals did not displace the previous concrete day-to-day relationship people had with their real animals. That relationship always remained central to the medieval economy; the symbolism was a newly added dimension.

I suggest that the increasing popularity of these exemplar texts had an influence deeper than simply adding a new metaphoric role for animals. When people can see an animal acting as a human, the metaphor can work both ways, revealing the animal within each human. This was, indeed, the message in ancient Greece and Rome, where these texts were written down in the form they would reach the medieval world. As we saw in the last chapter, by the high Middle Ages, people were no longer so confident about the distinctions between humans and animals, and they thus sought to legislate the differences. At the same time, however, churchmen (and at least one noblewoman) were circulating tales of animals that were supposed to urge people to high moral conduct. Ironically, these tales served to undermine the position that the church had taken at the beginning of the Middle Ages by repeatedly showing people that the lines between human and animal were fine. By immoral acts, people could descend to the level of the beasts, or in our twentieth-century terminology, people could allow the beast that was always within to emerge. In this chapter, I shall show the reintroduction into the medieval west of classical texts that wrote of the metaphoric relationship between humans and animals, consider ways in which these texts contributed to the transformation of the early medieval view of animals, and look at what view of animals is portrayed within them.

Classical Heritage

One of the earliest literary forms that used animals as human exemplars is the fable. Fables offer short fictional tales in which animals (and less often, inanimate objects) speak. From such tales of animal actions and speech, humans were to see their own flaws and draw morals for future action. The ancient Greek definition of a fable is "a fictitious story picturing a truth."[2] This definition accents one important aspect of fables, the moral truth that could be drawn from the predominately animal action. The seventh-century cataloguer of classical learning, Isidore of Seville, elaborated on this definition a bit to stress the quality of human exemplar that the tales possess. He wrote, "fables are told in order to produce a recognizable picture of human life through the conversations of imaginary dumb animals."[3]

Such stories have a remarkably long tradition. Archeologists have found clay tablets with Sumerian proverbs that seem to belong to an animal fable tradition. Within these proverbs, humans are compared to animals, and many have actions that involve interactions between humans and animals.[4] Fables have a highly developed tradition in India, and some authors have suggested an ancient Indo-European tradition of fables.[5] It is most likely that any society that sees a close relationship between humans and animals, that sees a parallel between species, will produce fable-type stories that explore the metaphoric relationship.

For the medieval west, the most influential fable tradition was that of ancient Greece. In about the sixth century B.C., oral fables circulated that were attributed to the slave Aesop. Aesop was a legendary figure about whom we know nothing with any certainty. In about the fourth century B.C., a *Life of Aesop* was written, and it circulated with many manuscripts of fables. Like so many such *Lives*, it was changed periodically and we have several extant versions. By the second century A.D., a long and elaborate *Life* was written, and we know this version was accessible in the Middle Ages because it survives in a tenth-century manuscript.[6]

The *Life of Aesop* describes the fabulist as a mute slave who is dwarfish, dark, and hopelessly homely. The goddess Isis awards the gift of speech to the slave in return for a kindness. A philosopher buys Aesop, and throughout the *Life*, Aesop shows himself to be more witty than the philosopher. After many demonstrations of Aesop's cleverness and wisdom (some of which he manifests by telling a timely fable), the philosopher frees Aesop, whose reputation for wisdom increases as he becomes counselor to kings. He is finally condemned to death by the priests at Delphi, who are offended by his scathing wit.[7] Since it is likely that all the elements of this biography are fictional, the author and those who continued the tradition selected certain points that seemed consistent with the fable tradition to which the *Life* was appended. First, the fact that Aesop was made a slave, and a slave who consistently outwits his betters, seems a social commentary. Indeed, many of the fables from the Greek world offer lessons that may be construed as at least democratic, and perhaps at times even revolutionary. Phaedrus (a first-century fabulist) explained this association between social criticism and fables:

Now I will explain briefly why the type of thing called fable was invented. The slave, being liable to punishment for any offence, since he dared not say outright what he wished to say, projected his personal sentiments into fables and eluded censure under the guise of jesting with made-up stories.[8]

Thus, Phaedrus saw a clear relationship between fables and social critique. (I shall show below that this relationship changes as fables enter the medieval world.)

A second important element in the *Life of Aesop* and one that is perhaps even more significant for my argument here is the description of Aesop. Throughout the *Life* he is described as so ugly and deformed that people could hardly tell whether he was human. The philosopher's wife calls Aesop a dog, and another person says, "Is he a frog, or a hedgehog, or a pot-bellied jar, or a captain of monkeys, or a moulded jug, or a cook's gear, or a dog in a basket?"[9] At the beginning of the tale, Aesop is mute, like a dumb animal. These associations reveal Aesop to exist on the border of human and animal, indeed to resemble an animal that speaks wisely. He is presented as a metaphor for the fables he tells, stories of animals that speak wisely. In fact, the description of Aesop can serve to point to what will happen in the Middle Ages when the society is drawn to looking at animals as human exemplars. They begin to see how humans are close to the animal world, just as Aesop himself was.[10]

The oral tales that were attributed to Aesop were written down in about the fourth century B.C. (although we do not have any manuscripts that preserve this version). In the first century A.D., the tales formed the basis for a Latin verse translation by Phaedrus. In the third century, Babrius composed a series of fables in Greek verse. A century later, Romulus wrote a Latin prose version based on Phaedrus and others, and shortly after that, Avianus wrote forty-two Latin verse fables based on Phaedrus and Babrius. The versions of Avianus and Romulus were the most influential in the Middle Ages.[11]

One of the features of the fables that contributed to their wide-ranging influence in the Middle Ages was the fact that they lent themselves so readily to illustration. These illustrations would eventually be separated from the written text and thus offer wider visibility. Scholars assume that many of the early editions of fables were illustrated, but there are only two surviving fragments of illustrated manuscripts from the late Roman period, and there is one sixth-century Avianus manuscript that is illustrated with line drawings.[12] After the twelfth century, the images of the fables spread almost as rapidly as the written texts and, at times, spread independently of them.

107

These fable collections contain most of the stories with which we are familiar. The town mouse and the country mouse reflect upon the relative merits of simple food eaten in safety or rich food consumed with danger. The owner of the goose that lays golden eggs learns the dangers of greed. The tortoise and the hare race to give a lesson of persistence, and the fox complains of sour grapes outside his reach. Although many of the stories are familiar, they were nevertheless changed as the fables were transmitted into the Middle Ages. I shall detail some of these changes below, but here I want to note the elements in the structure of the classical fables that lent themselves to subsequent transformation. (In fact, these fluid characteristics contribute to the continued popularity of fables.)

One of the characteristics of classical fables (that would be later changed) was that the animals did not exhibit stock characteristics beyond the fact that predators remained predators and prey remained consumed. For example, foxes were not always or only sly.[13] In a number of the fables, the animals could be changed and the moral remain the same. Babrius told the fable of a lizard who "burst apart in the middle when he tried to equal a serpent in length." The moral Babrius gave, "You will hurt yourself and accomplish nothing if you try to imitate one who is much your superior,"[14] could apply equally to the toad who tried to swell himself up to be as large as an ox.[15] The fable of the wild ass who prefered freedom with scarcity over the well-fed tame ass who labored for his owner yields the same message as the fable of the wolf who preferred freedom to the lot of his sleek, well-fed relative the dog, whose neck was rubbed bare by his master's collar.[16] The animal was less important than the lesson of freedom, and almost any animal could be used to portray that truth. Thus, the fable remains useful when a relationship between humans and *particular* animals changes.

A second characteristic of classical fables is that the morals were frequently left ambiguous. This has allowed the same fables to be used in different cultural contexts as the morals are modified to suit differing circumstances. This quality of fables seems to have been self-conscious, rather than accidental. Phaedrus wrote in one of his collections, "It was by design that antiquity wrapped up truth in symbols, that the wise might understand, the ignorant go astray."[17] Some fables we find familiar have morals that have a slightly different emphasis in the classical versions. One example is the story of the man who urges his sons to work together by demonstrating that they can not break a bundle of sticks unless the bundle is separated. We use this story to tell a general lesson of cooperation. Babrius's moral was more specific to families: "Brotherly love is the greatest good for men; even the humble are exalted by it."[18] Another instance of Babrius's inclination to make morals very specific is found in the story of a little boy who overeats of beef entrails during a feast. He goes home to his mother in pain, saying "It's awful, Mother, I'm dying; all my insides are stricken." The mother responds "Don't worry child, throw it up and don't hold anything back. It's not your insides that you are giving up but the bull's." One might draw lessons about gluttony or even about the ease of giving up another's property (easy come, easy go). Babrius, however, says, "One might apply this fable to a guardian who has squandered an orphan's inheritance and wails when he is obliged to pay it back."[19] If such stories depended upon the specific content of morals like Babrius's, they would not have survived.

Some fables seem to have been so ambiguous that even the fabulist had difficulties coming up with the moral. Phaedrus tells a short fable of a person who saw an ape hanging in a butcher's shop among the other food. He asked what its flavor was like, "whereupon the butcher replied in jest: It tastes as bad as it looks." Phaedrus, seemingly despairing of a moral, wrote, "This, I suppose, has been told more for the sake of a laugh than with regard to the truth; for I...have known many with ugly features to be the best of men."[20]

It is in fact this potential for fluid interpretation that has contributed to the longevity of the stories. On an abstract level, the open-ended characteristic of fables allows them to be applied (and relevant) to different contexts, thus increasing the probability for their continued popularity. On a practical level, this quality made them perfect tools for the study of rhetoric. Prose fables were included in rhetoric books in the classical period for young scholars to use in practicing arguing a point. By urging students to explain a truth that might be articulated in the story, teachers were creating a perfect vehicle for ensuring that the fables would remain viable literary creations. In this form, fables also passed into the medieval schoolroom.

Fables were produced in the classical pagan society that could easily see animals as human exemplars; that was consistent with their view that humans were close to animals. As we have seen, the Christian tradition had more trouble with that principle. In the second century A.D., however, a Christian composed a text that also used animals as human exemplars, but in a specifically Christian context. This was the *Physiologus*, ostensibly a scientific (rather than literary) work on animals that drew Christian morals from the animals portrayed.

Physiologus means "natural historian" and has come to be identified with both the title and alleged author of the work. This book was likely composed in Alexandria for two reasons. The most obvious evidence is that almost all the animals were native to North Africa, which suggests that the author came from that part of the world. On a more abstract level, the method used in the work was consistent with that of the Alexandrian school of Christian philosophy, which developed allegoric interpretations as a key part of the Christian experience. Alexandrian allegorists believed that the Creator had left clues to his own being in all elements of the creation, so by skillfully applying allegory to the natural world (including animals) one might begin to unlock the secrets of the Creator (or at least learn what messages he had left for humanity.)[21]

In general, the entries in *Physiologus* begin with a quotation from scripture. Then follow one or more facts of natural history about the habits or properties of the animal, followed by the moral to be drawn for human life. Finally, an entry might end with more biblical quotations.[22] The popular entry on the lion that begins the collection can serve to illustrate this method. The entry opens with a passage from Genesis: "Jacob, blessing his son Judah, said, 'Judah is a lion's whelp.'" Then the work goes on to discuss elements of the lion's "nature," observing that lions use their tails to cover their tracks so hunters may not follow them. The author then explains that from this example, we may learn that God, the Father, "hid his intelligible tracks (that is, his divine nature) from the unbelieving Jews."[23] Twelfth-century bestiaries add even more metaphoric weight to the lion. For example, they add that lions sleep with their eyes open, showing that when Christ was buried his Godhead remained awake. Finally, the bestiary writes that when a lioness gives birth to cubs, they are born dead and remain so for three days until their father brings them to life by breathing on them, just as the Father brought Christ to life on the third day.[24] The illustration in Figure 1 from a bestiary shows the lion bringing his cubs back to life. In this illustration, however, the lions are licking the cubs instead of just breathing on them. The illustrator joined many others in the Middle Ages in confusing the lion's resurrection of its cubs with the bear's reputed licking of formless cubs into shape.[25]

This free mixing of animal metaphors indicates the degree to which the metaphor was more important than the animal. Thus, one can see that while the work was intended to be a "scientific" study of animals, it was not scientific in the same way we understand the term. The author was less interested in describing an animal than in using the animal as a vehicle for understanding religious truth, the "science" the author was ultimately studying. As the author of a

Figure 1: *Lions Licking Cubs into Shape* Ms M. 81, f 8r.
Courtesy of The Pierpoint Morgan Library, New York

twelfth-century bestiary that built on *Physiologus* wrote after a description of an animal, "Now all this is to be understood in a spiritual manner, and you have to say it allegorically, to the higher sense."[26]

Like fables, *Physiologus* offered a way to understand animals as human exemplars.[27] Fables accented moral and ethical choices; *Physiologus* pointed to metaphysical truths. Both, however, contained the underlying assumption that animals could be used in this fashion. Like fables, *Physiologus* lent itself readily to illustration. Early manuscripts contained illustrations that attempted to capture the animal and its moral in one glance. Also like the illustrations of the fables, these visual lessons could be and were removed from the text to stand alone and thus reach more people.

The metaphoric richness of these *Bestiary* illustrations may be seen in the illustration of a crocodile shown in Figure 2. The crocodile is shown eating a man, reminding readers of its reputation as a hypocritical man-eater that cries "crocodile tears" after consuming the human. Notice, however, the snake emerging from the side of the beast. This is the hydra that had the *Bestiary* reputation of killing crocodiles by coating itself in mud and crawling into the beast's mouth to rip it apart from within and emerge unharmed.[28] In this one illustration, the artist shows vividly the moral lesson against hypocrisy, and shows the deep medieval fears surrounding eating and being eaten. A small,

111

lively image was full of meaning, and animals carry a heavy metaphoric weight of moral lesson.

Figure 2: *Bestiary Crocodile and Hydra* Harley MS. 3244, f. 43.
By permission of the British Library

Church fathers must have been placed in an interesting dilemma if they had thought carefully about their position regarding this body of thought. On the one hand, we have seen that they vigorously insisted upon the differences between humans and animals. On the other hand, *Physiologus* was a Christian work that had the highest moral goals, achieving them by using animals for teaching spiritual truth, and the fables contained moral lessons that could improve human behavior.

Medieval Rediscovery

The allegorical model in *Physiologus* provided a prototype for the early medieval preservation of works that offered animals as human exemplars and indeed spurred some of the church fathers to do some speculating on their own about how animals might be used to give lessons to people. Two fourth-century church fathers wrote treatises on the Creation (called *Hexaemeron*) in which they naturally discussed animals as part of the Creation. The Eastern father, Basil, rejected the heavy allegory of *Physiologus* in favor of "analogy." The results were similar, however, in that in his *Hexaemeron* he urged people to draw lessons from the animals of the Creation. For example, he wrote, "Notice how the swan plunges his neck into the depth of the water to draw his food from it, and you will understand the wisdom of the Creator in giving this creature a neck longer than his feet...."[29] In this example, Basil is urging the observer to appreciate the magnificence of the Creator by looking at His product. This is not as extreme as urging people to model their behavior after animals nor drawing complex (and at times preposterous) allegory from presumed animal behavior. But it does suggest that the human and his/her characteristics are part of some divine plan. Basil's work is an example of a conservative church father's approach to the question of the use to which people can put observations of animal behavior. His approach was likely a conscious choice that expressed the standard Christian view of a strong separation between humans and animals, not a lack of exposure to the classical view that accepted animals as human exemplars. This conclusion is warranted because Basil was aware of classical fables; he referred to two in his letters.[30] He chose not to take this approach, even in his tract that offered the most likely forum for such comparison, the *Hexaemeron*.

The fourth-century Western father who is also known for his *Hexaemeron* is St. Ambrose. Ambrose adopted more of an allegorical approach to animals than did Basil, to the extent that he urged people to pattern some of their behavior on animals. "There is in the nature of quadrupeds something which the language of the prophetical books exhorts us to imitate. We should follow their example."[31] Ambrose urged people to learn hard work from the example of the ant, to learn loving care for the young from the bear, and gratitude from dogs.[32] These simple lessons were precisely those that one could learn from fables or from the scientific works like *Physiologus*. The prestigious doctor of the church, who as I showed earlier, forwarded the early medieval notion that people and animals were dramatically different, here legitimized using animals as human exemplars, which offers a metaphor for drawing the species together.

This legitimacy was confirmed by the most influential Western church father of all, Augustine. He specifically defended fables against detractors who claimed they were untrue. Augustine said that the meaning of the fable (that is, the moral truth it offered for humans) was more important that its accuracy (that is, its information about animal behavior).[33] Augustine also accepted the approach to animals expressed in the *Physiologus* by urging people to study the "nature of animals" so they can understand the analogies with animals made in scripture.[34]

These examples drawn from some of the most influential church thinkers of the early medieval period serve only to show that the use of animals as human exemplars was given some legitimacy, but this view of animals was not unambiguous. Even Ambrose had to explain his interest in animals to Christians who believed that humans were the only proper area of inquiry for humans. Ambrose argued, "We cannot fully know ourselves without first knowing the nature of all living creatures."[35] It is not surprising that there would be some ambiguity in the early Christian texts. After all, Christianity was defining people as different from animals, yet it inherited morally uplifting texts that depended upon seeing parallels between people and animals.[36]

The early Christian ambiguity towards texts that used animals as human exemplars was resolved in two ways: the texts were saved and some copies were made in monastic libraries, but the texts were not widely used or disseminated in the early Middle Ages. As we have seen in the preceeding chapters, the predominant relationship between people and animals during the early centuries was concrete. Most people lived too closely to their animals to appreciate their value as metaphor.[37] This changed in the twelfth century, which coincided with the beginnings of the increased ambiguity between people and animals that we saw in the last chapter.

The oldest surviving manuscripts of *Physiologus* are from the ninth century, and there are only two of those. The text was preserved, but apparently was not particularly popular. In the twelfth century, however, the old classical text of *Physiologus* was expanded by the addition of chapters about many animals and birds, and the inclusion of information from Isidore of Seville's *Etymologies*. Information was later added from the thirteenth-century encyclopedia, *On the Nature of Things*, by Bartholomaeus Anglicus.[38] These expanded versions are called bestiaries, and they became among the most popular forms of literature in medieval Europe. These bestiaries were first and foremost products of medieval monasteries. English Cistercians copied and used the work,[39] and the allegorical methods of the bestiary were consistent with the new Platonism of the French school of Chartres.[40] Monasteries developed techniques to copy a number of illuminated copies of the popular work at a time to keep up with demand for it.[41]

This popular and influential form of literature has engendered a good deal of historical interest, perhaps largely because these were (and are) seen as works of science, in spite of the inclusion of some fantastic creatures like the phoenix, unicorn, and manticore and in spite of some of the improbable characteristics described (pelicans bring their young to life by piercing their own sides and drenching the babies with their blood.)[42] T. White has written, "It can hardly be repeated too often that the bestiary is a serious scientific work,"[43] and others who describe them see their new popularity in the twelfth century as a product of that century's "scientific revival."[44] Such analysis has led many to assume that the history of bestiaries represented a slow but steady progress from the dark swamp of *Physiologus* allegory to the high ground of science in the Renaissance. This approach suits our desire to understand the past in terms of our present, but it leads us to misunderstand the past. The twelfth-century resurrection of the bestiary was "scientific" only in medieval terms, when "science" meant the attempt to understand all truth, including in particular metaphysical truth. Bestiaries were first a part of that search for metaphysical reality. In fact, the twelfth century did not represent a movement away from the allegory of the second-century *Physiologus*, but a return to it. The twelfth century saw an increased popularity of the bestiaries, and for the next two centuries they exerted a profound influence on medieval thought and society.

Monasteries also preserved collections of fables, and like the bestiaries they were not as popular during the early Middle Ages as they later became. From the numbers of surviving manuscripts, France seems to have been the region where fables were most carefully preserved, and it was the region from which fables spread after they were repopularized.[45] Collections of fables were probably preserved in part for their use as educational tools in monastic schools. As I mentioned above, fables were seen as perfect tools for teaching rhetoric, but by the eleventh century there is evidence for fables being used as human exemplars for the morals they offered for human behavior. For example, in that century the catalogue of the monastery of Fleury shows that they had several manuscripts of fables, and in about 1030 the fables became the basis for a fresco on the wall of the monks' dining area. The writings below the fresco show the moral of the fable; for example, "bad consequences always ensue if one helps the wicked."[46]

The movement of fables from text to wall painting marks the beginning of an increasing trend in the late eleventh century when fable and bestiary illustrations appeared as independent decoration separate from the text.[47] Carvings of bestiary and fable animals appeared in churches[48] and became more common through the Gothic period. Perhaps the best example of the introduction of these metaphoric animals into the art and consciousness of the period may be seen in the eleventh-century Bayeaux Tapestry. This tapestry was produced in a monastery to commemorate the Norman victory in the Battle of Hastings in England. The central part of the tapestry retells the story of William the Conqueror's victory over Anglo-Saxon England. The borders of the tapestry, however, are full of fable and bestiary animals that have no direct relationship to the main narrative. There are at least twelve fables and thirteen bestiary animals portrayed in the border.[49] As early as the eleventh century, then, monks could be certain enough that fables and bestiaries were sufficiently familiar that they could portray images without any accompanying text to explain the moral. As a figure from the Bayeaux Tapestry shows, simply portraying a bird in a tree with a generic quadruped below could remind the viewer of the dangers of vanity that caused a raven to lose his bit of cheese to the fox.

Although moral lessons were consistent with monastic purpose, there were always critics who believed that portraying animals acting like humans was frivolous. Criticism of illustrating animal fables in manuscripts or in monastic art continued sporadically through the twelfth century, but the images were too popular to disappear. By the thirteenth century, such protests virtually ceased,[50] and the margins of manuscripts began to be populated with small animals in human parody. Like bestiaries, fables were preserved in monastic communities, became increasingly popular in the eleventh century, and by the twelfth century emerged from behind monastery walls to amuse and influence society at large.

At first glance, these two types of literature seem to belong to different spheres of interest. On the one hand, the bestiaries were scientific works designed to explain the nature of animals and what that revealed about the Creation. On the other hand, fables were often amusing tracts in which the nature of animals was ignored and animals were shown acting like people in order to teach moral lessons to humans. What these works have in common, however, is that in both the actual animals were secondary to the main purpose of teaching humans a lesson. Medieval compilers recognized this relationship to the degree that the two kinds of literary expressions influenced each other. Classical fable stories of the beaver that castrates itself, or the bisexual hyena, or the dog reaching for the reflection of cheese in the water entered bestiaries as expressions of "scientific" characteristics of these animals.[51] The degree of the integration may be seen in Italian bestiaries of the fourteenth century. One manuscript has 61 bestiary chapters followed by 16 animal fables. Another has 57 animals followed by 15 fables, and a third, 46 animals followed by 11 fables.[52] This kind of integration suggests strongly that any separation of genre into scientific versus literary is more likely to be a twentieth-century construct than any medieval distinction.

Fable literature and bestiaries also influenced each other in a more general way. By the thirteenth century, the profound allegory of *Physiologus* had given way to a more specific "moralizing tendency."[53] Instead of revealing the highest truths, bestiaries began to focus more on telling people how to behave (as the fables had done). Guillaume de Clerc, an early thirteenth-century author of a bestiary, included the statement that readers should "profit from the moral lesson" expounded in his bestiary.[54] This used to be the goal of fables. After the twelfth century, the fabulists began to move from strictly social commentary to more elaborate allegory in their stories.[55] When authors focused on the overarching function of these types of literature (to instruct human behavior), the lines between the two forms all but disappear. So much so that a French fabulist of the thirteenth century referred to his fables as a "bestiary."[56] I agree with this assessment. By the twelfth century, a new form of literary expression had been created that treated animals as human exemplars. This new form that grew from both the classical bestiary and the classical fable presented people and animals as more similar than other bodies of Christian thought had acknowledged, and this new way of looking at animals spread from the monasteries to the broader society.

One of the most important figures in the spread of the fable to courtly society was Marie de France. We do not know much about this twelfth-century literary figure who identified herself in her works by giving the barest information: "Marie is my name and I am of France." Her writings reveal her to be well educated in the classics (including classical fables). She probably lived in Norman England, and her works were likely read in the English court of Henry II and his educated and cultured wife, Eleanor of Aquitaine. Marie is known for three works, the *Lais* (short romances), the *Purgatory of St. Patrick* (a religious adventure), and most popular, the *Fables* (written between 1155 and 1189). Marie's collection of fables contains 103 verse fables with morals written at the end of each. Many of the fables are derived from a medieval collection of Phaedrus's fables. The rest seem to be derived from a number of literary and folk traditions.[57]

This collection was influential in bringing fable literature out from behind monastery walls into the wider society. Marie wrote her fable verses in French, when all the other collections were in Latin, looking backward to their classical roots. The popularity of this French collection is clearly evident from the number of manuscripts that have survived. More Middle Ages manuscripts of fables have survived from Marie than from any other author.[58] Marie's genius lay not only in her brisk verse style that made stories preserved largely for rhetorical excercises into vehicles for courtly entertainment, but she transformed the fables themselves into stories that belonged to twelfth century society rather than the classical world that had originally produced them.

Consistent with the strong sense of individualism in Greek society, classical fables had morals directed to the ethical conduct of individuals. Because of medieval preoccupations with classes over individuals, Marie changed the fables to make them comment on society, not on individuals. In a classical fable, a weak animal represented a weak person; for Marie, a weak animal represented powerless groups—peasants or servants. Phaedrus had a strong animal represent a strong person; Marie converted such an animal into a strong social class—the nobility or the rich.[59] In addition, and more subtly, Marie changed the moral of the tales. These are no longer products to be associated with a semibestial slave who was outside society and thus could be critical of it. Marie's fables were of and for the court, for people in power who were strongly committed to maintaining the social hierarchy that placed them in power. Marie's fables are socially conservative.

In Marie's world of fables, society is ruled by those born to do so. Lions and eagles are appropriate rulers because they are the strongest and most "noble" of the animals. In the fable of an evil king, problems arise when the proper king, the lion, has no heir, and though "The beasts requested, every one / That he provide another lion," the wolf becomes king, bringing troubles to the animal kingdom. In the classical version of this fable, the evil king is also a lion, but Marie changed it to show that those not "naturally" destined to rule are those that cause trouble.[60] The birds, too, are led into trouble when they follow other than the eagle, who is the rightful ruler. The eagle has all the qualities Marie saw in a rightful king:

> The eagle's grand and glorious,
> And he's especially valorous,
> And very staid and dignified.[61]

Marie believed that some were destined to rule, but she consistently reminded them they were to rule justly:

> A prince should be well-rested too;
> In his delights not overdo;
> Nor shame himself or his domain,
> Nor cause the poor folk undue pain.[62]

Beneath the rulers, the rich should govern society, but they too should govern with compassion for the poor. The fable of the lion who frees a mouse he had caught and in return is freed from ropes by the same mouse caused Marie to conclude:

> And so this model serves to show
> A lesson wealthy men should know
> Who over poor folks have much power.
> If these should wrong them, unaware,
> The rich should show them charity.[63]

Marie wrote that the spirit of noblesse oblige should guide those who govern, and she reinforced this lesson by indicating that the ruled would eventually take vengeance on an unjust ruler.[64] This moral, however, seems not a cry for social revolution, but a reminder to rulers not to abuse their power.

On their part, the ruled should be loyal to their proper lords. In the classical moral to the fable of the bat who during the war between animals and birds kept changing sides to try to be with the winner, an individual was warned that "anyone who wants to remain blameless in the eyes of two parties wins the favor of neither."[65] Marie made the moral specific to a feudal society in which loyalty to one's lord was central:

> He should give honour to his lord
> And should be loyal, keep his word.
> And when his master is in need,
> He should join others and bring aid.[66]

In her vision of a stable society, Marie advocated more than loyalty. People should keep their place, both socially and geographically. She repeatedly urged people to be content with their social class. For example, in the fable of the ass who wants to frolic with his master like a lap dog, the classical moral said "The fable shows that all do not have the same natural aptitudes."[67] Marie turned this fable of individual talents into social commentary, concluding:

> Those who to raise themselves aspire
> And who a higher place desire—
> One that's not fitting to their girth
> And most of all, not to their birth.
> The same result will come to pass
> For many, like the beaten ass.[68]

Perhaps even more strongly, Marie uses the fable of the hare who wants to have horns like a deer to comment:

> Folks covetous and miserly:
> They always start such projects as
> They think will raise their social class.
> What they attempt through foolishness
> Turns back on them, injurious.[69]

For Marie, then, people should not aspire above the station into which they were born. But further, they should not even aspire to move about. This monastic ideal of staying in one's space and being content with it permeates Marie's writings. For example, in the classical fable of the rabbits and the frogs, the author says the rabbits, despairing of their own cowardice, were going to commit suicide until they saw that the frogs feared them. The classic moral again was an individual one: "The misfortunes of others serve as consolations for our own troubles."[70] Marie changed the fable to have the rabbits search for a land in which they would feel safe, but seeing the frogs' fear, they decide to stay home. Marie concluded:

> Those folk who wish to move away,
> Abandoning their ancient home—
> They'd best take heed of what could come.
> No kingdom will they ever find
> Anywhere known to humankind
> Where everyone lives free of fear,
> Where toil and sorrow disappear.[71]

These socially conservative lessons would clearly have appealed to the courtly society for which Marie wrote. Furthermore, the audience would certainly have been amused by the many fables Marie told that poke fun at the ignorance of peasants.[72]

Marie's fables, however, are also noteworthy (and enduring) for their compassion for the poor, their appreciation for the domestic. She repeatedly sympathized with poor people who were abused by those in power. She reserved some of her strongest criticism for abuses in the lawcourts in which people used false charges to fleece the poor, as a dog did to a ewe:

> This example serves to tell
> What's true for many men as well:
> By lies and trickery, in short,

> They force the poor to go to court.
> False witnesses they'll often bring
> And pay them with the poor folks' things.[73]

Marie's repeated call for judicial reform likely appealed to her presumed patron, Henry II, a vigorous champion of legal reform in England.

Her compassion for those out of power also extended to an awareness of women's concerns. In the classical fable of the frog and mouse who are tied together, both the frog and the drowned mouse are eaten by a predatory bird. Marie changed the tale to make the mouse female and sympathetic and also changed the ending to save the mouse, leaving only the villainous frog to be devoured.[74] In her fable of a she-bear raped by a fox, she shows a remarkable (and generally unmedieval) sympathy for the female.[75] Finally, her concern for women is shown in the fable of the sow and the wolf in which a wolf wishes to attend the birth of the piglets and the sow wisely refuses. The classical fable offers the general moral, "You must make trial of a man before entrusting yourself to him," but Marie used the story to urge women to keep away from men during childbirth:

> All women suffer degradation
> If male hands should dare to touch
> At such a time, or even approach![76]

Thus, the world Marie envisioned was one of a static, well-ordered, hierarchic society. In this society, those of noble birth ruled, but their rule was to be a benign one, marked by integrity and compassion for the poor and the powerless in their charge. Subjects in this society were to be loyal and enduring, content with their lot and their place, and not aspiring to change. All would trust in God,[77] and the social order would be secure. When Marie used fables as a mechanism of social criticism, it was to criticize deviations from this order. She reprimanded nobility who abused their power, wealthy who were greedy and uncharitable, poor who were stupid or dissatisfied. Perhaps Marie's greatest accomplishment was to preserve the power of fables to use animals to criticize human behavior, yet this metaphoric tool was brought to the service of the established social order. In this form, fables were reintroduced into medieval society at large. The later medieval fabulists followed Marie's example, and fables became a popular new literary form.

At about the same time Marie introduced fables to the court, another form of animal parable was growing in popularity. Beast poems had been written in Latin for courts and especially monasteries from the eighth century. Since they were written in Latin, they were likely to have been written in monasteries by creative people who drew from fable tradition to shape a new form of exemplar literature. Jan Ziolkowski has made a complete study of these beast poems, and his careful work is not likely to be soon supplanted. Building on this beast poem tradition, a long epic was composed in about the eleventh century that had an animal as a protagonist.[78] This was *Ecbasis* (*Escape of a Captive*), in which a calf who has been captured by a wolf is saved by a group of animals, including a dog, a fox, and a bull. This tale is perhaps closest to the tradition of bestiaries in that it is a long allegory of the author's (the calf's) salvation from the hands of the devil (the wolf).[79] This poem offers a beginning of a model of beast epic that is only fully developed a century or more later.

In the middle of the twelfth century, two more Latin beast epics were composed, showing the increasing popularity of this form in monastic communities. One was the *Mirror of Fools*, written by Nigellus Wireker in England. This epic is a monastic satire whose hero is an ass, and it was written, according to Nigellus, so people "may learn to censure in themselves those things which they find reprehensible in others."[80] His satire was directed against those in religious orders who were hypocritical or dissastified.[81] Another epic, written in the Low Countries in the mid–twelfth century, was called *Ysengrimus*. It concerned a wolf named Ysengrimus and his ongoing rivalry with a fox named Reinardus.[82] By the late twelfth century, beast epics joined fables and bestiaries as another literary form that drew humans and animals together in people's minds by having animals act like humans.

Ysengrimus was an influential epic because it introduced the characters that would be featured in the most famous medieval beast epic, the *Romance of Reynard the Fox*. *Reynard* was written in vernacular languages rather than Latin, so it could reach a wider audience than the Latin beast epics had done. Between 1174 and 1250 the twenty-eight versions (or "branches") of the *Romance of Reynard the Fox* were written in France.[83] The authors of *Reynard* accomplished for the beast epic what Marie had done for fables: They took a form that had belonged to monasteries and brought it to court. This permitted the popularizing not only of the beast epic as a style, but of these animals in particular. Their popularity may even be seen in the language, for *reynard*, the proper name of the fox in the epic, becomes the generic French word for fox, replacing the older word, *goupil*. Various versions of this tale spread widely and variations were made in the popular story until the end of the fifteenth century.[84] The popularity and influence of this epic makes it worth our close attention.

The setting for the story of *Reynard the Fox* is the court of King Noble the Lion, where the lion presides over all the animals. The court is conducted with concern for all the niceties of medieval court life, including the concern for justice. The story opens with animals complaining to the king about wrongs they have suffered at the hands of Reynard. Isegrim the wolf, Curtois the hound, Tibert the cat, and Chanticleer the cock all bring charges against the fox. This provides the framework for Reynard's subsequent escapades, during which he is repeatedly called to task for his crimes and repeatedly by his quick wit saves himself from as many perils as the modern cartoon character, Roadrunner. The work culminates in a trial by combat between Reynard and Isegrim, written with the kind of detail that would surely have delighted the courtly audience. During the battle, the wit of the fox is dramatically contrasted with the power of the wolf. The different versions have variants of the ending, but in all the fox either survives to continue his rivalry with the wolf or emerges victorious, winning honors from King Noble.[85]

While this long narrative is an action-packed story that was designed to entertain courtly society, it has many things in common with the short fables that inspired it. With the opening lines, the poet reminds his audience that these animals are presented to teach humans "good lessons" by which they may learn about the "counsels of Lords and Prelates" and also about "merchants and other common people." People were also to learn about the deceits of the world to avoid "subtle false knaves."[86] Similarly, the poet closes the work by reminding readers to use it "for an example to the people that they may there learn better to use and follow virtue and to eschew sin and vices."[87] The beast epics, then, share with fables the desire to use animals to parody human behavior in order to teach moral lessons.

The story of Reynard also reveals its roots in fable by incorporating some fables directly into the work. The frogs who wanted a king and were awarded a stork appear in *Reynard*, as does a wolf who tried to read something on a horse's hoof and was kicked for his attempt.[88] The fox that appeared in Isidore of Seville's work and subsequently in the bestiaries that played dead with its tongue hanging out in order to catch birds also appears in *Reynard*,[89] showing again how closely connected are these works that use animals as human exemplars.

The poet of *Reynard* also shared Marie's social conservatism. While there are

123

satire, attacks on abuses of clergy, and criticism of human frailty in the poem, there is no critique of the institutions of society.[90] Like Marie, the *Reynard* poets were of the court and wrote for the court. They shared her contempt for lower classes, for example. Reynard says, "I don't count a villein of much worth, I would as soon touch a dirty pot with my hand as I would a villein." [91] In beast epics as in fables, we see animal parody serving the established order.

There are some differences between the beast epics, specifically *Reynard*, and the fables from which they grew. One of the major differences first appeared in the Latin epic *Ysengrimus*. In this work, animals were for the first time given names and personalities, a trend that was brought to its highest development in *Reynard*. This is a further development in anthropomorphism than existed in the fables. In this beast epic, it was not just any sly fox or any vicious wolf that served as a parody of human behavior, but a particular fox and wolf, Reynard and Isegrim. The other animals were also given names and personalities, and with this development one can see that people and animals were drawing closer together, at least in literature.

Another difference between beast epics and fables is that in the former the narrative begins to transcend the morals that had been the main feature of the fables. Despite the *Reynard* poet's claims that there are many lessons to be drawn from the animals' actions in the epic, there is really only one moral: wit may overcome power. In the text, the poet says of the fox: "This was all he studied: how he might put away his sorrow with wiles." In the conclusion, the poet summarizes and warns the reader, "For who that will not use Reynard's craft now is not worth in the world now in any estate that is of might."[92] This praise of wit or intellect is present in Marie's fables. According to Norman Shapiro, Marie's fables are "exemplifications of the use and abuse of the mind...generally of the capacity of the intellectual powers to rule the passions."[93] While Marie praised wit in many of her fables, the *Reynard* poet made it his overriding concern, with the result that the moral lesson was much subordinated to the plot. The real lesson of *Reynard* and the other beast epics, however, is that people began readily to imagine animals acting like people and vice versa.

There is not enough space here to follow the fortunes of fables and beast epics as they were retold after the twelfth century. The only other fable writer that I want to discuss is Odo of Cheriton. Odo, like Marie, used fables to offer messages of human behavior to preserve the medieval social order. While Marie brought fables to the attention and support of courtly society, however, Odo brought fables to the service of the church. Odo was born in about 1185 in

England, studied theology in Paris, and in the early thirteenth century, wrote many fables and stories for use by the clerical and monastic communities with which he had close ties.[94]

Like Marie's, Odo's stories were designed to give moral lessons, and these lessons were drawn from animals behaving as humans. Unlike Marie, Odo often used fables to draw morals for monks and clergy to tell them how to behave appropriately. In his hands, animals acted like ecclesiastics. A cat tonsured itself and dressed as a monk to catch a mouse. A wolf found it impossible to change his nature enough to enter a monastery, a cock became the unfortunate confessor to a hungry and not very repentent fox.[95]

Odo's ecclesiastical interest may also be seen in the ways he transformed familiar fables. The town and country mice became for Odo usurious churchmen living in luxury and not content with sufficiency. The frog and mouse tied together to their peril when a bird of prey came along became an evil churchman and his parishioner when the devil came and took both.[96] (As you see, Odo did not save the mouse at the last moment as Marie had done. That would have reduced the power of his religious message.)

As these two examples show, Odo began to move the fable morals to larger Christian morals. This is perfectly consistent with his ecclesiastical inclinations, but it is also consistent with and probably derivitive from Odo's familiarity with the allegory of bestiaries. Since bestiaries had been part of monastic culture for a long time and they were used there for people to take specifically Christian messages from animal tales, it is not surprising that Odo combined the two forms of exemplar literature, bestiary and fable, to offer his listeners strongly Christian morals. Odo included many more bestiary passages in his work than Marie had done; for example, a unicorn (a bestiary, not a fable animal) appears in one of Odo's stories.[97] His familiarity with the bestiary allegory caused Odo's morals to become more elaborate, more consistent with preaching than with simple storytelling.[98] The story of a stork fighting a serpent became in Odo's hands both an allegory of Adam's failure to defeat the first serpent and a call for people to fight evil in their day.[99] Finally, Odo incorporated material from the story of Reynard the Fox into his fables, completing a circle in which fables influenced beast epic and now were influenced in return.

Odo inspired many subsequent fabulists, and perhaps more importantly, preachers. The Franciscan Nicole Bozon in the thirteenth century and the Benedictine John of Sheppey in the fourteenth century were only two of many who drew the inspiration for their fables from Odo of Cheriton. Just as important as these preachers whose names we know were many anonymous preach-ers who used animal tales in their sermons to stimulate moral improvement.

Marie and the *Reynard* poet brought animals to court and showed how ani-mal behavior could offer examples to humans. Odo pointed the way to bring the same lesson to people in cities and countryside. As preachers went out armed with stories using animals as metaphors, it is very likely that the same metaphors began to change people's views of themselves. Certainly by the thirteenth century the use of animals as human exemplars in both fables and bestiaries had moved from monastic tracts to all parts of society, and the main vehicle for that movement was the preacher's *exemplum*.

In the twelfth century, churchmen increasingly believed that saving the souls in their charge required more than presiding over the sacraments. People need-ed sermons to educate them and lead them to a proper life. In the early Middle Ages, sermons had been an almost insignificant part of the life of the church; sermons in a Visigothic collection are about two to three minutes long.[100] In the twelfth century, a new kind of preaching developed,[101] and part of this popular new kind of preaching was the introduction of short narratives. During that century, Bernard of Clairveaux recommended that proverbs be used in ser-mons to "stimulate the mind of the listener."[102] It is likely that Bernard had in mind miracle stories and examples from saints' lives as the proverbs that could usefully be included in sermons. These were the kinds of examples that were found in collections from before the twelfth century.[103] But by the thirteenth century, churchmen increasingly used examples drawn from fables, *Bestiaries*, and beast epics to illustrate their sermons. It was customary for a preacher to conclude his sermon by reciting from one to five moralized exempla.[104]

Collections of appropriate stories (arranged alphabetically) that could be used to yield moral lessons to the faithful were compiled in the thirteenth century. In these collections of exempla, we can see the growing popularity of animals as human exemplars. Five main kinds of stories were included in the exempla collections: (1) stories of good and bad churchmen (these were by far the most numerous in most of the collections), (2) Biblical narratives, (3) historical incidents (including examples from saints' lives), (4) fables (both classical and original), and (5) *Bestiary* passages.[105] This list shows that animal tales were in very good company indeed in the exempla, and in this form they gained cred-ibility and spread widely.

Widespread use of exempla in thirteenth-century sermons was linked to the growth of the orders of preaching friars—the Dominicans and Franciscans. The foundations of both included a charge to preach to the faithful. The Dominicans were the most important in collecting compendia of exempla for other preachers to use,[106] but Franciscans like Nicole Bozon also collected such stories. Bozon's collection includes 37 fables, and they show that he drew from Marie's influential poetry.[107]

In the same way that Bozon brought Marie's fables to the people through his exempla, many of the classical fables and *Bestiary* stories became part of people's experience and of their mental makeup. Through a study of the exempla collections, it is possible to suggest which fables were most popular and therefore most likely used in the sermons. There are a total of 311 fables used in medieval exempla with varying frequencies. The most popular appeared 27 times, but some appeared only once.[108] The most popular classical fable was that of Androcles and the grateful lion, followed by the fable of the fox who appeals to a raven's vanity and thus persuades it to drop a piece of cheese. Equally popular were the fables of the frog and mouse tied together, as well as the fable of the ungrateful serpent that bites a man who saved its life. Bestiary material was also popular; the story of the ape mother with twins who accidently loses her favorite was as popular as the Androcles fable.[109] The most numerous of the classical fables were those that dealt with "foolish pride and arrogance and the assumption of equality between non-equals."[110] The popularity of these shows a continuation of the pattern established by Marie and Odo. Fables were brought into the service of a socially conservative society. The most popular stories were those that urged people to keep their place. While these were the favorites, the collections nevertheless preserved practically all the fables that were circulating in the monastic and courtly collections. (There were 311 fables included; Marie had only 103 in her collection.)

It is impossible to overestimate the influence of these exempla. The collections were widely used all over Europe,[111] and the number of preachers using them as reference tools was very high. The exempla also directly influenced the proliferation of illustrations in the margins of thirteenth and fourteenth century manuscripts by contributing subject matter and indeed the idea of marginalia. After all, the exempla added on to the sermons were "marginal" to the main text, just as were the illustrations in the borders of Gothic manuscripts.[112]

Anything that is so popular, particularly anything popular that is new, is bound to generate criticism, and the use of fables in sermons was no exception. The Council of Salzburg in 1386 condemned the friars' practice: "These false prophets [friars] by their sermons full of fables often lead astray the souls of their hearers."[113] Such criticism had little effect, and the exempla remained a popular part of sermons until the end of the Middle Ages. Fables, beast epics, and bestiary lore had been reclaimed from the classical past and had become central to medieval culture.

The Animals

The critics of the exempla were right on at least one point. The stories were significant in spreading a new vision of animals and humans, and this vision marked a radical departure from the early medieval patristic view. Medievalists see in the twelfth century a revolution in thought called the "twelfth-century renaissance" as a way to point out the significant growth in new directions of human intellectual development. This chapter shows that the twelfth century also marked a turning point in people's view of the relationship between themselves and their animals. Early Christians established a view of the world that posited a chasm of difference between humans and animals; the use of animals as human exemplars suggested, however, that the two species were sufficiently similar that animals could be imagined to act like people, to possess personalities like people, and thus to offer models for human behavior. Of course, it is impossible to draw a direct cause and effect relationship between these developments. Did the widespread use of animals as exemplars cause a shift in the way people looked at themselves and their animals, or had the change already occurred and was the popularity of fable-type stories only one expression of the change? The truth is probably in a combination of the two trends, each building and reinforcing the other, although I do give significant weight to the ability of metaphors to change people's perceptions.

By the thirteenth century, the metaphor of animals acting as human exemplars was accepted and popularized, and it joined the other functions animals served for medieval people. The graph "Animal Functions in Illuminated Manuscripts" (Figure 3) gives one indication of these various uses of animals. I created this graph based on counting the appearances of animals in illuminations in over 6,000 illuminated manuscripts in the Hill Monastic Library collection.[114] As you can see, the functions of animals as labor and food continued to dominate the medieval imagination. Portrayals of animals as human parody (which is essentially what the fables did) appear late, and although the graph does not indicate it, most of the human parody portrayals appeared in the margins of the manuscripts, not in the featured illustrations. Additionally, one can see in the graph the appearance and sudden popularity of the portrayal of human/animal hybrids (again mostly in the margins). I will discuss this further in the next chapter, but here we can see yet another indication of the blurring of the lines between humans and animals in the medieval imagination after the twelfth century.

Fig. 3

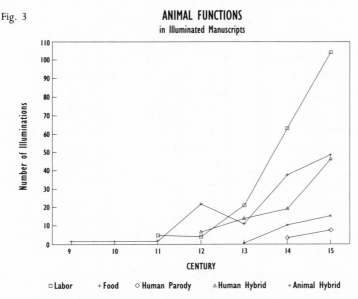

ANIMAL FUNCTIONS
in Illuminated Manuscripts

As human exemplars, animals become metaphors, and metaphors of the worst and best that is within humans. As we look more closely at the animals that appear in the exemplar literature, we see that we are increasingly examining not animals, but humans.

When Marie of France modified the classic fables to suit the courtly audience, she selected those animals that she could use to mirror the medieval society to which she belonged, the society that she wanted to perpetuate. Most of her animals fall clearly into three categories: predators (the ruling classes), prey (commoners as victims), and domestic animals (also commoners and treated as mostly supporting characters). As we have seen, for Babrius and the other classical fabulists an animal was not portrayed for its stock set of characteristics; for Marie and the other medieval fabulists, however, the animals exhibited stock characteristics that offered an image of society.

The metaphoric society of the medieval fabulists was ruled by the noble lion, a popular figure in all the exemplar literature. He appears in the earliest fables; he is the lead animal in *Physiologus* (see Figure 1) and retains that posi-

tion in the subsequent bestiaries. This is a curious animal to keep such prominence, because for most of the regions we are discussing, the lion was not
native. There were probably lions in Greece as late as 300 B.C.,[115] and the
North African authors (from *Physiologus* to Augustine) could have seen lions in
the wild. In other areas, however, lions were more abstract, biblical, subject
to interpretation. Until the twelfth century when all the fable animals began to
be treated as stock characters, lions were portrayed in a variety of ways. The
early church fathers recognized lions' fierce nature. Ambrose said the lion was
marked by "ungovernable anger and unbridled rage," and Augustine called the
devil a lion because of his ferocity.[116] Most often in Babrius, lions were shown
as hunters or hunted, only occasionally as kings. Thus, for Babrius as in reality,
lions could be both predator and prey. This ambiguous role did not suit Marie's
vision of society, for her (and the subsequent fabulists), the lion was always the
king. Not only was he king, but he was almost always portrayed as a just,
noble king, sometimes an aging king, but usually sympathetic. (As I noted
above, when Marie needed an evil king for her fable, she changed the lion in
the classic fable to a wolf, thus preserving the social order, which saw lions as
just and proper kings.) Marie's portrayal had little to do with lions and everything to do with her ideal of kings. They were noble, just, above the fray, and
perhaps, like lions, somewhat distant and unknowable.

The noble king was above most of the turmoil in the fabulists' society, but
other predators (noble animals too) caused the injustice in society. These
vicious animals were wolves, and the medieval fabulists from Marie onward
focused on this creature. He was shown as an evil, greedy, gluttonous, murderous thief. The heart of the problem with the wolf was greed. He was dissatisfied with his lot in society and wanted more. This is what caused disruption
in the social order. In medieval society, it was noble to be a predator. After
all, war—the predatory occupation—was the privilege of the noble class; it
was their reason for existence. That class favored their hunting animals over all
others, and on a symbolic level they placed the lion, the master predator, above
all others.

Courtly fables turned the wolf into the villain not because he was a predator, but because he was excessively greedy. In fables, wolves become a
metaphor for nobility gone astray. The fable of the preacher and the wolf
shows how appetite dominated the character of the fable wolf. In this tale, a
preacher attempts to teach the wolf the alphabet (perhaps to try to improve his
character). The wolf concentrates long enough to get to the letter C, but when

he is asked what that might spell, he answers "lamb," revealing that his mind has not been raised from his stomach.[117] Such greed threatened the hierarchy that placed nobility on top, and that threat was what the fabulists criticized in their portrayal of men acting as wolves. They did not advocate violating a social order in which noble predators ruled, but they tried to insist on moderation, which after all would be the only way to preserve such a social order.

The next most popular animal in all the exemplar literature was the fox. The fox as a predator represented someone of high social status, although not as powerful as lions or wolves. Foxes in fact and fable were known for their cunning. When they were hunted, foxes could outwit many dogs, and this reputation entered the exemplar lore from bestiaries to fables to beast epics, making foxes symbolize wit and trickery. With this emphasis on the fox's wit, the animal quickly came to represent those in society who lived by their intellect, frequently the clergy or courtly counsellors. Like wolves, foxes were not necessarily evil. As in the Reynard stories, the fox living by his wits was a sympathetic figure. Of course, since many of these stories were produced in monasteries by people living by their intellect, they recreated themselves in the foxes of their tales.

A society with rulers who were strong and counselors who were wise was not complete. The tales, as society itself, were populated with the meek, the poor, the victims. The proportion of the rich to the poor in the exemplar literature never matched real society. The storytellers were always much more interested in the doings of the powerful. The victims or domestic animals were there to provide opportunity for the powerful to exert their power. Chanticleer the Cock existed for Reynard to exploit; lambs existed for Isegrim to eat. Within this category of animals that includes everything from lambs to hares to asses to dogs, there are no fully sympathetic animals. Even in the fables of Marie, which show a great deal of sympathy for the powerless, none are particularly admirable creatures. Many like the ass are stupid, especially when they aspire to a higher estate than their birth. Many of the fables of people that circulated with the collections of animal fables deal with lower classes and mirror the image of the powerless animals. Just as Marie told the story of a foolishly upward-aspiring ass, she told of a peasant who was not content with one horse, but prayed for two and lost the one he had. Marie concluded unsympathetically: "Nobody ought to pray, therefore / To have more than his needs call for."[118] Marie told another tale in which a peasant has an inflated sense of his own importance. He has abdominal pains because of a beetle that has crawled up his anus, and is convinced that he is going to give birth to an important child. Marie warned:

> This example serves to say
> The ignorant are oft this way;
> Believing that which cannot be,
> They're swayed and changed by vanity.[119]

In this case, the peasant was as deluded as the flea in another of Marie's fables that presumed to think it disturbed the camel on which it rode.[120] Thus, even though Marie is best known among the fabulists for her compassion for the poor, it nevertheless was a compassion that assumed a static social order with an obedient lower class. Her stories certainly mirrored society.

One particularly striking example of the degree to which the fabulists held the lower classes in disdain may be seen in their usual treatment of lambs. From the earliest Christian years, lambs were heavily laden with symbolism. Christ was both the lamb of God and the good shepherd gathering the faithful into the flock. The lamb remained the symbol for the best in self-sacrifice in the Christian tradition. St. Francis (always sympathetic to all animals) was particularly fond of lambs because as his biographer, St. Bonaventure, wrote, lambs "present a natural reflection of Christ's merciful gentleness and represent him in Scriptural symbolism."[121] For St. Francis, the symbolic quality of lambs led him to be kind to individual real lambs. This represents a logical application of Christian symbolism. Medieval people, however, seldom bothered to follow the logical consequences of their metaphors, and in a literature that makes a wolf a hero of sorts, a lamb was a natural victim.

Lambs (and the poor) were "fleeced" by unscrupulous wolves:

> The wolf then grabbed the lamb so small,
> Chomped through his neck, extinguished all.
> ....
> They [rich people] strip them [the poor] clean of flesh and skin,
> As the wolf did to the lambkin.[122]

However, if innocent lambs were somewhat an object for sympathy, they were not admired. Sheep (and lambs) were considered stupid and cowardly, almost deserving whatever they received.[123]

If even the most sympathetic of the nonpredators was portrayed in a way that only the most pious or self-effacing would want to emulate, other domestic animals had no chance to be shown in any but a negative light. Dogs, the faithful servants (and the key word here is servant), were loyal. The entry for dogs in the *Bestiary* includes a series of anecdotes that demonstrate dogs' loyalty to their masters, and in one of Marie's fables a dog refuses to accept a bribe from a thief to relax his vigilance in guarding sheep.[124] This loyalty is shown in only one of Marie's fables. In the rest, dogs are shown as greedy, litigious, and garrulous. One of the most repeated medieval fables (included in both Marie's collection and in the *Bestiary*) was that of the dog who loses the cheese he is carrying by reaching for his reflection in the water, and dogs' were vilified for the greed that drove them to return to their own vomit (a characteristic that preoccupied medieval commentators).[125] Early medieval thinkers consistently attributed disagreeable characteristics to man's best friend. Tertullian wrote that dogs were impure, and Boethius said they were restless and always barking.[126] Thus, in medieval metaphoric ranking, dogs had lost the high status accorded them for being carnivores because they were also servants. In the medieval social order that became the model for the animal world, dogs were placed in a lower social class than the free predators.

These anecdotal examples suggest that by the twelfth century, animal exemplar stories were increasingly about human society, and a study of the total numbers of animals used in various collections bears this out. The graph "Frequency of Animals in Fable Collections" shown in Figure 4 compares the animals used most frequently in three fable collections: the classical fables of Babrius and the medieval fables of the courtly Marie de France and the cleric, Odo of Cheritan. In Babrius's fables, the "lower class" animals—ox, dog, and ass—are represented with almost as much frequency as the noble predators. With Marie this changes dramatically in favor of the courtly noble animals. Odo continued Marie's preference for the nobility, but he perhaps reveals his clerical bias by being less interested in tales of the regal lion than was Marie.

Even though *Bestiaries* purposely intended to be more inclusive than fables, they paralleled the tendency of medieval compilers to prefer wild predators. The original *Physiologus* included no domestic animals, perhaps because the author believed that wild animals, by being closer to nature could more easily reveal the Creator's plan. The fullest bestiary in the thirteenth century still preferred wild animals to tame 36 to 21. In this case, the motivation was also probably to reflect the ruling society's interest in itself and in the animals it thought most readily mirrored the ruling groups.

The animals depicted in the exemplar literature were initially used to teach

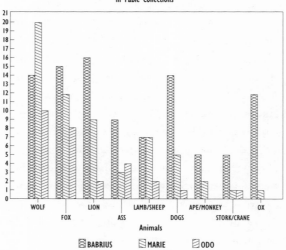

Fig. 4

FREQUENCY OF ANIMALS
in Fable Collections

BABRIUS   MARIE   ODO

lessons to humans. This had been the explicit intention, for example, as far back as the *Hexaemeron* of Basil, which had attempted to stay close to the reality of animal behavior to give lessons to people. By the twelfth century, however, such literature was really written about human society and behavior, and simply used animal bodies to express that behavior. There is nothing animal-like about their behavior; it is purely human. One can see the logical result of the popularity of literature that showed animals as human exemplars. The separation between animals and humans seemed to be lost even as contemporary influential thinkers like Thomas Aquinas were asserting the absolute difference between the species.

One can see the blurring of the lines between humans and animals in the exemplar materials from the thirteenth into the fourteenth centuries. The graph "Late Medieval Animals" in Figure 5 shows the frequency of animals mentioned in the Exempla collections. These figures were drawn from lists of 5400 exempla found in the 37 central collections.[127] While this list continues to show the influence of the important fables in the frequency of the portrayals of wolves, foxes, and lions, some new trends nevertheless begin to appear. The frequency of toads and serpents is due to their use as symbols of death and the devil in ecclesiastical warnings. Notice, however, the ape that appears 46 times. Apes were hardly mentioned in fable literature, but as people became more interested in (and more familiar with) seeing humans as animals, apes as the closest in appearance to humans were shown more often. Dogs, too, increase because they were also seen as being similar to people, albeit servants. Finally this interest in creatures existing on the borders between human and animal may be seen in new creatures added to the bestiary collections in the twelfth century. The original *Physiologus* had only one monkey as the closest human creature. *Bestiaries* added the Satyr, Sphinx, Cynocephalus (a dog-headed human), and other semihuman mythological creatures.

Fig. 5

LATE MEDIEVAL ANIMALS

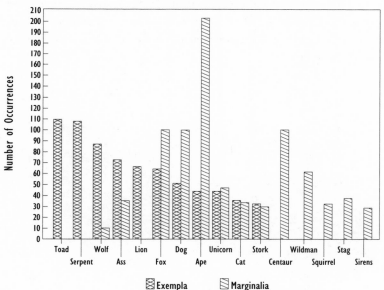

The animals portrayed in the margins of Gothic manuscripts from the thirteenth through the fifteenth centuries also show a greater tendency toward portraying animals as humans. As you can also see in the graph in Figure 5, of the five most popular animals, three were directly associated with humans. Apes, centaurs, and wild people (half human/half animal) are unambiguous examples of the portrayal of a blend of human and animal. The other two most popular animals, dogs and foxes, were also heavily associated with people, the first for its long association with humans and the second from the popular beast epic of Reynard the Fox.

All this evidence demonstrates that if medieval animals could be shown as humans, then the reverse of the metaphor was not far away. People could take the place of animals. The medieval fable collections as a whole mirrored the social order, but increasingly on an individual level people began to wonder about the animal potential within the individual. In some instances, humans replaced animals in fables. Caesarius of Heisterbach in the thirteenth century told a story that was clearly drawn from one of the fables. He related how a (particularly human-acting) wolf grabbed a young woman by the arm and dragged her to another wolf who had a bone caught in his throat. The woman removed the bone and was led back to her home.[128] In Caesarius's version the traditional crane that removed the bone had been replaced by a woman; the species have become interchangeable, at times indistinguishable. As the lines between humans and animals blur in literature and in medieval people's imaginations, we can look at the perceptions of humans as animals, to the beast within each person.

5

Humans as Animals

AS PEOPLE BEGAN TO GET USED TO
the metaphor of animals acting as human exemplars in fable and bestiary literature, it was a small intellectual step to accepting the notion of half-human
creatures or of shape-shifting between species, whether animal to animal or
even humans to animal. In a world where such changes seemed possible, it was
harder to preserve the original Christian construct of qualitative separation
between humans and animals.

Humans are uncomfortable with ambiguity. The way we use language
(which of course reflects the way we think) shows that we define things as
much in terms of what they are not as what they are. This animal is a horse,
not a pig. Such clear categories order our environments and our lives. Edmund
Leach has written an illuminating article in which he considers human discomfort with ambiguous categories. He shows that ambiguous, marginal things that
fall between two separate, distinct categories are always considered supernatural and taboo.[1] For this reason, sex, for example, is infused with taboos and
special significance because through sexual intercourse, the clear boundaries

between individuals are lost. Other category violations bother us to varying degrees. We might find a squirrel or chipmunk appealing to watch outdoors, yet if the same animal enters our house, violating the boundaries between wild and domestic, we are distressed. But simultaneously, the human mind seems compelled to cling to, to force itself to fixate on these ambiguities. In the late Middle Ages, we can see an increasing preoccupation with ambiguous creatures.

When early Christian thinkers established what they believed to be clear categories that separated animals from humans, they were not only making a theological statement of humanity's dominance over the natural world, but they were actually defining what it meant to be human. And as in so many things, it was easier to define humans by what they were not—animals—than by what they were. This definition of humans as definitively not animals lasted for centuries (from about the fifth through the eleventh). However, as I discussed in the last chapter, in the twelfth century things began to change. The increasing popularity of the metaphoric linking of humans and animals seems to have opened the possibility for redefining humanity in a way that eliminated the categoric separation of the species. If humans and animals could share the same characteristics in people's imagination (as they did in fables and related literature), then it seems that people were more prepared to see comparable blurring of the lines in life. This is not to say that in the Middle Ages people were ever comfortable seeing humans as animals. The taboos that were established to protect the boundaries between humans and animals remained in place enough to cause at least discomfort with creatures that existed on the imagined borders between species. Yet, not surprisingly, these creatures exerted all the fascination for people that usually accompanies the forbidden, the taboo.

The first part of this chapter looks at the animals (and humans) that existed on the borders between humans and animals. Such creatures became increasingly popular and increasingly feared in the Middle Ages from the twelfth century onward into the Renaissance, revealing an increased movement away from the early church's position of separation toward the modern position that categorically states that people *are* animals. This preoccupation is another indication of the slow but steady blurring of the lines that separated people from animals.

Creatures on the Borders

Just as they were uncomfortable with animals that approached the borders of humanity, medieval people (just as ourselves) were concerned with animals that violated clear categories of differences. One example of such a borderline animal is the bat. Bats were considered properly neither bird nor beast, and the suspicion that came with this status can perhaps be seen most clearly in the fables about bats.

In one Aesopian fable, a bat saves itself from two different weasels. The first weasel is looking for a bird to eat, the second a mouse. The bat explains it is a mouse to the first and a bird to the second, thus escaping from both.[2] This fable plays with the borderline status of bats but does not show the discomfort that is emphasized in the medieval fables. The most popular bat fable in the Middle Ages describes the war between birds and beasts, with the bat repeatedly changing sides to try to stay with the winner. Marie of France strongly objected to this behavior, calling it treasonous,[3] but it was not just the behavior that was treasonous, but the bat's very existence on the borders between beasts and birds. The classical world was much more comfortable with interspecies ambiguity than was the medieval world, which wanted each thing in its place.

An indication of people's growing preoccupation with the blurring of categories is the increasing appearance of hybrid animals in the late Middle Ages. Aristotle, the great medieval authority on almost everything, denied the possibility of hybridization of animals not closely related, arguing quite practically that the differing gestation periods would preclude a successful hybridization. He concluded, "It is impossible for a monstrosity of this type to be formed."[4] But even the authority of Aristotle was not enough to prevent an upsurge in the appearance of these creatures in art and literature. The "Animal Functions" graph in Figure 3 of Chapter 4 shows the appearance of hybrid animals in illuminations in the thirteenth century and the increase of these creatures through the fifteenth century. Many of these illustrations show the *Bestiary* griffin, with the body of a lion and the wings of an eagle, and others show less popular *Bestiary* animals like the leucrota, which has the "haunches of a stag, the breast and shins of a lion, the head of a horse," and the Parandrus, with the head of a stag and a coat like a bear. The yale, a *Bestiary* animal hybrid with the tail of an elephant and the jowls of a boar, entered society's mainstream and became a popular heraldry animal.[5]

These popular exotic creatures were products of imaginations that began to envision a world in which categories were not so clearly defined. We may contrast this late medieval view of hybrids with that of Isidore of Seville in his *Etymologies*, which were written in the seventh century and influenced strongly by the early medieval mindset. Although in his work Isidore mentions many of the fantastic creatures of classical literature, his direct description of hybrids comes from the barnyard, not the imagination. He defines hybrids as animals born from two different species, such as mules, hinnies (a cross between horse and burro), hybrids of boars and pigs, or of sheep and male goats, or of female goats and rams.[6]

These animals were not particularly threatening to the categorization imperative because they were created by and for humans as part of their dominance over nature. Furthermore, these hybrids were between closely related animals, so they were not particularly threatening to medieval understandings of categories. Albert the Great explained these nonthreatening hybrids in scientific terms as he detailed the same sort of list of hybrids as Isidore and explained, "those animals which have similar terms of pregnancy, wombs that are comparable in size and physical forms that are not very different, are able to crossbreed."[7] Yet by the late Middle Ages, people believed in a kind of out-of-control hybridization that created monsters. For example, bestiaries warned of an Ethiopian monster called a crotote, born from the mating of a lioness with a hyena,[8] but such wild hybrids could also appear in places less remote from the European medieval world.

From the twelfth century, animal hybrids begin to flourish in historical and literary sources. In his *Journey Through Wales*, the chronicler Gerald of Wales described a mare who had mated with a stag and produced an offspring with its "front part being like that of a horse and its haunches resembling those of a deer." Even more incredibly, Gerald reported on a "bitch who had a litter by a monkey and produced puppies which were ape-like in front but more like a dog behind." The litter did not last long, for "their deformed and hybrid bodies revolted this country bumpkin" and he killed them.[9] The rural fellow no doubt expressed many medieval people's response to perceived unnatural hybrids.

Such hybrids as monkey/dog are, of course, impossible. Therefore, the significance of such accounts was that by the twelfth century at least some people believed they were possible. With such belief, any animal that seemed out of the ordinary might be perceived to have been the product of an unnatural blurring of the species. As I discussed in Chapter 3, this fear of cross-impregnation contributed to the late medieval strengthening of legislation against bestiality. But even without the extreme case of human/animal crossing, the increase in references to animal hybridization in the late Middle Ages suggests that the clear categories that had ordered the early Christian world were no longer so secure.

Unusual hybrids were reason enough to reflect upon the order in the natural world, but even more confusing and dangerous was the possibility of shape-shifting animals, those that turned from one thing into another. The hyena was despised because people believed that it shifted its gender: "Its nature is that at one moment it is masculine and at another moment feminine, and hence it is a dirty brute."[10] Creatures that could change species seemed even more threatening. The exempla of the late medieval preachers offer warnings of animal shape-shifting. In one, a chicken turns into a snake and "entwines itself permanently around the man's neck" to punish him for stinginess.[11] These exempla also offer warnings revealing the old concern about becoming what one eats, describing horses that absorb the nature of an ass by drinking asses' milk.[12] These examples again give insight into the concern for the blurring of categories in people's minds.

Finally, by the late Middle Ages the most threatening form of animal-to-animal shape-shifting occurred when demons appeared as animals. In the early twelfth century, Guibert of Nogent described a badger "who was actually the devil in the shape of a badger."[13] A century later, Caesarius of Heisterbach warned of demons that appeared as horses, bears, and pigs.[14] Roger of Hovedon in the late twelfth century described a woman possessed by devils, and his tale contains a bewildering sequence of animal shape-shifting that reveals the diabolic presence: "she vomited two black toads, which turned into two huge dogs then into asses."[15]

Jeffrey Burton Russell has discussed the animals whose shape the devil took in the Middle Ages, and the list is so extensive it is easier to say what shape the devil never took. He would never be a lamb because of the association with Christ as the Lamb of God, and he was never an ox because the ox attended the Christ child's birth.[16] (Beyond its associations with Jesus' birth, the ox was probably too mundane an animal, too associated with property, to be linked to diabolical presence.) An important aspect of demons appearing as animals is that in the legends the behavior of these demonic animals was perfectly consistent with behavior of normal animals. It was people's interpretation of the behavior that endowed an animal with supernatural possession.[17] It was the perception of perfectly normal-seeming animals being demons in disguise that was most insidious in people's imaginations.

The concern with demons appearing as animals may be also seen in the "Late Medieval Animals" graph that appears as Figure 5 in Chapter 4. In this chart one may see the sudden and frequent appearance of toads and serpents in the exempla collection. These were the most popular animals for demonic possession, and their prominence in these collections is revealing of late medieval preoccupation.

One could never be sure the late medieval world was what it seemed. Animals could change their shape, demons could appear as animals, and species could blur in hybridization with an instance of misplaced sexual expression. This was not the world as defined by the church fathers. Such ambiguity in the animal kingdom was bad enough, but not surprisingly the blurring of clear categories extended to the human species as well.

The animals that seemed closest to humans were monkeys and apes. The *Bestiary* said that monkeys were named "simia" because "people notice a great similitude to human reason in them."[18] As this descriptive reference indicates, people's interest in apes was largely due to their perceived similarity to humans. Therefore, the popularity of and speculation about apes increased after the twelfth century when people began to reflect upon the possibility of similarity between animals and humans. In his comprehensive study of apes in the Middle Ages, H. Janson has observed that there are no surviving representations of apes in early Christian art and no portrayals of apes parodying human behavior before the twelfth century. After the twelfth century, however, apes were increasingly shown "as the image of man, but a deformed image representing man in a state of degeneracy."[19] The "Late Medieval Animals" graph showing animals in marginalia in Figure 5 of Chapter 4 demonstrates this trend and indicates the sudden dramatic appearance and popularity of apes in late medieval marginal art.

The growing popularity of thinking about apes (and therefore about humans) may also be seen in post-twelfth-century literature. Apes had not been particularly featured in classical fables, nor in the rediscovery of the fables in the early twelfth century (see the graph of "Frequency of Animals in Fable Collections" in Figure 4 of Chapter 4). As new fables were created for the exempla of medieval preachers, however, apes were popular protoganists. Two of the most frequently used of the top six newly developed exempla in the medieval collections concerned apes. For example, the most popular was that of a foolish ape that threw away a nut because of the bitter rind.[20]

Even in the earlier human exemplar literature, however, apes were treated somewhat differently from the other animals. While other animals were portrayed with human qualities and behavior, apes were shown as themselves, pale imitations of humans.[21] Therefore, in the exemplar literature they were disdained as more bestial and thus inferior to other animals that were portrayed as human. For example, in the Reynard epic, when the human-like Reynard meets an ape, he refers to the simian as "a foul beast."[22]

This treatment of apes in the fable literature parallels the disdain shown bats, another borderline animal. Instead of being raised above other beasts because of their perceived similarity to humans, apes and other simians were portrayed as ridiculous. Lacking dignity of their own, they were shown imperfectly imitating their betters, humans. The most popular ape tales show this reputation for simian foolish imitation. In the popular exemplum, an ape tries to imitate the human behavior of eating a nut, but is unable to do so properly since he does not understand the complexity of removing a bitter rind. The bestiary tale of the foolish mother ape who drops her favorite twin is a lesson of imperfect human mother love.

Fable stories of how to catch an ape are even more direct examples of imperfect imitation. An often repeated classical tale said that a hunter who wanted to catch an ape could put on a pair of boots weighted with lead in the presence of a watchful ape. The shrewd hunter would then pretend to leave, abandoning the boots. The curious ape would imitate the hunter's actions and try on the boots. Unable to run in the weighted boots, the ape would be easily caught.[23] This classical tale is entertaining and lacks a malicious tone, but other similar tales with a stronger warning against imitative behavior were even more popular in the Middle Ages. Alexander Neckham in the twelfth century tells about catching an ape by pretending to rub bird-lime in the eyes, which blinds the imitative ape. A prospective hunter had even less work to do in a tale seemingly invented by Alexander. A cobbler, annoyed by an ape, drew the blunt side of a knife across his neck. The foolish imitative ape cut its own throat.[24]

As you see, these tales are not stories of foolish human behavior, but they are tales of foolish ape behavior. And apes were foolish because they were perceived to resemble humans. There seem to be two general morals to be drawn from these stories: 1) Do not try to be something you are not. This reinforces the socially conservative stance of the medieval fables as developed by Marie. 2) Creatures that do not fit clearly into categories are at best foolish, at worst dangerous. Both these morals and the increasing popularity of apes point to the growing concern with ambiguity between humans and animals.

This increasing ambiguity may be seen most clearly in scientific writings of the twelfth and thirteenth centuries. The two most important and original writers on the subject of apes and people were Hildegard of Bingen, the twelfth century abbess, and Albert the Great, the thirteenth-century scholastic. In her medical tract, *Physica*, Hildegard wrote of the ape, "his behavior is neither completely human nor completely animal."[25] Here in a scientific tract, we have the expression of a category somewhere between humans and animals. This idea was developed more fully by Albert the Great. Albert was the first to establish three distinct "species" in the hierarchy of creation: humans, "man-like creatures" (*similitudiens hominis*), and beasts.[26] Albert's establishment of this third category that included apes, Pygmies, and other ambiguous border creatures may have seemed to solve an intellectual problem about the nature of these creatures, but it opened the door for a new paradigm.

These two writers represent a striking turning point in the vision of the relationship between humans and animals. As Janson writes, "Their main significance...lies in the fact that they established a theoretical bridge, however frail, between man and the rest of the animal world, with the ape serving as a kind of pillar in midstream."[27] Of course, this observation of the possibility of a link between humans and animals did not immediately change the early Christian paradigm of the separation of the species. We have seen that Thomas Aquinas, who followed Hildegard and Albert, strongly reaffirmed the unbreachable separation of the species. The history of ideas does not proceed with steady progress, but the twelfth century marked the beginnings of an idea that would ultimately evolve into our present view of ourselves as animals.

Late medieval preoccupation with apes imitating human behavior indicated increasing uncertainty about the essential category of humanity. Even more threatening was the appearance of monsters that further defied clear categorization. The term monster, derived from the Latin word *monstrum*, meaning to show, was used in the classical world to describe births of unusual form, and the significant thing about such births was that they were portents, "showings," signs of God's will.[28] A famous classical example (popular in the Middle Ages) of such a prophetic birth comes from the *Life of Alexander*, in which a child was born with the upper torso of a human and the lower parts of composite beasts. This birth was interpreted to foretell the death of Alexander.[29] Of course, like all omens, it was extremely difficult to determine what one was to make of such a sign, but the ancients were quite certain that monstrous births boded no good. The Roman Laws of the Twelve Tables from 450 B.C. said, "A father shall immediately put to death a son...who is a monster, or has a form different from that of members of the human race."[30]

The early Christian position was more compassionate. Augustine wrote that all births, even if they seemed abnormal, were part of God's inscrutable plan. He stated that people should not criticize the Creator when they saw children born with more than five fingers or toes, or "even if a greater divergence from the norm should appear." Augustine described Siamese twins born "with a double set of upper parts, but a single set of the lower limbs" as such a monstrous birth, monstrous not in the sense of evil, but as showing God's diverse plan.[31] In some texts, the largest problem posed by births of unusual humans was how to baptize them. For example, a fourteenth-century canon lawyer wondered whether a creature born with two heads and one body ought to be baptized as one person or two.[32]

Monstrous births were not always viewed with benign concern for the state of the child's soul, however. Depending on how one looked at the birth, one could see different things in the result. After the twelfth century, as people showed increasing preoccupation with the blurring of lines between species, including humans and animals, an observer could see in a deformed child evidence of the blending of species. Gerald of Wales in the twelfth century described a man who had been born with disfigurements:

> From the joinings of the hand with the arms and the feet with the legs, he had hooves the same as an ox. He had no hair on his head....His eyes were huge and were like those of an ox both in colour, and in being round. His face was flat as far as his mouth. Instead of a nose he had two holes to act as nostrils, but no protuberance. He could not speak at all; he could only low.

If we assume for a moment that Gerald's description was fairly accurate, it would seem that the poor man had as many features different from an ox (flat face, lack of nose) as those that seemed to resemble the animal (large eyes and misshapen hands and feet). Yet Gerald's conclusion (as well as that of the local populace) was that the man was the result of a man's intercourse with a cow, thus the creature was half-animal. Gerald reports on several births of human/cow hybrids.[33] This descriptive trend continued throughout the late Middle Ages, and in the sources one can read of such things as a "man...born with a cow's head,...or the feet of a lion."[34]

Increasingly through the late Middle Ages, people seem to have understood "monstrous" births as revealing a hybridization. This interpretation of such births is another example of the growth of the idea (and fear) of the blurring of the lines between humans and animals. Since people often see that which they fear, it is perhaps not surprising that increasing reports of hybrid births were recorded. Once people accepted the description definition of these "monsters" as half-human and half-animal, the sources turned to an explanation of how such an event might have come about, what this "portent" might indicate. As I described in Chapter 3, the most common explanation was that of Gerald of Wales; these births were the result of "unnatural" intercourse between humans and animals. Vincent of Beauvais in his *Speculum Naturale* in the thirteenth century perhaps states it as concisely and "scientifically" as anyone:

> This may have the head of a boar or a bull, or else in a similar way a calf with the head of a man is engendered, or a lamb with the head of a bull. This type of monstrosity sometimes occurs in this way, that is, by means of coitus between different species, or by means of an unnatural type of copulation.[35]

Less often, the birth of a human/animal hybrid was attributed to incaution on the part of a pregnant woman. For example, she might have been careless about her diet. We have seen how strongly medieval people believed in the influence of food on the body, and this hypothesis continues that preoccupation. In the fourteenth century, Reinfrid von Braunschweig seems to have drawn from rabbinic writings to explain that there were some herbs that people were forbidden to eat: "Adam forbade all his daughters to eat these herbs, but they ate them nonetheless, and it came about that they bore half-men who were conceived from these herbs and therefore had souls like those of beasts."[36] A pregnant woman might even be careless about her environment or her thoughts. The *Bestiary*, in its section on hybrid births warns "women not to look [at] any of the very disgusting animals in the face—like dog-headed apes or monkeys—lest they should give birth to children similar in appearance to those they met." The paragraph continues, warning further what women "imagine...in the mind...just so do they procreate the progeny."[37]

Thus, by the late Middle Ages, it seems that one's claim to humanity could be more and more easily lost. By sins of the flesh (food or sex), one's offspring could slip over the line from human to beast. From the collection of exempla for preachers, we can see the warning, all the more chilling in its brevity: "A woman gives birth to a snake which kills her."[38]

These individual examples of the loss of humanity occasionally appeared in Western European society (and texts). But as medieval people became preoccupied with the phenomenon, there was an increase in their preoccupation with

146

whole "races" of people who seemed to exist on the borders of humanity. As early as the seventh century, Isidore of Seville applied the word "monster" to groups of people who seemed deformed in the same ways as individual "monsters." In his comprehensive compilation of classical knowledge, Isidore had to address the question of monstrous races since the medieval world had inherited a good deal of literature on these unusual beings. John B. Friedman's *Monstrous Races in Medieval Art and Thought* remains the finest analysis of these creatures, and he calls them collectively Plinian races, noting the profound impact of the Roman author Pliny the Elder's *Natural History* upon subsequent descriptions. These races include wondrous creatures that seem to embody the full range of diversity available to human imagination. There were the Blemmyae, who lacked heads and necks and bore their facial features on their chests, and the Astomi or "Apple-Smellers," who lacked mouths and lived from smells, dying in the presence of a foul odor. Even more anatomically improbable were the Sciopods, one-legged with a giant foot, who although extremely swift, preferred to spend their time lying on their backs using their foot as a parasol against the sun, or the Panotii, whose ears were so large they could be wrapped around the body like a blanket. Among the most popular of the Plinian races were the Cynocephali, human-formed with heads of dogs. These exotic creatures joined the Cyclops, Amazons, and Pygmies, with which we are more familiar in the catalogue of monstrous races.[39]

The key to understanding people's belief in these races is to consider their perception of themselves and their world. Friedman points out that the descriptions of many of the races derive from interpretations of observed behavior. Perhaps the Sciopods were Hindus practicing yoga, the Blemmyae an African tribe who wore decorative body armor, the Apple-Smellers a Himalayan tribe who warded off disease by sniffing onions.[40] The ubiquitous Cynocephali were probably baboons and were described in the *Bestiary* as "numbered among monkeys."[41] When confronted with such anomalies, observers had several choices. They could assume they were individual "monstrous births," or collective "monstrous races," or animals. By the Middle Ages, the preponderance of classical references argued against the first choice, leaving questions about the humanity or bestiality of the races.

Creatures that seemed to mix the categories of human and animal, to exist on the borders of what were supposed to be qualitatively different species, could certainly have caused difficulty to early church fathers establishing a new paradigm of the relationship between humans and animals. The influential doctor of the church Augustine confronted this question in the *City of God*. He described the races that derived from Pliny and addressed the question of whether or not they were human. In the course of this discussion, he astutely warned his readers to be cautious about the descriptions:

> This assumes, of course, the truth of their stories about the divergent features of those races, and their great difference from one another and from us. The definition is important; for if we did not know that monkeys, long-tailed apes and chimpanzees are not men but animals, those natural historians...might pass them off on us as races of men, and get away with such nonsense.

Augustine continues, however, to allow for the possibility that God permitted monstrous races to exist in the same way he allowed monstrous births, and if they were indeed human, they were completely human, rational, mortal, and descended from Adam.[42] Augustine is representative of the early Christian view in that he may not have been certain about the exact existence of monstrous races, but he was certain that there was no ambiguity between the species; one was either animal or human.

The references in Augustine and Isidore show that the monstrous races were available to the medieval imagination from the earliest years, but their popularity was mitigated, perhaps by a mind-set that did not like species ambiguity. An eighth-century text shows this early medieval tension. The *Book of Monsters* (*Liber Monstrorum*) describes many monsters, most inherited from the classical tradition, including the Plinian races. The author shared Augustine's desire for clarity on the human status of these monsters and clearly defined the monstrous races as human.[43] In his introduction, however, the author cautions that he describes "marvels which have some claim to be believed, and each can make up his own mind." He continues his skeptical introduction by explaining away some of the classical texts by saying that in his time "monsters are less frequently produced in the sublunary world, and through nearly every corner of the globe we read of them as entirely eradicated and destroyed."[44]

The author's skepticism shows early medieval caution about such creatures, but after the twelfth century, skepticism seems to have been cast away, and the monstrous races captured the medieval imagination.[45] Many of the creatures were included in the Bestiaries of the thirteenth century, and the entries in this "scientific" work reveal the extent to which people could imagine the blurring of the species. For example, the *Bestiary* mentions the manticore, a fierce "beast" with the face of a man. But the texts show that people were not only concerned with surface characteristics that seemed to blend species; their preoccupation showed concern for a mixing of the actual essence of human and animal. For example, the *Bestiary* says of centaurs that "the nature of men and horses can be mixed."[46]

We can trace the increasing popularity of borderline creatures not only in the bestiaries but also in late medieval travel literature. A fourth-century life of Alexander the Great was translated into vernacular languages after the twelfth century and spread widely,[47] no doubt fascinating readers with tales of Alexander's encounter with Amazons and "dog-headed men and men without heads who had eyes and mouths in their chests."[48] Another extremely popular travel story was *Mandeville's Travels*, which was written in French in about 1360, then translated quickly into every major European language.[49] Mandeville's work is rich in detail drawn from many earlier medieval sources and represents almost a compendium of exotic creatures that inhabited late medieval imaginations. All the Plinian races from the dog-headed Cynocephali to giants to Sciopods appear in the travelogue, and many of the creatures are described with the kind of detail designed to accent their bestiality. For example, Mandeville said that the Cynocephali, giants, and other monsters were cannibals, and thus attributed to them the quality that most defined animals, the desire to eat humans.[50] The popularity of *Mandeville's Travels* expresses the late medieval preoccupation with monsters.

There have been a number of suggestions about why monsters became popular in the High Middle Ages. It may have been a function of increased expansion and travel, which feeds a curiosity for exotica. Norman Smith has argued that times of greatest discord call forth a fascination with grotesque monsters,[51] and the late Middle Ages was a time of great turmoil. These explanations do not address why preoccupations took this particular form. For example, one could be intrigued by a previously unseen baboon without assuming it was a dog-headed human. I suggest that the new preoccupation with these monstrous races by the thirteenth century was part of the same preoccupation that focused on hybrids. People were reconsidering the early medieval categories of human and animal.

Whatever the reason for the new popularity, one can see evidence of it in literature and art throughout the High Middle Ages. Art parallels the growth in the popularity of travel literature. In the "Animal Functions" graph in Figure 3 of Chapter 4, one can see the increase of human/animal hybrids after the

149

fourteenth century, and in the "Late Medieval Animals" graph in Figure 5 of Chapter 4, one can see the popularity of new animals in the marginal illuminations. Centaurs, wild men, and sirens joined the animals that frequented the medieval imagination. Serpents with human heads appear as a "startling innovation in art" in the thirteenth century.[52] Bernard of Clairveaux as early as the twelfth century warned against this new preoccupation in art, in the same way people warned in vain against artistic portrayal of fables:

> To what purpose are those unclean apes,...those monstrous centaurs, those half-men...? Here is a four-footed beast with a serpent's tail; there a fish with a beast's head. Here again the forepart of a horse trails half a goat behind it, or a horned beast bears the hind-quarter of a horse.... For God's sake, if men are not ashamed of these follies, why at least do they not shrink from the expense?[53]

Such warnings were in vain. Monsters had captured the medieval imagination by the late twelfth century. Descriptions of monsters offer insights into late medieval definitions of humanity and bestiality. As we have seen, the separation between the two could no longer be taken for granted. As categories blurred, people began to use behavior as the criterion that defined bestiality (or, of course, humanity). When the texts wrote of humans, giants, and Cynocephali that eat raw meat, and indeed raw human meat,[54] people immediately thought of these creatures as animal. Preoccupation with definitions of bestial behavior increased as people became more fascinated with creatures that existed on the borders of humanity.

The encyclopedists of the thirteenth century introduced their discussion of the Plinian races by the heading "Monstrous Men," seemingly arguing for their humanity. That conclusion was not universal, however. The Franciscan Alexander of Hales in a rather peculiar argument claimed that they were human because such deformity could only be the result of sin and only humans could sin. By contrast, the Dominican Lambert of Saint Omer included all as animals, and this position is at least implied by their inclusion in medieval "bestiaries." Thomas of Cantimpré separated the Plinian races from animals, but made them not quite human.[55] They existed on the borders of humanity. These three thinkers express the range of options for considering these creatures, and they reveal the range of ambiguity.

By the end of the Middle Ages, from about 1450 onward, people seemed to have acquired some skepticism about the existence of the monstrous races. That is not to say that people had become so certain of their humanity that they no longer feared ambiguous creatures on the border. People began simply to consider monsters as a form of hairy wild men who inhabited woods far from civilization.[56]

From classical mythology, the Middle Ages inherited belief in creatures that were part fertility figures, part ghosts,[57] and seemingly only part human. These creatures appeared to be the exact antithesis of humans. They were covered with hair, lived away from the civilization of settlements, lacked speech, used only a primitive club as a tool, and ate a bestial diet, usually of raw meat. All these actions defined the creatures as animals. Civilized people perceived the wild folk to be "like animals, slaves to desire and unable to control their passions."[58]

Medieval people, longing for clear distinction among species, had trouble determining whether wild people were human or animal.[59] The early medieval cataloguers of classical knowledge like Isidore of Seville simply recorded the existence of these creatures along with fauns and satyrs. Jerome acknowledged their presence in his commentary on the Bible in which he explained about "pagan hairy woodland demons."[60] One of the most famous literary monsters, Grendel in *Beowulf*, resembles these wild folk. Grendel seems to belong to the human race, for he was described as descended from Cain. (The medieval sine qua non of humanity was to be descended from the first man.) Furthermore, Grendel had a human anatomy, albeit extremely strong, as the prototypical wild man. But his behavior defined him as monstrous: he ate human flesh, and he ate alone, he did not belong to a society of the mead hall, so he envied that society and was bent on its destruction.[61] Grendel was an early medieval example of the creation of an antihuman monstrosity that was a threat to society.

In the twelfth century, however, wild men and women joined monsters and other borderline creatures that flourished in medieval art, literature, and consciousness. Wild people inhabited the forests in many of the twelfth-century romances and offered the perfect foil for chivalrous, civilized knights. For example, in *Yvain, or the Knight with the Lion*, knights wandering in a dark wood meet a giant caring for wild bulls. The giant is huge, hairy, dressed in skins, and armed with a club.[62] This brief description shows him to possess all the elements of the archetypical wild man.

In the middle of the thirteenth century, wild people appeared in art and theatrical performances, and they reached their peak of popularity late in the fourteenth century.[63] They remain in modern imagination as abominable snow people and Big Foot, half-human creatures that are said to reside in areas where humans do not.

What did this ubiquitous figure mean to late medieval people (and, perhaps to us)? Probably the most important function for wild people was to help humans define their humanity, particularly important in a time when that humanity seemed threatened, or at least ill-defined.[64] The concept of a negative human, one who embodied everything humans did not, must have presented a strangely comforting figure because it threw into focus precisely those qualities that defined humanity: rational thought, social behavior, cleanliness, clothing, etc. Another function that wild folk served was as "a projection of repressed desires and anxieties."[65] People seemed to have taken those qualities that they tried to suppress, the beast within, and projected them on the wild man outside. Thus, a belief in subhuman wild folk became both a rejection of some traits humans possessed and a reaffirmation of those things people defined as human.

Of course, these explanations of what functions wild people served grow from our twentieth-century interpretations of medieval attitudes. Obviously, the question of why the human mind would believe in a semihuman woodland creature was not a medieval question. Instead of speculating on the creature's existence, they simply questioned whether it was human or animal. Their response was most often that the creatures were degenerations of humans.[66] They began as humans but slipped into the realm of irrational beast. In the same way, lunatics fell into the category of wild people.[67] Medieval romances were full of heroes like Yvain who experienced a crisis, lost their minds, and lived in the woods as semihuman wild people. In the romance, Yvain underwent a period of madness during which he retreated to the woods, hunted animals and "ate their flesh uncooked, completely raw, like a wild man."[68]

The medieval explanation that wild people were degenerate humans grew out of a desire to preserve separate categories for humans and animals. That desire prevented medieval thinkers from defining wild people as something in between, as a "missing link." However, by defining them as humans who degenerated into the bestial, who allowed the beast within to emerge, they actually reduced the boundaries between humans and animals, because humans could now slip over into the bestial world. Wild people may have been created out of a desire to clarify that which defined humanity, but their popularity contributed to the growing uncertainty of humans in their separation from animals. When confronted with wild folk, it seemed that the only way to differentiate human from animal was by behavior, not simply by species.

As people began to define humanity by behavior, the possibility was opened for redefining people who had previously been accepted as human. Early Christian thinkers had categorically stated that all people were human. By the late Middle Ages, however, some groups of people seemed to be less human than others. During the early Middle Ages, the poor and women may have been considered lesser humans, but by the late Middle Ages, they were considered closer to animals. This reduction in status was made possible by the increasing blurring of lines in people's minds between humans and animals.

Marie of France's influential twelfth-century fable collection shows an increasing bestialization of the poor. To the traditional collection of animal fables, Marie added stories with a folk tradition, and many of these stories featured people, mostly peasants. She has fourteen peasants in her tales and only four "rich men." The rich men were usually portrayed sympathetically, but the peasants were uniformly shown as stupid. A male peasant foolishly believes he can give birth, and peasant husbands believe the most transparent excuses given them by their adulterous wives.[69] As I noted in the Introduction, one of the defining qualities of animals in the Middle Ages was their irrationality. Humans had reason, animals did not. By showing peasants as uniformly stupid and irrational within a context of animal fables, Marie subtly, yet powerfully, reduced their status to the borders of the bestial.

In addition to rationality, we have seen that sexuality defines an animal. From the twelfth century onward, peasant sexuality was linked more closely to that of animals than to the more cultured love of the nobility. (Of course, remember it was members of the upper classes who were making this definition.) Andrew the Chaplain in his *Art of Courtly Love* clearly sets up his hierarchy of humanity and bestiality based on one's capacity for refined love and sex. He writes of men with too much lust:

> Men of this kind lust after every woman they see; their love is like that of a shameless dog. They should rather...be compared to asses, for they are moved only by that low nature which shows that men are on the level of the other animals rather than by that true nature which sets us apart from all the other animals by the difference of reason.[70]

For Andrew, the defining element of humanity—reason—was linked to the expression of love and sex. When he considers peasants, however, he says that peasants cannot really love because they have sex "naturally, like a horse or a mule."[71] Therefore, he, like Marie, reduces peasants as a whole group to a position lower than human by denying them rationality and seeing the proof of that denial in his perception of the nature of their sexuality.

Finally, as we have seen, humans defined themselves by diet. In this respect as well, upper-class writers reduced peasants and the poor to a level more bestial than their own. As I indicated in Chapter 2, by the late Middle Ages, diet defined social status, and as one came to the bottom of the social hierarchy the diet of the poor blended into the diet of animals. In the fourteenth and fifteenth centuries, "horsebread" was baked out of the less desirable grains, and this was prepared for consumption by horses, dogs, and paupers.[72] While this practice may seem a practical way of cheaply feeding the poor, and indeed may have begun as such, the association between paupers and animals would not have been lost on people who believed so profoundly in the notion that you are what you eat. We may react with sadness when we hear of today's poor being driven to eat cat food, but people in the Middle Ages most likely mixed disdain with any feelings of compassion.

Not only did the poor accept animal food as part of charity, but because of their poverty they were driven to eat other bestial things. We have seen that holy people feared allowing their hunger to turn them into animals, and they believed they could look to God for help in their fast. But many people faced hunger with no hope for spiritual reward. Piero Camporesi has written a forceful and moving work describing the hunger that was an ever-present part of the lives of the poor in early modern Europe, and this pervasive, life-numbing hunger also existed in medieval times.[73] Too often people observed the poor driven by their hunger to behavior that was considered bestial. The most striking example of such behavior is cannibalism.

There are references to the poor resorting to cannibalism in times of famine throughout the Middle Ages. Procopius of Caesarea in the sixth century told of two women who killed and ate seventeen strangers to whom they offered lodging for the night.[74] Similar stories are repeated of the ninth-century famine and of the famines of the eleventh and fourteenth centuries.[75] People believed hunger could drive people to such desperation that even the human ties of family could not save people from descending to the worst kind of bestial behavior. John of Salisbury in the twelfth century wrote of a woman who was driven to such desparation by hunger that she ate her own son.[76]

Such stories may have generated compassion in medieval minds, but they also generated fear. What would such "bestial" people not do when confronted with hunger? And, indeed, noble fears seem to have had some basis because during peasant revolts, rebels seem to have occasionally expressed their anger by converting their oppressors to food and eating them. As Juvenal, the classical satirist observed of a revolt in ancient Egypt, "On the other side was hate, and the hate was hungry." The victorious Egyptian rebels expressed their hate and hunger by eating the landlords.[77] The same kind of retribution was reported in the Middle Ages. The chronicler Froissart claimed to have observed the fourteenth-century Jacquerie, a peasant revolt in France. Froissart described with horror the form taken by the anger of peasants: "among other things they slew a knight and after did put him on a broach and roasted him at the fire in the sight of the lady his wife and his children; and after the lady had been enforced and ravished with a ten or twelve, they made her perforce to eat of her husband."[78] In this instance, peasants act in bestial ways both sexually and by forcing cannibalism. We cannot be sure whether rebellious peasants actually expressed their anger by cannibalism, but we can be certain that the nobility feared that they did. In the late Middle Ages, this fear linked peasants to the animal world that seemed lurking ready to make a meal of a human.

Once the early medieval paradigm of a strict separation of human and animal species began to blur, it seems people were quick to add social status to the criteria of full humanity. The close association between poverty and social status may be seen in the writings of Jordanus Catalani, the fourteenth-century Franciscan traveler who described the wonders of India. He remarked that the lowest caste, the Dumbri, "do the drudgeries of other people, and carry loads." This much he likely observed. He further claimed, however, that these people lowest on the social scale "eat carrion and carcasses."[79] Since low-caste people did not eat carrion, Jordanus must have assumed it, and the most likely reason for his assumption was the late medieval association of poverty with bestiality. Peasants and the poor slid down the human scale to a level closer to the edges of humanity, nearer the monsters that inhabited the borderline regions.

Once medieval thinkers began to consider which people were more "human" than others, women, too, were moved down the scale. In many pre-Christian societies, goddesses and by extension women were associated with animals. Buffie Johnson in her detailed study of images of the ancient goddess writes: "At the core of prehistory loom the animal archetypes,... that stand beside the Great Mother. Her animals are neither totems nor the independent divinities of polytheistic beliefs. They embody the deity herself, defining her personality and exemplifying her power."[80] As Christians defined the new paradigm for people's view of animals, this explicit association of woman, animal, and deity was of course split. But even from the earliest years of the Middle Ages, church thinkers defined women as more earthy, more sensual then men.[81] With this view, it did not take much for women to slip to the bestial level. Medieval medical texts no doubt helped forward the view of women as more bestial than men, because these texts explained the birth of females as an accident. Doctors believed that if the womb were imperfectly heated the fetus would not develop fully into a male, so it would become a girl. Thus the very existence of women was similar to that of monsters, an accident of nature.[82]

In the "scientific" bestiaries, it is possible to see continued hints at the archetypical elements of femininity that were traditionally linked to animals.[83] For example, the bestiary tiger that embodied mother love in its fierce pursuit of a hunter stealing its child, also became associated with female vanity because the tiger was distracted from the chase by a mirror. In the initial tellings of the tale, the tiger was said to believe the cub was in the mirror; later the mirror was assumed to characterize the mother's vanity, which distracted her from rescuing her cub.[84] In both cases, the tiger was linked with femininity, and over time with increasingly negative associations.

In addition to subtle archetypical associations of animals with women, thinkers presaged linking women and beasts through a joint association with food. Carolyn Walker Bynum has brilliantly detailed the ways medieval people saw women's bodies as food. Women from lactating mothers to saints miraculously exuding fluids transformed their bodies into food.[85] The association of women with food sounds a little peculiar in the medieval Christian context linking women, food, and religious expression, but this association continues in people's modern imagination. Nick Fiddes, in writing about modern attitudes toward meat, shows how women today are portrayed as meat, and he indicates how this portrayal links women to the animal world: "The portrayal of women, by men, as meat is an instance of the wider caricature of woman as animal."[86] In chapter 2, I showed how one of the defining functions of animals is to be food. Thus, a syllogism emerges that says if animals are food, and women are food, then women are animals. This association increased from the twelfth century on as literary references linked women to animals.

Literary references to an interchangeable nature between women and animals begin to appear in the twelfth century. The first reference to blending between women and snakes occurred in the twelfth century when Peter

Comestor wrote that a serpent had a "virginal face, because like things applaud like."[87] In this case women were physically (not simply metaphorically) linked to serpents.

Such associations linking women and animals continue with increasing frequency. Often the references were in the form of similes comparing women's behavior to that of animals. For example, thirteenth-century exemplars say women are like wild cats and like peacocks, so people should take moral lessons from the similarity of female and animal behaviors.[88] The fourteenth-century Spanish *Book of Good Love* further develops the comparisons between women and animals in similes in order to explain how one should treat women. Women were like horses, so they should be forced into sexual intercourse; women were like hares, who get confused when hunted.[89] Juan Ruiz, the author of the *Book of Good Love*, went beyond similes in his description of bestial women. He described a "mare-girl" in detail, and his description shows the blending of human and animal that characterized this woman, this lower-class woman:

> Her ears were greater than the ones that from a donkey sprout;
> Her neck was black, thick-set, and short, and hairy all about;
> Her nose was beaked and longer than the great flamingo's snout;
> ....
> Her mouth was fashioned like a hound's with muzzle thick and short;
> With long and narrow horse's teeth of every crooked sort;
> ....
> And like a yearling heifer's, great big ankles you would see.[90]

His description continued along those lines until every part of the woman was equated with an animal. He was obviously playing with the notion that intercourse with this creature was bestiality, and he shows how quickly and easily women could be reduced to the animal world. Many of the images Ruiz used to describe this woman were drawn from descriptions of semihuman "wild women" described above,[91] but they were attributed to a real woman, showing a blurring of the lines between "wild women," a different species, and all women.

Later in the Middle Ages, references increasingly shift from similes to metaphors. Perhaps the most compelling example of a metaphoric treatment of women as animals is in the late thirteenth/early fourteenth century French poem, "The Vices of Women." Within a misogynist poem is a list of metaphors associating women with various animals:

> Woman is a snake to be venomous.
> Woman is a lion for imperiousness.
> Woman is a leopard to devour.
> Woman is a fox to deceive.
> Woman is a bear to be combative.
> Woman is a dog to have sharp senses.
> Woman is a cat to bite with teeth.
> Woman is a rat to destroy.
> Woman is a mouse to be sneaky. [92]

This list reinforced the idea that women were in fact bestial, borderline creatures like the monsters that captured the same imaginations.

Another example of literature that treats women as animals is Richard of Fournival's *Bestiary of Love*. In Richard's creative work, he compares women's love and women themselves to various animals: wolves, vipers, crows, weasels, panthers, lions, pelicans, beavers, crocodiles, monkeys, to name only a few. Richard claims that when involved with love, men, too are are like animals: cocks, wolves, crickets, swans, dogs, baby partridge, and others.[93] The most original aspect of Richard's work is not any one of the comparisons, however. By structuring the whole work as a bestiary, Richard increased the metaphoric blurring: this bestiary was *about* women; animals were used simply to illustrate a woman's character. Richard quoted Aristotle in the opening lines, "One may learn the nature of one animal from the nature of another."[94] By using this quotation, Richard meant that one could learn about the female by understanding other animals. Women had been reduced to the bestial.

Richard's work points to a shift in the treatment of women and women's love in the late Middle Ages. Bruno Roy calls this change one from an idealistic erotic to a realistic one, and this change could be seen in an increasing emphasis on a new erotic expression: the hunt of love, in which women become the prey. From the thirteenth century to the end of the Middle Ages, women were described as deer and other animals who served as quarry.[95] At this point, the literary treatment of women comes to match the religious imagery noted by Carolyn Bynum: women were food to be hunted, and as such were more bestial than men. The boundaries between humans and animals were becoming so thin by the late Middle Ages that women joined peasants in slipping over that line.

During the high Middle Ages, then, people perceived a number of creatures that existed on the edges between clear humanity and obvious bestiality. Things from apes to monsters to paupers to women called into question the clear division between humans and animals that had defined early Christian thought. This blurring of lines reached its full expression in the belief in metamorphosis, the transformation of human into animal.

Metamorphosis

The classical world had envisioned a universe in which all elements were connected. Things were joined through connecting causes or through Platonic emanations that permeated all beings, whether human or animal. The classic myths reveal this connectedness most clearly through metamorphosis, changes in form. Transformations of humans into animals permeate the classical texts with such ease that they reveal a belief in a universe in which boundaries were much more fluid between species and categories than we have seen since.[96] The Roman poet Ovid collected many of the myths and stories and wrote the most influential work on transformations. He began his *Metamorphoses* with the concrete statement, "My purpose is to tell of bodies which have been transformed into shapes of a different kind"[97] and then proceeded to retell many tales of shape-shifting. By the time we reach the final transformation, Julius Caesar into a star, we are uncertain about the permanence of any form. This same bewildering world is visible in Apuleius's *The Golden Ass*, a story of the metamorphosis of a man named Lucius into an ass and his subsequent journey as that animal in his quest to return to his human form. In *The Golden Ass*, not only was Lucius transformed, but the story is full of rapid transformations of fortune and form that mark a world with fluid boundaries.

In these stories, metamorphosis usually occurred because people exhibited the characteristics of an animal to an extreme degree. The transformation only made manifest the bestial nature that had been within.[98] Lucius acted like an overly curious ass before he experimented with the magic cream that turned him into one; Arachne showed her skill in weaving before she was turned into a spider to spin perpetually.

The early Christian Middle Ages also inherited the idea of metamorphosis from northern pagan tradition. For example, early Irish myths show frequent examples of shape-shifting. A beautiful woman spends every other year as a swan, and the man who loves her changes into a swan to possess her. Another woman is impregnated by a man appearing as a bird, and another couple turns into swans to escape an irate husband.[99] These transformations link the human and animal worlds at moments of sexuality, a time when the animal side traditionally emerges. The metamorphoses into birds may also recall an ancient mythological association of women, fertility and birds.[100]

The Nordic tradition of shape-shifting that survives in myths and sagas points to another bestial side of people—violence. People in these stories most often magically turned into bears or wolves to acquire the animals' strength and luck in battle. The fiercest Scandinavian warriors, the berserks, seem to have owed their strength to their ability to take on animal characteristics, or rather to allow the animal within themselves to emerge. The name "berserk" may have derived from the wearing of bearskin, a hypothesis strengthened by the alternate name for berserks—"wolf-coats." The *Volsunga Saga* offers a dramatic example of transformations brought about by wearing wolf skins. Sigmund and his son, Sinfjotli, put on wolfskins but are unable to remove them. With the skins on, they "spoke with the voice of wolves," yet they understand each other. In this form they are fierce and invincible until they are able to remove the skins and take back their human form. Testimony in Norwegian witch trials echoes the tradition of wearing skins of animals into battle, because it tells of men and women wearing wolf belts to transform themselves into the savage animal.

These stories show an awareness of the animal that is within each of us. Sometimes the animal traits were undesirable ones—lust, cannibalism, or violence. At other times, animal traits like strength or cunning were sought out. Either way, however, pagan metamorphosis myths expressed the emergence of animal traits at the expense of the human. This perception required a belief in humans as a mingling of both animal and human, a belief in a continuum of life that linked human and animal. Early medieval thinkers were too concerned with separation of species, however, to integrate these tales into their world view.

When confronted with pagan tales of metamorphosis, early church fathers were vigorous in their denial of the possibility of such shape-shifting. As early as the second century in Roman North Africa, Tertullian rejected the possibility of Ovidian metamorphosis, saying that just because people exhibit the "habits, characters, and desires" of beasts, it does not mean they can actually turn into an animal.[101] The fourth-century doctor of the church Ambrose stated the early Christian case even more strongly: "those made after the likeness and image of God cannot be changed into the forms of beasts." He further summed up the early Christian explanation, saying that metamorphosis was impossible because "the nature of beasts [is] so opposed to that of mankind."[102] Thus, he restates the Christian paradigm of separation of species and uses it to reject the pagan vision of a more fluid world.

As with so many topics, Augustine developed the early church position most fully regarding this subject. Augustine allowed for the possibility of God in his omnipotence effecting a metamorphosis of a human into an animal. Beyond that, however, Augustine claimed it was impossible and that the pagan stories were untrue. He argued that the pagan gods, who were demons in his system, could not transform people from the form in which they had been created by God. Therefore, belief in metamorphosis was only illusion. People might imagine they had been transformed into an animal, but they were not actually changed.[103]

Augustine's position remained the prevailing Christian view throughout the Middle Ages. It was reaffirmed by Thomas Aquinas and continued through the sixteenth century with theorists of demonic possession like Henri Boguet, a judge in werewolf trials who said the "much-talked-of examples of metamorphosis,...were true in appearance only, but not in fact."[104] Of course, this view of metamorphosis as illusion or self-delusion continues today with psychological studies of people who believe they have been transformed into animals and act on that belief.[105] The medieval church attempted to enforce this skeptical view of metamorphosis in penitential literature from Regino to Burchard which forbad belief that a man "can be transformed into a wolf, called in German a Werewolf, or into some other form."[106] This ecclesiastical legislation influenced secular law as well such as the Norwegian law code that stated: "No man shall utter slander...or tell impossible tales about another. Impossible is that which cannot be true...like calling him a werewolf."[107] However, as we have seen throughout this book, the early medieval paradigm of the separation of humans from animals could not last.

As in so many other elements of medieval thought about animals, in the twelfth century we may see a significant turning point in medieval perceptions of metamorphosis. One clear indication of the increase in popularity of the idea of human to animal transformation is seen in the fortunes of Ovid's book, *Metamorphosis*. Before the twelfth century, there were very few copies made of this classic transformation text. Between the twelfth and the fourteenth centuries, there was an explosion of popularity of the text, shown both in the numbers of new manuscripts and in the many commentaries on the work.[108] Many of the commentators on Ovid and other metamorphosis stories interpreted the tales allegorically,[109] so that traditional stories of shape-shifting could be read as moral lessons in the same way fables and bestiary lore were read.

Thus, pagan ideas of metamorphosis thus reentered European consciousness in the same way as stories of animals as human exemplars.

The growing popularity of metamorphosis literature surely contributed to a reconsideration of the possibility of shape-shifting. In addition, there was a subtle shift in the medieval mind-set that facilitated a renewed belief in metamorphosis in spite of ecclesiastical reasoning to the contrary. From the twelfth century on people, believed there were many things that were not as they seemed. For example, medieval science was preoccupied with transformations in nature, such as looking for the philosopher stone that could transform base metals into gold.[110] Even the central mystery of the church, the eucharist, was increasingly viewed as a miraculous transformation. In 1215 the church declared transubstantiation doctrine, claiming that the bread and wine were transformed into the actual body and blood of Christ. By this declaration, the church was acknowledging that things may be miraculously changed beyond human powers to perceive. In the twelfth-century narrative of Gerald of Wales, we can see the way the medieval mind could link transformation of the eucharist with metamorphosis of humans. Gerald listed a series of reputed transformations from Apuleius's curious ass to people being changed to pigs and hares. He then repeated and reaffirmed Augustine's statement that demons cannot change people, but he went on to say that with God's permission people can change their outward appearance, if not their essence. He concluded this section by mentioning transubstantiation, saying he chooses not to discuss it, "its comprehension being far beyond the powers of the human intellect."[111] But his acceptance of the incomprehensible miracle of the Mass was joined in his mind with an acceptance of seemingly improbable shape-shifting.

In Gerald, we can see the recovery of the belief in metamorphosis. Gerald's examples reveal, however, uniquely Christian transformations, different from those described in pagan literature. In pagan metamorphosis, an external appearance changed into that of an animal to make visible the interior animal-like characteristics. In Christian metamorphosis, the exterior changed to reveal some animal-like characteristics of the human, but the human essence, the interior, remained unchanged. This was consistent with the patristic position that humans cannot be changed into animals, so it offered a way to accept a compromise form of metamorphosis.

Another element in the high medieval world view that helped recover a belief in metamorphosis was people's increasing tendency to define humanity and bestiality by actions. As we saw above, people (like peasants) who were perceived to act like animals were considered bestial. The criterion of action probably more often served to suggest that a particularly smart animal was actually a person who had shifted his shape. We have seen that by the late Middle Ages animals were readily perceived as being demons in disguise. This same thinking persuaded people that an animal that showed cunning greater than one might expect from an animal was really a human.[112] After all, reason was a defining quality of humans, so an animal possessing that quality might really be human. Late medieval accounts of particularly intelligent wolves frequently raise the question of whether it actually was simply a wolf, or a human in wolf shape. This was the case in 1148 when a huge wolf killed thirty people in Geneva.[113] Presumably, such skill in killing was considered beyond normal animal capacity.

There seem to have been two ways to understand the behavior of extraordinary wolves. One was practical, looking backward to the early medieval world when animals were just that. A late medieval definition of "werewolf" shows this view. In a treatise on hunting, Edward the Duke of York wrote, "There be some [wolves] that have eaten children or men,...and they are called werewolves, for men should beware of them."[114] Here we see a definition of werewolf that is totally devoid of any supernatural context. In most of the texts of the late Middle Ages, however, the supernatural was attributed to intelligent wolves, showing the second way to understand the behavior. The *Malleus Maleficarum*, the Renaissance tract for discovering witchcraft, addressed the question of wolves that were so fierce and smart they seemed unlike other wolves. The *Malleus* explained that they were wolves, indeed, but they were possessed by devils.[115] An exceptional wolf was transformed into a supernatural creature. This attempt to explain the actions of a wolf then contributed to a view in which species could blend and werewolves could exist.

Finally, perhaps the change that was most influential in the growth of belief in metamorphosis was the blurring of lines between humans and animals. As people began to recognize, wonder about, and fear the beast within themselves, they began looking for this animal. Belief in metamorphosis, and particularly in werewolves, reveals a fear of the beast inside overwhelming the human qualities of rationality and spirituality, leaving only the animal appetites of lust, hunger, and rage. This fear, and the related discovery of transformed humans, reached its high point during the Renaissance and early modern periods and is outside the scope of this study. Nevertheless, in the late Middle Ages there were more frequent references to humans as animals. These stories point to the growing discovery that we too are animals.

It seems that many of the tales of transformation from human to animal reentered European literary tradition from the Celtic regions. It may be that old pagan traditions remained closer to the surface in those regions and less transformed by Christian views of humanity. We have seen above how Gerald of Wales was intrigued by the concept of transformation as he brought tales back from his travels in Wales and Ireland. He told of a beautiful woman who turned into a "hairy creature, rough and shaggy" while in the embrace of a man.[116] He also described old women in Wales, Scotland, and Ireland who changed themselves into hares so they could steal people's milk by sucking the teats of cows.[117] Gerald's most involved tale concerns a couple who are cursed and forced to become wolves every seven years. The wolf speaks to a priest, asking for last rites for his wife. When the wolf peels back the wolfskin to reveal a woman, the priest gives the woman/wolf communion. This tale caused Gerald to reflect upon what was a human and what was an animal.[118] Gerald was quite right to wonder. As soon as medieval thinkers allowed for the possibility of such shape-shifting, the early medieval paradigm was breaking down. But Gerald's werewolf also shows the new Christian view of metamorphosis in which the interior remained human while the external appearance was transformed.

A thirteenth-century chronicler, Gervaise of Tilbury, also showed a new belief in werewolves. He preserved a Christian perspective on metamorphosis by expressing the opinion that a person's nature could not be converted to a bestial one. However, at the same time he claimed to have known at least two British werewolves, one of whom "devoured infants," highly bestial behavior.[119] Like Gerald's, Gervais's chronicle shows the Christian compromise with shape-shifting: the externals were changed, behavior was bestial, but the essence remained human.

The historical chroniclers show the beginnings of Christian transformation and acceptance of metamorphosis, but writers of literature probably were more influential in forwarding this view. We saw in the last chapter how Marie of France was important in popularizing fables. She also drew from Celtic tradition and wrote a collection of short romances, *Lais*, one of which was about a werewolf called Bisclavaret. Marie tells us that "people used to say—and it often actually happened—that some men turned into werewolves and lived in the woods."[120] Marie then proceeds to tell a tale of one such werewolf, and her story is instructive because it sheds a good deal of light on medieval views of metamorphosis.

Marie tells the tale of a man who is condemned to become a wolf and spend three days of every week in the woods. This unhappy man confesses his plight to his beloved bride. The faithless woman cannot accept the beast within her husband: "She never wanted to sleep with him again."[121] She reveals the secret to a knight who wishes to be her lover. The two conspire to steal the man's clothing, which is the mechanism of his conversion back to human form, and thus condemn him to remain a wolf. While in the woods, the wolf is befriended by a king, who notices the animal's exceptional abilities and says, "It has the mind of a man....This beast is rational—he has a mind."[122] Unlike the faithless wife who cannot see beyond the beast in the man, the wise king can see the man within the beast.

The wolf's human qualities are confirmed when he attacks the knight who has taken his wife, clothing, and humanity, and when he attacks his vain wife and bites off her nose. The king forces the wife to restore the wolf's clothing. The wolf becomes a man again, the wife is banished (to bear noseless daughters), and the friendship with the king continues.

Marie concluded her tale by saying that the Lay "was made so it would be remembered forever."[123] What morals were implicit here that should be remembered? There was the obvious moral, of course, that one had better select one's wife wisely, and perhaps not trust a woman with a secret. Beyond this, however, we learn something about Marie's views of humans and animals. The man, sympathetically as he is portrayed, has the beast within him.[124] Before his wife becomes involved in his plight, he is an animal half the time. In this we see most clearly the beginnings of the twelfth-century acceptance of an animal side of people. The animal side consumes the human through the agency of a woman, more carnal and closer to animals than even the half-wolf man. Through the woman, he loses almost all outward trace of his humanity actually and symbolically through the loss of his clothing. However, consistent with Christian belief, the wolf retains his humanity within because he does not lose his rational, human thought. Finally, he is restored to humanity again through the agency of a friend and lord, a higher spiritual being. Marie shows us that we are all subject to a loss of humanity if we focus on the wrong things. Faith in one's lord, a spiritual tie, should be placed above carnal attraction.

The same lessons appear in the fourteenth-century tale of Arthur and Gorlagon. King Arthur, wanting to understand the female mind, is led to Gorlagon, who tells him a story of female betrayal and a werewolf. In this story, a king who guards a secret sapling that broke through the ground when the king was born. This sapling has the power to convert the king to a wolf. As in Marie's story, a faithless wife discovers the secret, uses it to her advantage, and the wolf is ultimately restored through friendship with another king.[125] Once again, the man is identified with his animal potentiality through the sapling, and he is reduced to a bestial state through love of a woman. He never fully loses his interior nature, however, and it is restored through good lordship.

There were many late medieval examples of literary werewolves who like these two had many fine qualities. These examples introduce a "sympathetic werewolf": the audience was led to feelings of pity for the human trapped within an animal exterior.[126] This compassion seems to have extended beyond feelings for a literary creature. People in the late Middle Ages may not have come to feeling much compassion for the real animals that shared their world. But through the animals that existed in their imagination, from half-human monsters to occasionally human werewolves, they had become aware of, feared, and found empathy for the beast they discovered within us all.

Conclusion:
What Is a Human?

WHAT IS A HUMAN? ONCE THE clear distinctions between the species had blurred, humanity became not what you are, but how you act. We define our humanity as the rational, the logical, and the compassionate. Whenever we transcend our animal inclinations—our appetites, our passions—then we embrace what was defined in the Middle Ages as the human. I began this book by exploring the early Christian definition of animals that showed them to be profoundly different from humans. In the course of this work, I have looked at the functions of animals in the medieval world and explored the increasing ambiguity that surrounded the initial confident definition. By the late Middle Ages, the animal that prowls within each of us became increasingly evident. Thinkers moved more closely to the Greco-Roman view that saw humans along a continuum with animals, with the potential of lowering themselves to the bestial level by their actions. This view that we can see emerging in the twelfth century dominated Renaissance thought.[1] Yet, the Christian Middle Ages never fully embraced this attitude, however. In medieval texts, one can see the uncertainty that shadowed the definition of animals. Of course, as I noted in the Introduction, people's definitions of animals really amounted to a definition of what it meant to be human. Therefore, it seems appropriate to conclude this look at animals with a more direct look at a medieval definition of humanity in contrast to bestiality. This will offer a last summary of medieval attitudes towards animals by looking at the negative image of an animal, the human.

There are a number of ways to approach a definition of humanity. Certainly, medieval philosophers from Augustine to Albert the Great to Thomas Aquinas wrote about humans, a topic they considered much more central than any reflections on animals. Their reflections, however, came from Aristotle and the schoolrooms of logical thinking. These men were profoundly influential, but there is perhaps a better measure of what most people believed was the ideal human, indeed a superhuman,[2] and that is the saints.

Saints in the Middle Ages were extraordinary human beings, serving as examples of the best in human behavior and transcending the flaws that plagued normal humans.[3] As exemplars, saints helped define an ideal humanity to which people aspiring to be holy could strive. For example, Saint Francis's biographer says, he was "a man so venerable and worthy of imitation."[4] In their relations with animals, however, medieval saints served to define the nature of the animal world, or rather, to express vividly society's definition. As these saints were products of medieval Christian society, they reflected, expressed, and indeed perpetuated the Christian view of animals.[5] We can trace their interactions with animals (and the beast within themselves) in all the ways I have discussed in this book. But further, since they were considered saints, the stories throw into focus a definition of humanity. This conclusion can thus both summarize the themes I have explored and begin to answer the question of medieval perceptions of humanity.

At first glance, saints seem to offer the least information about humans in relation to their animal property. After all, one of the hallmarks of many saints was poverty. They were not bound to worldly needs the way most of us are. Saints never became property either, so they separated themselves from the animal quality of being owned. In fact, holy people acquired more freedoms than most people had through their holiness.[6] They were even free from the fear of wild animals that marked most humans. As a desert holy man explained when he carried two lion cubs in his cloak: "If we keep the commandments of our Lord Jesus Christ, these animals will be afraid of us; but through our sins we have become slaves, and it is we, rather, who are afraid of them."[7] Animals were marked by bondage, humans by freedom, and superhuman saints by the most freedom of all. This definition of humanity is familiar to us, for American slaves were defined as only semihuman because of their status of property.[8] This property status placed them closer to animals in the eyes of many.

Saints, as was appropriate to their humanity, did use animals in the functions we saw in the chapter on property. Saints used animals for labor and wore clothing of animal products. In the saints' lives, however, these relationships are miraculously without the tension and difficulties that marked the working ties between normal humans and animals. Perhaps the most famous story of this sort is that of the lion that was willing to work for Saint Jerome, first guarding his donkey, then serving as a beast of burden for the saint.[9] This story, however, was not unique. The saints' lives are full of animals eager to serve. Wild asses mildly carry burdens, cows obediently come home on their own to be milked, bears serve as shepherds.[10] The saintly moral of all this is that it is human to use animals to serve, and it is the nature of animals to serve. It is the height of humanity to have animals serve willingly in one's presence.

Clothing, too, is central to the definition of humanity. Only humans were self-conscious enough to cloth themselves,[11] and the wearing of clothes was one of the things that medieval people thought separated real humans from some of the monstrous races that were nude. A thirteenth-century author, Ratramnus of Corbie, argued against the idea that the dog-headed Cynocephali were human because they wore clothing, even though they had animal heads and did not speak.[12] In our age of the predominance of cotton and synthetic fibers, it is easy to forget how closely linked clothing was to the animals that provided it. Wool, furs, and skins made up most of the clothing in the Middle Ages, and that meant some association with animals. For saints, clothing often served to mark their sanctity. Melania the Younger changed her clothing to ever more plain garb as she marked her progress to sanctity.[13] Wulfstan of Worcester was known for wearing simple clothes, preferring "to keep out the cold with the fleeces of sheep rather than with other kinds of skins."[14] Such examples of holy people wearing simple cloth (or coarse hair shirts) as marks of sanctity are very common. Even in their world-renouncing humility, saints share the defining human quality of wearing clothing. At times, animals were said to provide for this human need freely, as the lioness who was so grateful to Saint Macarius for curing her cubs that she brought him a huge ram skin for his use.[15]

The only property function of animals that does not appear in the saints' lives is that of status. This is not surprising given the saintly goal of humility and unconcern for worldly things. But it also shows that while seeking a status higher than that of one's fellows may be a common human trait, it was not perceived to be a defining quality of being human. Ordinary people used their animal property to enhance their own position, but perfect humans did not. Just as the relationship with animals as property was the one most free from ambiguity for most people, it seemingly posed few problems for the saints. When people begin to define some actions as bestial, however, the relationship between humans and animals becomes more complex. Saints affirmed and defined humanity by renouncing such actions. As we have seen, one of the most complex definitions of humanity was by diet.

In Chapter 2, I showed how food and eating were surrounded by rules and customs that served to differentiate humans from animals. Both humans and animals eat, but is there a specifically human way of eating that can help define the species? Medieval people thought so. On the bestial side of dietary practices, people frequently identified monstrous races as animal by their eating habits. Pygmies were said to be animals in part because they were believed to eat no bread, "but rather herbs of various kinds and milkfoods, as do beasts."[16] Human eating meant eating refined foods and cooked foods. The dietary inclination that most defined an animal, however, was a taste for human flesh. The Cynocephali that people believed shared many human qualities were securely defined as animals because they ate humans.[17] The manticore may have been portrayed as profoundly human in that most important area, the head and face, the location of human reason, but the *Bestiary* definitively locates it in the animal kingdom, saying "It hankers after human flesh most ravenously."[18]

If food served to define the bestial kingdom, it also defined the human in saints' lives. As I showed in Chapter 2, vegetarianism was seen as a more perfect state than a carnivorous life. Many saints adhered to vegetarianism as a way of emphasizing the human rather than the bestial within themselves. The account of the sixth-century Irish saint Brendan makes a point of saying that from the time Brendan had become a priest, "he ate nothing in which there had been the breath of life."[19] St. Francis at times mixed his food with ashes to be sure he would not enjoy it, and once St. Francis performed severe public penance because he had eaten meat to restore his strength when he was ill.[20]

Some saints' lives even tell of animals who were moved to renounce their carnivorous ways in the presence of saints. A desert holy man fed dates to a wild lion, much to the astonishment of his observers. Paul the Greek persuaded a lion to eat only bread for a while, but when the lion went back to its ways, the holy man drove him away, saying, "You have disobeyed me and have eaten flesh! By the blessed Lord, you flesh-eater, I shall no longer give you the food of the fathers!"[21] By eating flesh, the lion removed itself from being allowed to associate with sanctity, so the lesson implied that it was even more important for humans to renounce flesh-eating in their quest for perfection.

Renouncing meat was only a beginning for many holy people. Fasting, and in many cases excessive fasting, marked saintly struggles with bestial appetites. Renouncing food temporarily in a fast had been part of Christian practice and symbols from the earliest centuries of Christianity.[22] Thinkers from Jerome to Aquinas and many in between recommended it as a way to conquer the bestial inclinations and to allow human reason to rise to the fore. Many saints earned their reputation in part by their remarkable ability to go without food.[23] Carolyn Walker Bynum has shown, however, that saints' relationship to food is more rich than simple renunciation. She shows that women saints in the late Middle Ages used and controlled food and their eating habits to convert their flesh to God-like suffering flesh. Food symbols were a way of understanding the mysteries of religion. Bynum writes, "Medieval people saw food and body as sources of life, repositories of sensation. Thus food and body signified generativity and suffering."[24] This is true when it came to the purified bodies and food of the saints. Medieval people also saw food and bodies as potentially bestial. The miracle of saints was that they brought out the profoundly human, and thus for medieval people, spiritual, qualities in the flesh. Food and eating was made human, not bestial by the saints. For this they were canonized.

Of course, most of us in our diets fall between the extremes of bestial and holy. We eat a mix of things, and we are horrified at extremes in dietary habits. We recoil from extreme renunciation, and anorexia is a severe social and personal problem.[25] We are appalled by reports of cannibalism, whether from hunger or political excess.[26] Between these extremes, however, we still struggle for a balance, a peace, with an appetite that many still identify as bestial.

Renouncing, controlling, and remaking food into something appropriate for humans was complicated by the fact that people cannot do without it. Sex, however, was a bit easier to deal with. Renouncing sexual activity was difficult, but it was possible. Thus, sexuality remained defined as a bestial activity, as I showed in Chapter 3. To define their superhumanity, saints needed to renounce their sexual lives, and they did so in large numbers. As Weinstein and Bell point out in their study of saints, "The *sine qua non* of an ascetic life was renunciation of sexual activity."[27] The struggle for a life of perfect chastity with no trace of bestial intercourse was not easy. The lives of the saints are full of tales of saints fighting lust by rolling in sharp nettles, burning the flesh with hot coals, or other bodily mortifications.[28] In their victory, they helped hold out the ideal of chastity as the perfect way of life. In Chapter 3, we saw that the church wanted to keep humans from crossing forbidden boundaries in bestial intercourse. The lessons from saints' lives went further; perfection required struggling against the bestial passion within, to avoid becoming like an animal. As Saint Aelred warned, there were people "whom obscene lust has transformed into animals."[29]

In this narrative so far, one can see that saints' lives help define humanity by highlighting the functions of humans in relationship to the ways the first three chapters showed humans interacting with animals. In the last two chapters, I showed how animals of the imagination in literature helped reveal the animal within humans, thus helping to break down the paradigm of separation of species. When one compares the descriptions of the relations between saints and animals in the early Middle Ages with the later narratives, saints' lives can also reveal the growing ambiguity between humans and animals.

In the early medieval saints' lives, the prevailing miraculous interaction between saints and animals was that saints frequently demonstrated the power to suspend the bestial nature of animals in their presence. Early medieval saints who retreated from society into the wilderness, whether to the eastern deserts or the northern forests, reveal similar talents with regard to the animals' world. In the presence of sanctity, animals renounced their bestial nature, which was defined as "irrational" and violent, with no capacity for human "friendship,"[30] and frequently marked by the desire to eat humans. There are two main forms of interactions between saints and animals in the saints' lives before the twelfth century. Animals either simply suspended their bestial behavior or went beyond that and acquired some human qualities.

The transformation of bestial behavior in the presence of sanctity had biblical precedent with Daniel in the lions' den and appears regularly in martyr stories. In only two out of many examples, a lion refuses to harm St. Thecla,[31] and scavangers resist eating the corpse of St. Vincent.[32] The theme continues after the age of martyrdom: wolves and bears do not harm St. Columban in the woods, and animals recoil from hurting desert hermits.[33] Animals also suspend their natural inclinations to eat things other than the nearby saint. For example, St. Cuthbert forbids ravens to eat grain or steal thatch for their nests.[34] For a saint to generate such behavior on the part of animals is miraculous, but only requires suspension of animal behavior (viciousness and hunger). It is a higher level of miracle for animals to take on some human traits, and that transformation appears in the second form of animal story.

Some animals take on human emotions in the presence of early medieval sanctity. The most common and familiar theme of this sort is contained in tales of grateful animals. The examples I have given above of Jerome and his lion and the grateful lioness that brought a fur to the holy man are of this type. In addition to gratitude, animals in the presence of sanctity can feel guilt (a wolf that steals a hermit's loaf)[35] or prescient sadness at the imminent death of a holy person (Colomba's horse).[36]

Sometimes a saint could cause animals to take on the human trait of kindness (or at least helpfulness). Some animals in the *Vitae* offered help spontaneously to saints, for example, serving as guides,[37] or helping to bury dead saints.[38] Otters came out of the sea to dry and warm Cuthbert's feet after he was chilled from extensive prayer.[39] Spontaneous behavior of this sort was a higher level of miracle than gratitude, because animals take on the human quality of compassion simply in the presence of a saint without any precipitating kindly action.

Finally, examples of animals acting most like humans in the early medieval saints' lives occurred when animals brought food to saints.[40] In these cases, animals completely reversed their natural inclination to consume the human, in favor of feeding him or her. In this circumstance, in the presence of a saint a prelapsarian relationship was once again established between humans and animals. They peacefully coexisted, and animals recognized and placidly accepted the human dominion that early Christian thinkers believed was endowed by God in Genesis.

Thus in the early Middle Ages the predominate stories of the interactions between saints and animals reflect the strong Christian position of a dichotomy between the species. Saints miraculously transformed the bestial where they saw it most clearly, in animals, and animals were so different from people that any human-like behavior on the part of the animal was considered miraculous in itself.

In the twelfth century, as I have shown, the early medieval paradigm of separation began to break down, allowing for some perceived ambiguity between humans and animals. Saints after the twelfth century continued to overturn beastly behavior as they had done earlier. Birds were forbidden to eat crops, and rats were expelled from towns.[41] However, if animals were no longer viewed as dramatically different from humans, then these activities were not as miraculous as they had been earlier. New interactions between humans and animals appear that point to a new definition of humanity.

One manifestation of a perceived increased ambiguity between species is the appearance of animals that act distinctly human, that is, show evidence of reason, not just compassion. The *Life of St. Bartholomew* (who died in the late twelfth century) gives one such example. A duckling falls into a cleft of a rock, and the mother duck comes to the saint for help. As she appeals to the saint, the *Vita* says, "let no one doubt but that she was then endowed with human reason." She tugs at Bartholomew's hem "as if to say plainly: 'Get up and follow me and give me back my son.'"[42] Of course, the saint complies and restored the duckling to the mother, but the significance of the story with regard to animals is that the duck manifested human qualities before contact with Bartholomew. The saint only needed to recognize the presence of human reason, not create it in an irrational beast. Furthermore, we are not left with a grateful duck to serve the saint in a non-bestial fashion. Instead the bird returns to its own duck-like pursuits, untransformed by contact with the saint.

This story of avian intelligence is related to a more common miraculous intervention of post-twelfth-century saints, the inclination of saints to save animals' lives. This does not appear in the early Lives, and it would have been virtually inconceivable in a world that saw animals as useful only for human purpose. To save the life of an animal without expecting a human return for it assumes that the animal's life has some intrinsic value beyond its service for humanity. This, of course, is the modern environmental position, but it was a new concept in the twelfth century, and saints, who so often were barometers of cultural values, expressed this new view.

The twelfth-century chronicler Gerald of Wales told of St. Kevin in whose upheld hand a blackbird laid its eggs. The saint remained immobile out of concern for the eggs until the young birds hatched and left the saintly nest.[43] The twelfth-century Saint Godric saved a stag and a hare from hunters and rescued other animals from the effects of cold and hunger.[44] Again, as in the case of Bartholomew's duck, the animals were saved with no purpose other than to return them to their animal existence. They did not do any particular favors for the saint after their salvation. This miraculous concern for animals may be contrasted with a similar story from the *Life of St. Malo*. Malo died in the seventh century, but his *Vita* was written about 1100, right at the beginning of the changing sensibility toward animals. Malo brought a sow back to life that had been inadvertently killed by a careless swineherd. The *Vita* says the saint performed the miracle out of compassion for the swineherd; there was no evidence for any concern for the sow.[45]

A final example of saintly concern for animals that led to a miracle as complex as any in the hagiographical records is found in the *Life of Werburga* written by William of Malmesbury. The saint had performed a traditional miracle of overturning bestial behavior by forbidding geese to eat some grain. Her steward, however, ate one of the obedient geese. Werburga gathered up the bones and restored the goose alive to the rest of the flock.[46] Even though the goose simply returned to this world, this resurrection of an animal violates the spirit of Thomas Aquinas's analysis of no afterlife for animals and points to the growing ambiguity in the early medieval paradigm for the separation between humans and animals.

The most extreme example of a saint's cult that completely eliminates the lines between humans and animals is that of Saint Guinefort, a greyhound that was venerated in a region of France near Lyons. The fame of the greyhound Guinefort derived from a legend that has ample precedent in Indo-European folklore. In the tale, an infant is left alone in a house with a dog. A serpent enters and approaches the baby's cradle. The faithful greyhound attacks the serpent, and in the ensuing fight is covered with the serpent's blood. The dog is victorious, throws the body of the serpent far from the cradle and lies down next to the cradle to continue its vigilance. When the family returns, they discover the dog covered with blood, and thinking the dog has killed the child, the master kills the dog. When they find the child safe and the serpent dead, the facts become apparent. The innocent dog is vindicated as a martyr.[47] Jean-Claude Schmitt shows that in the twelfth century a cult grew up venerating the greyhound as a saint that could be called upon to protect children.[48] If saints were supposed to embody perfect humanity, worshipping a dog offers the most profound violation of what the church considered sanctity, and in fact, in the thirteenth century the Inquisition attempted to stamp out the veneration.[49] But the example of the cult of the greyhound offers a vivid example of the way that impressions of sanctity show the growing ambiguity between species.

The greyhound cult, as well as the stories that show saints being kind to animals for the sake of animals themselves, point to the beginnings of the perception that animals were closer to humans. In addition, however, we can see in saints' lives humans moving closer to animals. Saints transcend the bestial that becomes increasingly apparent within humans. Saints like Kevin show no trace of violence in their solicitude for small creatures. Furthermore, by saving animals from hunters or from hungry stewards, saints overcome the bestial actions and appetites of their fellow humans. By these actions, saints look back to the spirit of Saint Ambrose, who described the power of the Holy Spirit as having the ability to remove the bestial from humanity: "We, then, were wild animals....But now through the Holy Spirit the madness of lions, the spots of leopards, the craftiness of foxes, the rapacity of wolves have passed away from our affections."[50]

In the early Middle Ages, people had taken for granted that humans and animals were profoundly different. Saints could, therefore, focus their miracles on transforming the animals they encountered in their spiritual quests. After the twelfth century, that separation no longer seemed so secure, so saints miraculously recreated the action of the Holy Spirit, saving people from the bestial within themselves.

In this spirit, late medieval saints look back to the allegorical interpretations of Origen in the second century. Origen interpreted many biblical references to animals allegorically, including the famous verse in Genesis in which God gave humans dominion over animals, saying that the "animals" were human passions that needed control.[51] In the actions and attitudes of these saints, we can begin to see a reemphasis of the classical Platonism that had shaped Origen's thought and had linked humans and animals together more closely than most early Christian thinkers allowed.

The late medieval tendency to blur the lines between humans and animals may be most clearly seen in the thirteenth century in the *Life of St. Francis*. St. Francis recognized and acknowledged the animal part of himself. As his biographer wrote, "He used to call his body Brother Ass, for he felt it should be subjected to heavy labor, beaten frequently with whips and fed the poorest food."[52] His mistreatment of the animal within himself did not lead, however, to a similar maltreatment of other animals, for St. Francis saw some humanity in animals that deserved compassion.

St. Francis expressed a Platonic belief that all creatures contained something of the Divinity; thus in the words of his biographer, St. Bonaventure, he called "creatures, no matter how small, by the name of brother or sister, because he knew they had the same source as himself." While St. Francis was compassionate to many animals, his favorite were lambs, "which present a natural reflection of Christ's merciful gentleness and represent Him in Scriptural symbolism."[53] Thus, St. Francis erased the lines between symbol and reality, and

176

expressed his piety by "ransoming" lambs that were being led to slaughter. He was instrumental in training sheep and lambs to attend church service.[54] These interventions were nonmiraculous expressions of compassion, but St. Francis, like the earlier saints, showed his sanctity by miraculously overturning animal qualities. When a "ferocious sow," in behavior standard for the animal, killed a new-born lamb, St. Francis cursed the sow, saying, "may no man or beast ever eat of her." The curse came true, and the sow died, lay in a ditch, and "did not serve as food for any hungry animal."[55] The nature of the sow was to be food; St. Francis overturned that nature, making the animal inedible.

St. Francis also transformed the bestial in wild creatures. Timid rabbits did not fear him, fish played by his boat, and birds obeyed his commands for silence.[56] These miracles were in the same tradition as those performed by the early Christian saints whose sanctity was marked by their ability to transform the nature of wild beasts and restore at least on a small scale the prelapsarian peaceful coexistence of the Garden of Eden. St. Bonaventure poetically described this quality of St. Francis: "it subdued ferocious beasts, tamed the wild, trained the tame and bent to his obedience the brute beasts that had rebelled against fallen mankind." The difference between St. Francis and the early saints was that these miracles were marked by a different interpretation of the relative position of humans and animals. Such miracles in the *Lives* of the early saints were demonstrations of the differences between humans and animals. In St. Francis, they demonstrated the connections between the species. Again, in St. Bonaventure's words: "Truly this is the virtue that unites all creatures in brotherhood."[57]

St. Bonaventure's words and St. Francis' actions can be contrasted with the more traditional position of the thirteenth-century church articulated by Thomas Aquinas. Thomas wrote a good deal about the irreconcilable differences between humans and animals, but his position might be succinctly summarized in his words "[the] life of animals...is preserved not for themselves, but for man."[58] In this philosophy, it would have made no sense for St. Francis to save lambs from slaughter; lambs had no purpose other than to serve humans' needs. St. Francis' sanctity was shown in his ability not only to transcend the bestial in animals, but to overcome animal inclinations within humans by showing compassion for animals when there was little cultural support for such compassion.

This brief summary of the kinds of interactions between humans and animals that were described in medieval saints lives tells us good deal about the way people looked at animals. In the early Middle Ages, animals were seen as so separate from humans that any suspension of bestial behavior was miraculous. In the twelfth century, the lines between the species were not so clear, and saints interacted with animals that were less bestial to begin with and began to be credited for the miraculous overturning of the beast within. St. Francis (and many of the saints that followed his model) brought this development to a fuller expression, seeing humans and animals as joined in a chain of God's love.

Thus saints defined humanity by contrast with bestiality, and we can draw positive conclusions about what is a human. Many texts offer defining elements of humanity: humans wear clothes, use fire, speak and laugh.[59] Beyond these things, however, humanity was defined as that which was rational. In humans, the mind can govern the passions and appetites that govern the animal world. Saints as perfect humans were defining humanity by their ability to transcend the bestial, the irrational, wherever they found it, whether in the wilderness or within the human mind.

In our modern view, we do not separate our human selves from our bestial selves by the clear divisions of rational versus irrational. For us the human animal is just that, linking both reason and passion. For the most part, we expect our reason to be able to override passion, thus we join our medieval ancestors in marking ourselves human by our intellect. Our modern view of ourselves as animals and the related concerns that emerge from this view had their roots in Western Europe in the twelfth century. The metaphors people used to understand themselves and their actions caused them to link themselves with animals in their own imaginations. From that point, it was a matter of time until someone like Darwin would find a scientific explanation to complete the union. Of course, all this has taken a long time. We do not change our identity easily. It was difficult for early Christian thinkers to persuade people that they were different from animals, and it was an idea that did not hold up under the pressures of new texts and competing images. In our definition of what it means to be human, it seems we cannot deny for long the beast within us.

Appendix

Relative Animal Values

The charts on the following pages show some rough comparisons of animal values as revealed in the early medieval law codes. While it is difficult to compare different societies with differing monetary values, it is possible to do some general comparisons, particularly by comparing the gold in the coins. The value of the solidus ranged from 4 to 4 1/2 grams of gold in Spain (and in Byzantium). The value in Italy and western Europe was lowered in A.D. 367 to 3.89 grams of gold. In the eleventh century, the Franks created the sou, based on the solidus, which had 3.78 grams of gold. In England in 1066 the shilling was worth 16.2 grams of silver.[1]

---

[1] F. Pick and R. Sedillot, *All the Monies of the World—A Chronicle of Currency Values* (New York, 1971), 525, 538, 553, 539.

Continental Laws — Animal Values

	Visigothic: 476-654	Burgundian: 483-532	Alamannic Laws: ca. 718	Bavarian Laws: ca. 745	Lombard Laws: 643-755
1 Tremisis	-Stealing bell from ram -confining another's animal	-Tracker for lost goat	-Stealing cow or draft horse -killing doe	-Stealing bell from small animal -cutting tail off horse -breaking horn from ox	-Causing miscarriage in pregnant cow
2 tremises	-Stealing bell from cow		-Damaging draft horse	-Stealing bell from cow	
1 solidus	-Stealing bell for mare or ox -freeing horse from hobbles -overworking animal	-Tracker for lost cow, sheep or pig -killing a dog	-Killing cow, guard dog -wounding shackled stag	-Stealing bell from horse or ox -killing guard dog -killing small hawk or tame songbirds	-Causing miscarriage in pregnant mare
1½ to 2 solidi		-Tracker for lost ox, mare	-Killing ox -cutting tail off horse		-Riding someone else's horse
3 solidi	-Branding stray animal	-Tracker for lost horse	-Killing someone's deer -killing draft horse -killing bull -stealing hunting dog	-Killing hunting dog -sheep dog	
5 solidi		-Stealing hunting dog			
6 solidi		-Stealing falcon	-Stealing lead cow or hog -killing someone's deer -killing mare or bull -killing horse -stealing milk giving mare -killing lead cow or hog	-Killing hunting dogs -tracking dogs -hawks	-Stealing immature domesticated stag -stealing falcon -cutting tail off horse
12 solidi			-Stealing or killing bison, stag, or best mare -killing stallion or lead horse of draft team		-Striking domesticated mature stag -stealing lead boar

British Laws — Animal Values

Laws of Ine: ca. 685	Aethelstan: 925-940	Ethelred: 991-1016
2 pence -Breaking off cow's horn		**2 pence** -Killing goat
5 pence -Cutting cow's tail -damaging eye of ox		
1 shilling -Damaging ewe with lamb -damaging tail of ox -damaging eye of cow	**1 shilling** -Killing sheep	**1 shilling** -Killing sheep
		8 pence -Killing swine
10 pence -Damaging horn of ox	**10 pence** -Killing pig	
	20 pence -Killing cow	
		24 pence -Killing cow
		30 pence -Killing ox
		12 shillings -Killing unbroken colt
		20 shillings -Killing mare
		30 shillings -Killing horse
	1 mancus -Killing ox	
	¹/₂ pound -Killing horse	
		1 pound -Killing man

Continental Laws — Human Values

Visigothic: 476-654	Burgundian: 483-532	Alamannic Laws: ca. 718

Alamannic Laws: ca. 718

2 Solidi -Striking a freewoman, drawing no blood

5 Solidi -Breaking teeth of non-noble person

12 Solidi -Cutting off a thumb

15 Solidi -Breaking teeth of noblemen

20 Solidi -Injuring an eye

40 Solidi -Cutting off arm or foot

200 Solidi -Killing a person between ages of 50 and 70

250 Solidi -Killing a freedman

300 Solidi -Killing a non-noble person between ages of 20 and 50

500 Solidi -Killing a nobleman

Notes

Notes to Introduction: WHAT IS AN ANIMAL?

1. Augustine, *City of God* (Middlesex, 1972), xviii, 18, 783.
2. Gerald of Wales, *The Journey Through Wales / The Description of Wales* (New York, 1988), 116.
3. J. Rachels, *Created from Animals: The Moral Implications of Darwinism* (New York, 1991), 4. See also K. Thomas, *Man and the Natural World: A History of the Modern Sensibility* (New York: 1983), 122.
4. J. Berger, "Vanishing Animals," *New Society* 39 (31 March 1977), 665.
5. N. Fiddes, *Meat: A Natural Symbol* (New York: 1991), 132-43.
6. The best work tracing this changing sensibility is Thomas, *Man and the Natural World*.
7. L. Rosenfield, *From Beast-Machine to Man-Machine* (New York, 1968), 54.
8. Genesis 1:28.
9. J. Cohen, *"Be Fertile and Increase, Fill the Earth and Master It": The Ancient and Medieval Career of a Biblical Text* (Ithaca, 1989), 5.
10. Cohen, *"Be Fertile and Increase,"* 224.
11. For an analysis of classical attitudes towards animals, see Tilley, "Martyrs, Monks, Insects, and Animals," in *The Medieval World of Nature*, ed. J. Salisbury (New York: 1993), 96-8. Other works also stress the difference between classical and

Christian attitudes. See H. Te Velde, "A Few Remarks upon the Religious Significance of Animals in Ancient Egypt," in *Numen* 27 (1980), 76-82, which shows animals and humans viewed as partners in the world. See also Thomas, *Man and the Natural World*, 75; H. White, "The Forms of Wildness: Archaeology of an Idea," in *The Wild Man Within: An Image in Western Thought from the Renaissance to Romanticism*, ed. E. Dudley and M. Novak (Pittsburgh, 1972), 24; and A. Elliott, *Roads to Paradise: Reading the Lives of the Early Saints* (Hanover, 1987), 196.

12. B. Perry, ed., *Babrius and Phaedrus* (Cambridge, 1965), 469.

13. Albertus Magnus, "Quaestiones Super de Animalibus," in *Opera Omnia I*, ed. by E. Filthaut (Austria, 1955), Q 8, 113; Q 17-18, 247.

14. Albert the Great, *Man and the Beasts*, trans. J. Scanlan (Binghamton, 1987), 2, 1, 68.

15. Albert the Great, *Man and Beasts*, 2, 1, 69.

16. T. White, *The Bestiary: A Book of Beasts* (New York, 1960), 7.

17. Thomas Aquinas, *Summa Theologica*, Q 159, 2, 1845.

18. This contrasts with the modern post-Darwinian position that intellectual differences between humans and higher mammmals are a matter of degree not kind. For an excellent, concise discussion of modern views about whether humans are the only rational animals, see J. Rachels, *Created from Animals* , 132-47.

19. Ambrose, "On Faith in the Resurrection," *Funeral Orations by Saint Gregory Nazianzen and Saint Ambrose*, trans. L. McCauley et al. (Washington, D.C., 1953), 256.

20. Augustine, "Divine Providence and the Problem of Evil," trans. Russell, in *Writings of Saint Augustine*, vol. 1, *Fathers of the Church* (New York, 1948), 326.

21. Aquinas, *Summa Theologica*, Q 93, 2, 470.

22. Thomas Aquinas, *On the Power of God*, trans. English Dominican Fathers (Westminster, Md., 1952) 2, 9, 141. For a modern argument in favor of animals in paradise, see "The Question of Animal Redemption," in A. Linzey and T. Regan, *Animals and Christianity: A Book of Readings* (New York, 1988), 79-110.

23. Aquinas, *Summa Theologica*, Q 17, 2, 657; Q 16, 2, 654.

24. Aquinas, *Summa Theologica*, 1-2, 13.2. See P. Sobol, "The Shadow of Reason," in *The Medieval World of Nature*, 120, for a discussion of this position.

25. Albertus Magnus, "Quaestiones Super de Animalibus," Q 3, 189. For an analysis of the complexities of the wolf/sheep question for scholastics, see P. Sobol, "The Shadow of Reason," 112-15.

26. H. Wolfson, "The Internal Senses in Latin, Arabic, and Hebrew Philosophic Texts," *Harvard Theological Review* 28 (1935), 89. Wolfson explains: "It would...be necessary to introduce another faculty which would act upon the imagination of animals as the rational or deliberative faculty acts upon the imagination of man."

27. See Wolfson, "The Internal Senses," 69-133, for a discussion of these internal senses.

28. Sobol, "The Shadow of Reason," 121, claims that the medieval inability to really

study animal behavior was due to the link between reason and immortality; by eliminating animals from the latter, it was impossible to grant them the former. This is, of course, true, but it avoids the larger question of how people looked at animals at all. Rachels, *Created from Animals*, 143, shows that Darwinism "...insists that human psychology and animal psychology are continuous." Thus after Darwin, one can study animal psychology for what one can learn about humans. This marks the shift in the way people looked at animals that shaped scientific inquiry.

29. Aquinas, *Summa Theologica*, Q 17, 2, 657.

30. J. Baker, "Old Testament Attitudes to Nature," in Linzey and Regan, *Animals and Christianity*, 12.

31. Isidore, *Etymologies*, 1, 1, 57.

32. Isidore, *Etymologies*, 2, 25, 75.

33. L. White, Jr., "The Historic Roots of Our Ecologic Crises," *Science* 155 (1967), 1203-7; and "Continuing the Conversation," in *Western Man and Environmental Ethics: Attitudes Towards Nature and Technology*, ed. I. Barbour (Reading, Mass., 1973), 55-65.

34. For example, different thinkers have interpreted the text to mean humans were given responsibility to care for creatures. This analysis yielded ideas "...much more akin to the aims of...environmental conservation." J. Baker, "Old Testament Attitudes to Nature," 16.

35. In a general work on animals in the ancient Roman world, Toynbee concludes that the prevailing attitude towards animals was for the most part one of insensitivity to cruelty. J.M.C. Toynbee, *Animals in Roman Life and Art* (Ithaca, 1973), 23.

36. M-D. Chenu, *Nature, Man, and Society in the Twelfth Century: Essays on New Theological Perspectives in the Latin West* (Chicago, 1968), 4-5. See also J. Cohen, *"Be Fertile and Increase, Fill the Earth and Master It,"* 279-80, for a discussion of the new approach to nature.

37. The degree to which these issues continue to be current may be seen in the 1993 issue of the *Journal of Social Issues*, which devoted the issue to considering the role of animals in human society. The editor noted that one of the recurrent themes is the ongoing "tension between animals as property and animals as individuals." S. Plous, "The Role of Animals in Human Society," *Journal of Social Issues* 49, no.1 (1993), 6.

38. A. Kinsey, *Sexual Behavior in the Human Male* (Philadelphia, 1948), 671.

39. Aquinas, *Summa Theologica*, Q 25, 3, 1287-88.

40. See Thomas, *Man and the Natural World*, for the development of animals as pets and sources of affection in the early modern period.

41. As Keith Thomas has observed, "it is impossible to disentangle what the people of the past thought about plants and animals from what they thought about themselves." *Man and the Natural World*, 16. See also *Animals and Christianity*, xiii, for the same recognition: "the path to self-understanding must proceed through an

understanding of 'the other,' even when the other is not human."

Notes to Chapter One: ANIMALS AS PROPERTY

1. See J. Clutton-Brock, *Domesticated Animals from Early Times* (Austin, Tex., 1981) for an excellent discussion of the process of domestication of animals. *Ancient Europe* (Chicago, 1965), 35-37, discusses specifically the paleolithic animals of Western Europe.

2. Ambrose, "Paradise," in *Saint Ambrose: Hexameron, Paradise, and Cain and Abel*, trans. by J. Savage (New York, 1961), 328.

3. Isidore of Seville, *Etymologías* (Madrid, 1933) 57-123.

4. J. Clutton-Brock, "The Animal Resources," in *The Archaeology of Anglo-Saxon England*, ed. D.M. Wilson (London, 1976), 384.

5. See J. Clutton-Brock, *Domesticated Animals*, 106-13, for his discussion of the cat and its non-domestic status. See also B. Newman, "The *Cattes Tale*: A Chaucer Apocryphon," *The Chaucer Review* 26, no.4 (1992): 411-23.

6. *English Rural Life in the Middle Ages*, Bodlein Picture Book no. 14. (Oxford, 1965), figure 1b.

7. Thomas Aquinas, *Summa Theologica*, trans. the English Dominican Fathers (New York, 1947), Q 72, 351.

8. Clutton-Brock, *Domesticated Animals*, 22-24.

9. Clutton-Brock, *Domesticated Animals*, 24.

10. See S. Budiansky, *The Covenant of the Wild: Why Animals Chose Domestication* (New York, 1991), 17. Indeed, the whole book makes a fine case for the mutual evolution of domesticated species, including us.

11. See Budianski, *Covenant of the Wild*.

12. M. Fornasari, ed., *Collectio Canonum in V Libris (Lib. I-III)*, Corpus Christianorum VI, (Turnholt, 1970) III, 345, 496.

13. Aquinas, *Summa Theologica*, Q 96, 1, 486.

14. Aquinas, *Summa Theologica*, Q 64, 1, 1466.

15. The Visigothic Code as early as the fifth century specifically said that the laws that applied to animals that were on loan would apply to any other "property which has been loaned." S. Scott, *Visigothic Code* (Littleton, Colo., 1982), 171.

16. Aquinas, *Summa Theologica*, Q. 96, 1, 487.

17. Clutton-Brock, *Domesticated Animals,* 63

18. Clutton-Brock, *Domesticated Animals*, 63.

19. See especially K. Drew, trans., *The Burgundian Code* (Philadelphia, 1972), 84; K. Drew, trans., *The Laws of the Salian Franks* (Philadelphia, 1991), 70-71, 207; L. Larson, *The Earliest Norwegian Laws: Being the Gulathing Law and the Frostating Law* (New York, 1935), 369-70.

20. T. White, *The Bestiary: A Book of Beasts* (New York: 1960), 62.

21. Scott, *Visigothic Code*, p. 282, T. Rivers, *Laws of the Alamans and Bavarians* (Philadelphia, 1977), 91.

22. Scott, *Visigothic Code*, 285, 287.

23. Drew, *Salian Franks*, 71, for example.

24. Walter of Henley, "Husbandry," in E. Lamond, trans., *Walter of Henley's Husbandry* (London, 1890), 111.

25. The sixth-century Ostrogothic laws refer to thefts of animals from "stable or field." "Edictum Theodorici Regis lvi," in S. Riccobono and Johannes Baviera, eds., *Fontes Juris Romani Antejustiniani* (Florence, 1940), 694. See also R. Trow-Smith, *A History of British Livestock Husbandry to 1700* (London, 1957), 113-15, for a description of housing of livestock in medieval England.

26. Walter of Henley, "Husbandry," 113.

27. O'Callaghan, *A History of Medieval Spain* (Ithaca, 1975), 478.

28. Larson, *Norwegian Laws* , 92.

29. Walter of Henley, "Husbandry," 13. See also, Trow-Smith, *Livestock Husbandry*, 116.

30. Trow-Smith, *Livestock Husbandry,* 98.

31. M. Postan, *Cambridge Economic History of Europe*, vol. 1. (Cambridge, 1966), 172-73.

32. Larson, *Norwegian Laws*, 69.

33. Larson, *Norwegian Laws*, 369.

34. See Scott, *Visigothic Code,* 287; Rivers, *Bavarian Laws*, 144; Drew, *Salian Franks,* 88.

35. Trow-Smith, *Livestock Husbandry*, 70.

36. Drew, *Salian Franks*, 68, for example.

37. Larson, *Norwegian Laws*, 69.

38. Walter of Henley, "Husbandry," 95.

39. Walter of Henley, "Husbandry," 13.

40. Rivers, *Laws of the Alamans and Bavarians*, 37.

41. J. Coy, "The Animal Bones," in J. Haslam, "A Middle Saxon Iron Smelting Site at Ramsbury, Wiltshire," *Medieval Archaeology* 24 (1980), 46.

42. Drew, *Salian Franks*, 73, 88.

43. See Langdon, *Horses, Oxen and Technological Innovation: The Use of Draught Animals in English Farming from 1066 to 1500* (Cambridge, 1986) and Lynn White, Jr., *Medieval Technology and Social Change*, (London, 1964).

44. Trow-Smith, *Livestock Husbandry*, 92.

45. Postan, *Cambridge Economic History,* 143.

46. Langdon, *Horses, Oxen*, 175.

47. Langdon, *Oxen, Horses*, 112. See also, Postan, *Cambridge Economic History*, 154.

48. Langdon, *Horses, Oxen*, 162.

49. Walter of Henley, "Husbandry," 13.

50. D. L. Farmer, "Some Livestock Price Movements in 13th Century England," *Economic Historical Review*, 2d ser., 22 (1969): 11.

51. Benjamin Thorpe, *Ancient Laws and Institutes of England* (London, 1840), 297.

52. Drew, *Salian Franks*, 125-26.

53. K. F. Drew, *The Lombard Laws* (Philadelphia, 1973), 117.

54. Larson, *Norwegian Laws*, 69.

55. Walter of Henley, "Husbandry," 93, 111, 117.

56. R. Reed, *Ancient Skins, Parchments and Leathers* (New York, 1972), 32.

57. Reed, *Ancient Skins*, 36-37.

58. See Reed, *Ancient Skins,* 133-44, for some translations of the medieval manuscript recipes for parchment production.

59. Reed, *Ancient Skins*, 40, 126.

60. J. Gantz, *Early Irish Myths and Sagas* (Hammondsworth, 1981), 200.

61. Reed, *Ancient Skins,* 167.

62. Drew, *Salian Franks*, 69.

63. Drew, *Salian Franks*, 88, 100.

64. Postan, *Cambridge Economic History*, 171.

65. Postan, *Cambridge Economic History*, 634.

66. Postan, *Cambridge Economic History,* 380, 425.

67. M. Postan, "Village Livestock in the 13th Century," in *Essays on Medieval Agriculture and General Problems of the Medieval Economy* (Cambridge, 1973), 227, 229.

68. See Dyer, *Standards of Living in the Later Middle Ages* (Cambridge, 1989) for a detailed analysis of the holdings of peasants in the late Middle Ages.

69. Trow-Smith, *Livestock Husbandry*, 60-61.

70. Drew, *Salian Franks*, 70.

71. P. Crabtree, "Zooarchaeology at Early Anglo-Saxon West Stow." in *Medieval Archaeology*, ed. Charles L. Redman (Binghamton, N.Y., 1989), 204, 210.

72. Coy, "Animal Bones," 51.

73. Trow-Smith, *Livestock Husbandry*, 74-75, 79-80.

74. Postan, *Cambridge Economic History*, 439.

75. Trow-Smith, *Livestock Husbandry*, 95.

76. See, J. Klein, *The Mesta* (Cambridge, Mass., 1920) for the best description and analysis of this extraordinary transhumance.

77. Postan, *Cambridge Economic History*, 439.

78. Postan, *Cambridge Economic History*, 380.

79. Trow-Smith, *Livestock Husbandry*, 114. See also Walter of Henley, 115, for recommendations about putting sheep in folds.

80. K. Thomas, *Man and the Natural World* (New York, 1983),273 describes how once the wolf was extinct in England, shepherds could walk behind their flocks.

81. Trow-Smith, *Livestock Husbandry*, 159.

82. B.Lees, ed., *Records of the Templars in England in the Twelfth Century* (British Academy Record, ix) (London, 1935), 51.

83. K. Ponting, *Sheep of the World* (Dorset, 1980), 11-12.

84. *An Illustrated World History of the Sheep and Wool Industry* (Pretoria, 1970), 67, 25. Ponting, *Sheep of the World*, 68, 77.

85. Trow-Smith, *Livestock Husbandry*, 170.

86. See Postan, "Village Livestock," 243, 247, for a discussion of the conversion of

German pastures to arable land under the pressures of population, and for the description of how sheep farming in England was becoming a rich man's occupation in the thirteenth century.

87. Klein, *Mesta*, 25-26, Trow-Smith *Livestock Husbandry*, 143.

88. T.Lloyd, *The English Wool Trade in the Middle Ages* (Cambridge, 1977), 4.

89. Lloyd, *English Wool Trade*, 1.

90. Klein, *Mesta*, 18.

91. Klein, *Mesta*, 303.

92. Klein, *Mesta*, 162.

93. Drew, *Salian Franks,* 70.

94. Reed, *Ancient Skins*, 41.

95. Walter of Henley, "Husbandry," 114-15.

96. Drew, *Salian Franks*, 66-69, 88.

97. Trow-Smith, *Livestock Husbandry*, 51. For Visigothic village laws governing pigs, see Salisbury, *Iberian Popular Religion, 600 B.C. to 700 A. D.* (New York: 1985), 23.

98. Clutton-Brock, "The Animal Resources," 378.

99. Clutton-Brock, *Domesticated Animals*, 22.

100. Piggott, *Ancient Europe*, 235-36.

101. "The Cattle Raid of Cooley," in T. Cross and C. Slover, eds., *Ancient Irish Tales* (New York, 1936), 281-327.

102. Trow-Smith, *Livestock Husbandry*, 80.

103. R. Davis, *Medieval Warhorse* (London, 1989), 107-08.

104. J. Coy, "Animal Bones," 46.

105. Davis, *Medieval Warhorse* , 69.

106. Isidore, *Etymologies*, 1, 43, 65. White, *Bestiary*, 85.

107. See Davis, *Medieval Warhorse*, 135-37, for a glossary of kinds of horses.

108. Davis, *Medieval Warhorse*, 82

109. M. Alexander, trans., *Beowulf* (New York, 1973), 83.

110. Davis, *Medieval Warhorse*, 58.

111. Hermann Pálsson, trans. *Hrafnkel's Saga* (New York, 1971), 38.

112. Drew, *Salian Franks*, 65-98; Larson, *Norwegian Laws,* 92, 168-69.

113. Drew, *Salian Franks*, 71.

114. "Edictum Theodorici Regis," 694. In the thirteenth century the same principle was elaborated by adding recommendations for inquiring into people transporting other people's animals. Henry de Bracton, *On the Laws and Customs of England*, trans. S. Thorne (Cambridge, 1968), 443-49.

115. "Penitential of Columbanus," ed. L. Bieler, *The Irish Penitentials: Scriptores Latini Hiberniae*, vol. 5. (Dublin, 1963), 101.

116. For examples, see Rivers, *Laws of Alamans and Bavarians*, 53-56.

117. Drew, *Salian Franks*, 72, 213-14.

118. Drew, *Lombard Laws,* 113-14.

119. Bracton, *On the Laws*, 42.

120. Drew, *Burgundian Code*, 84. The law requires highest payment (3 solidi) for anyone who can track a lost horse. Rivers, *Alamans and Bavarians*, 83. The *pactus* of the Alamans valued stolen deer at 54 solidi (53-54). The Alammanic laws valued a stallion and a good dog at 12 solidi (90, 95). The Bavarian laws value hunting hawks and tracking dogs both at 6 solidi, the highest value accorded any animal. Rivers, *Alamans and Bavarians*, 169-70. In the Anglo-Saxon laws, the Laws of Aethelstan give the horse the highest value of 1/2 pound. F. Attenborough, trans., *The Laws of the Earliest English Kings* (Cambridge, 1922), 161. The Laws of Ethelred also rank the horse the highest at 30 shillings. Benjamin Thorpe, *Ancient Laws and Institutes of England* (London: 1840), 357.

121. Rivers, *Alamans and Bavarians*, 37.

122. Drew, *Salian Franks*, 99.

123. Scott, *Visigothic Code*, 284-87; Drew, *Burgundian Code*, 83; Drew, *Salian Franks*, 68, 99; Drew, *Lombard Laws*, 116-17; Rivers, *Alamans and Bavarians*, 57, 156-57; Attenborough "Laws of Aethelstan," 161; Thorpe, "Laws of Ethelred," 357.

124. Rivers, *Alamans and Bavarians*, 91-92.

125. Rivers, *Alamans and Bavarians*, 91-92. Drew, *Burgundian Code*, 83.

126. Drew, *Salian Franks*, 66, 68, 71.

127. Drew, *Burgundian Code*, 83.

128. Attenborough, "Laws of Aethelstan," 161.

129. Thorpe, "Laws of Ethelred," 357.

130. Scott, *Visigothic Code*, 284.

131. Davis, *Medieval Warhorse*, 57.

132. Davis, *Medieval Warhorse*, 67.

133. See Drew, *Burgundian Code*, 83, and "Laws of King Ethelred," in Thorpe, *Ancient Laws*, 357.

134. A. Poole, "Live Stock Prices in the Twelfth Century" *English Historical Review* 55 (April 1940), 285.

135. Postan, "Village Livestock," 248.

136. Farmer, "Livestock Price Movements," 14.

137. Scott, *Visigothic Code*, 289.

138. Drew, *Salian Franks*, 92, 99.

139. Drew, *Burgundian Code*, 41.

140. Rivers, *Alamans and Bavarians*, 49.

141. Scott, *Visigothic Code*, 279.

142. Scott, *Visigothic Code*, 289.

143. Drew, *Salian Franks*, 98.

144. "Lex Romana Burgundium," xiii, in S. Riccobono and Johannes Baviera, eds., *Fontes Juris Romani Antejustiniani*, 726-27; Drew, *Salian Franks,* 74.

145. Larson, *Norwegian Laws*, 288.

146. Rivers, *Alamans and Bavarians*, 55.

147. Rivers, *Alamans and Bavarians*, 54.

148. Rivers, *Alamans and Bavarians*, 54-55.

149. Drew, *Lombard Laws*, 115.

150. Larson, *Norwegian Laws*, 134.

151. Attenborough, "Laws of Alfred," 75.

152. E. Bonkalo, "Criminal Proceedings Against Animals in the Middle Ages," *Journal of Unconventional History* 3, no.2 (1992), 26.

153. Bonkalo, "Criminal Proceedings," 27.

154. Larson, *Norwegian Laws*, 103.

155. Drew, *Burgundian Code*, 84.

156. Drew, *Burgundian Code*, 84. the law reads the meat shall be placed "super testones." The term is unclear, and I have taken the translator's opinion.

157. Bracton, *Laws and Customs of England*, 418.

158. Davis, *Medieval Warhorse*, 18.

159. For associations between male sexuality and power see Joyce E. Salisbury, *Church Fathers, Independent Virgins* (London, 1991), 21-23.

Notes to Chapter Two: ANIMALS AS FOOD

1. Thomas Aquinas, *Summa Theologica*, trans. English Dominican Fathers (New York, 1947), Q 64, 1466.

2. Bakhtin, *Rabelais and His World*, trans. Hélène Iswolsky (Cambridge,Mass., 1965), 281.

3. Aquinas, *Summa Theologica*, Q 119, 1, 578.

4. Boswell, *Christianity, Social Tolerance and Homosexuality* (Chicago, 1980), 356.

5. Aquinas, *Summa Theologica*, Q 119, 1-2, 578-80.

6. For a fine description of medieval hunting that details the intimate partnership between humans and animals that made up this pastime, see Cummings, *The Hound and the Hawk* (New York, 1988).

7. *Sir Gawain and the Green Knight*, trans. Burton Raffel (New York, 1970), 85-86.

8. *Sir Gawain and the Green Knight*, 90.

9. See Cummings, *Hound and the Hawk*, 32-60, for detailed descriptions of these two methods of hunting.

10. Gottfried von Strassburg, *Tristan* (Baltimore, 1960), 78.

11. *Sir Gawain and the Green Knight*, 86.

12. L. Larson, *The Earliest Norwegian Laws: Being the Gulathing Law and the Frostating Law* (New York, 1935), 103-4.

13. Descriptions of all the many kinds of hunting dogs can be found in the following sources; K. Drew, trans., *The Laws of the Salian Franks* (Philadelphia, 1991), 70-71, 207; K. Drew, *The Burgundian Code* (Philadelphia, 1972) 84; T. Rivers, *Laws of the Alamans and Bavarians* (Philadelphia, 1977), 95, 169; "Laws of King Cnut" in B. Thorpe, *Ancient Laws and Institutes of England* (London, 1840), 429-30.

14. Gottfried von Strassburg, *Tristan*, 80.

15. Cummings, *Hound and the Hawk*, 26.

16. *Sir Gawain and the Green Knight*, 91, 98.

17. Gottfried von Strassburg, *Tristan*, 81.

18. Rivers, *Alamans and Bavarians*, 53-54.

19. Cummings, *Hound and the Hawk*, 84.

20. J. Coy, "The Animal Bones" in J. Haslam, "A Middle Saxon Iron Smelting Site at Ramsbury, Wiltshire," *Medieval Archaeology* 24 (1980), 49.

21. Cummings, *Hound and the Hawk*, 57.

22. Drew, *Lombard Laws*, 114; Drew, *Laws of Salian Franks*, 95-96; and Rivers, *Alamans and Bavarians,* 53-45;

23. Drew, *Salian Franks*, 95-96.

24. Gerald of Wales, *Journey Through Wales*, 199.

25. H. Waddell, trans., *Beasts and Saints* (London, 1949), 132.

26. Cummings, *Hound and the Hawk*, 60.

27. *Complete Field Guide to North American Wildlife, Eastern Edition* (New York: Harper and Row, 1981), 301, describes this Old World swine that was imported from Europe into parts of New Hampshire and North Carolina for sport hunting.

28. *Sir Gawain and the Green Knight*, 97.

29. Cummings, *Hound and the Hawk*, 102, 104. This ritual is described in *Sir Gawain and the Green Knight*, 98.

30. For example, see M. Schleissner, "Animal Images in Gottfried von Strassburg's *Tristan*: Structure and Meaning of Metaphor," in *The Medieval World of Nature: A Book of Essays*, ed. J. Salisbury (New York, 1993), 80-38, for a discussion of the boar symbolism in *Tristan*.

31. *Sir Gawain and the Green Knight*, 99.

32. Cummings, *Hound and the Hawk*, 113.

33. Cummings, *Hound and the Hawk*, 119.

34. J. Clutton-Brock, *Domesticated Animals from Early Times* (Austin, Texas, 1981), 147.

35. Frederick II, *The Art of Falconry: Being the De Arte venandi cum avibus of Frederick II of Hohenstaufen*, trans. and ed. Casey A. Wood and F. Fybe (Stanford, Calif., 1969), 6.

36. Cummings, *Hawk and the Hound*, 195-99.

37. Rivers, *Alamans and Bavarians*, 37.

38. See Cummings, *Hound and the Hawk*, 214, for a full description of this kind of hunt.

39. Frederick II, *Art of Falconry* 290, 330.

40. Frederick II, *Art of Falconry*, 306-07, 330, 335.

41. Henry de Bracton, *On the Laws and Customs of England*, trans. by S. Thorne (Cambridge, 1968), 43.

42. Braudel, *Civilization & Capitalism: 15th-18th Century*, vol.1 *The Structures of Everyday Life* (New York, 1979), 104.

43. Fiddes, *Meat: A Natural Symbol* (New York, 1991), 2.

44. See Montanari, "Gli animali e l'alimentazione umana," in *L'Uomo di Fronte as Mondo Aminale Nell'Alto Medioevo: 7-13 Aprile 1983* (Spoleto, 1985), 621-22, for a discussion of the varied diet in medieval Europe from the sixth through the tenth

centuries.

45. P. Crabtree, "Zooarchaeology at Early Anglo-Saxon West Stow" in *Medieval Archaeology*, ed. by Charles L. Redman (Binghamton, N.Y., 1989), 209-10.

46. See Montanari, "Gli Animali," 623-28.

47. Heusler, "The Story of the Völsi, an Old Norse Anecdote of Conversion," trans. Nelson, in *Sex in the Middle Ages*, ed. J. Salisbury (New York, 1991), 187.

48. Crabtree, "Zooarchaeology," 209.

49. Theodore of Canterbury, "Canones Gregorii," in F. Wasserschleben, *Die Bussordnungen der abendländischen Kirche* (Halle, 1851), 176.

50. J. Coy, "The Animal Bones," in J. Haslam, "A Middle Saxon Iron Smelting Site at Ramsbury, Wiltshire," *Medieval Archaeology* 24 (1980), 46.

51. M. Postan, *Cambridge Economic History of Europe*, vol.1 (Cambridge: Cambridge University Press, 1966), 528.

52. Montanari, "Rural Food in Late Medieval Italy," in *Bauerliche Sachkultur des Spatmittelalters: Internationaler Kongress Krems an der Donau 21 Bis 24. September 1982* (Wien, 1984), 308. See Langdon, *Horses, Oxen and Technological (Innovation: The Use of Draught Animals in English Farming from 1066 to 1500* (Cambridge, 1986), 263 n. 43, for the sale of horsemeat during famine.

53. J. Clutton-Brock, "The Animal Resources," in *The Archaeology of Anglo-Saxon England* ed. D. Wilson (London, 1976), 378.

54. Montanari, "Rural Food," 318.

55. See Montanari, "Rural Food," 316, for an excellent discussion of this process.

56. Dyer, *Standards of Living in the Later Middle Ages* (Cambridge, 1989), 134-35. See R. Trow-Smith, *A History of British Livestock Husbandry to 1700* (London, 1957), 74, for a discussion of the beginnings of the use of cows for milk in the thirteenth century.

57. Trow-Smith, *Livestock Husbandry* 122-23.

58. Walter of Henley, "Husbandry," in *Walter of Henley's Husbandry* trans. Lamond, (London, 1890), 27.

59. J. Gantz, "The Exile of the Sons of Uisliu," in *Early Irish Myths and Sagas* (Hammondsworth, 1981), 260.

60. Dyer, "English Diet in the Later Middle Ages," in *Social Relations and Ideas: Essays in Honour of R. Hilton* (Cambridge, 1983), 191-93.

61. Dyer, "English Diet," 58-60.

62. Dyer, "English Diet," 195.

63. Dyer, "English Diet," 158-59.

64. Bell, *Peasant Life in Old German Epics* (New York, 1968), 60-61, 67, 80.

65. B. Henisch, *Fast and Feast: Food in Medieval Society* (University Park, Pa., 1976), 130.

66. Henisch, *Fast and Feast*, 129.

67. Einhard, *Life of Charlemagne*, quoted from Henisch, *Fast and Feast*, 137.

68. See Braudel, *Civilization & Capitalism: 15th-18th Century*,vol 1, *The Structures of Everyday Life* (New York, 1979), 187 ff.

69. See, J. Salisbury, *Iberian Popular Religion, 600 B.C. to 700 A.D.* (New York: 1985), 27-29, for the importance of feasting to village communities in the Middle Ages.

70. See, J. Friedman, *The Monstrous Races in Medieval Art and Thought* (Cambridge, Mass., 1981), 26-27, for a discussion of how diet marked medieval and ancient categories of different races of people.

71. M. Douglas, *Purity and Danger* (Middlesex, 1966), 67.

72. Douglas, *Purity and Danger*, 70.

73. Leviticus 11:6, 7, 8, 10, 27, 35.

74. L. Bieler, "Irish Canons I," in , *The Irish Penitentials: Scriptores Latini Hiberniae* vol.v, (Dublin, 1963), 161, 259.

75. Ambrose, "The Holy Spirit," in *Saint Ambrose: Theological and Dogmatic Works*, trans. R. Defararri (Washington, D.C., 1963), 119.

76. Montanari, "Gli animali," 654.

77. Bieler, "Canons of Adamnan," in *Irish Penitentials*, 177, 181, 260.

78. Ambrose, *Saint Ambrose: Hexameron, Paradise, and Cain and Abel*, trans. John J. Savage (New York, 1961), 233.

79. Ambrose, *Hexameron*, 246-47.

80. John Myrc, quoted in Henisch, *Fast and Feast*, 16.

81. Ambrose, *Hexameron*, 233.

82. Larson, *Norwegian Laws*, 398.

83. Brown, *The Body and Society* (New York, 1988), 220.

84. Genesis 1. See J. Baker, "Old Testament Attitudes to Nature," in *Animals and Christianity: A Book of Readings*, ed. A. Linzey and T. Regan (New York, 1988), 15, for a discussion of vegetarianism in paradise.

85. Brown, *Body and Society,* 93.

86. Fiddes, *Meat*, 141.

87. Frederick II, *Art of Falconry*, 31.

88. Bieler "Canons of Adamnan," in *Irish Penitentials*, 177, 179.

89. Gerald of Wales, *The History and Topography of Ireland*, trans. J. O'Meara (London, 1988), 101.

90. Bieler, "Canons of Adamnan," in *Irish Penitentials*, 179. Fiddes, *Meat*, 89, explains that by cooking their meat, humans set themselves apart from other carnivores. Cooking is a defining element of humanity.

91. Chrétien de Troyes, *Yvain: The Knight with the Lion*, trans. Ruth Harwood Cline (Athens, Ga., 1975), 79 and 96.

92. Bieler, *Irish Penitentials: Scriptores Latini Hiberniae*, 63, 113, 125, 131.

93. See for example, Henry, *The Book of Kells* (New York, 1974), 207, or Calkins, *Illuminated Books*, 85-86. Both simply refer to an assumed symbolic meaning for the illustration.

94. Exodus 22:31, Leviticus 7:23,24.

95. Bieler, "Canons of Adamnan," in *Irish Penitentials*, 181.

96. Bieler, "Canons of Adamnan," in *Irish Penitentials*, 177.

97. Theodore of Canterbury, "Canones Gregorii," in F. Wasserschleben, *Die*

Bussordnungen der abendländischen Kirche (Halle: 1851), 175.

98. Bieler, "Canons of Adamnan," in *Irish Penitentials*, 181.

99. Theodore of Canterbury, "Canones Gregorii," in Wasserschleben, *Die Bussordnungen*, 176.

100. Bieler, "Bigontian Penitential" and "Irish Canons I", in *Irish Penitentials*, 161, 163, 217.

101. Bieler, "Old Irish Penitentials" in *Irish Penitentials*, 261.

102. Larson, *Norwegian Laws*, 242.

103. Bieler, "Canons of Adamnan" in *Irish Penitentials*, 177.

104. Edward, Duke of York, *The Master of Game*, ed. W. and F. Baille-Grohman (London, 1904), 33-34.

105. Snorri Sturlson, *King Harald's Saga*, trans. Magnus Magnusson and H. Pálsson (New York, 1982), 140.

106. Drew, *Burgundian Code*, 53.

107. Bakhtin, *Rabelais and His World*, 301.

108. Augustine, "In Joannis Evangelium tractatus," in *Patrologiciae Cursus Completus, Series Latina*, ed. Migne (Belgium: Brepols, 1844–55), 35: 1385; (hereafter *PL*).

109. Piero Camporesi, *The Incorruptible Flesh: Bodily Mutation and Mortification in Religion and Folklore*, trans. T. Croft-Murray and H. Elson (Cambridge, 1988), 106-30.

110. M. Lehnert, *Poetry and Prose of the Anglo-Saxons* (Halle [Saale], 1960), 97.

111. M. Letts, trans., *Mandeville's Travels* (Nendeln/ Liechtenstein, 1967), 141.

112. Letts, *Mandeville's Travels*, 137.

113. Sophocles, "Antigone," in *The Theban Plays*, trans. E. Watting (New York: 1980).

114. See J. Salisbury, "The Origin of the Power of Vincent the Martyr," in *Proceedings of the PMR Conference* 8 (1983), 97-107, for an analysis of this martyr's passion.

115. Ignatius of Antioch, *Epistle to the Romans*, trans. A. Roberts and J. Donaldson in *Ante-Nicene Fathers*, vol. 1 (Edinburgh: 1885), 75.

116. Michael J. Curley, trans., *Physiologus* (Austin, Tex., 1979), 24.

117. Gregory of Tours. *History of the Franks* trans. E. Brehaut (New York, 1969), III, 7, 57.

118. Aquinas, *Summa Theologica* Q 159, 2, 1845.

119. Revelation 19:17-21.

120. Augustine, "The Christian Combat," trans. Russell, in *The Writings of Saint Augustine*, (New York, 1947), 317.

121. Gardiner, *Visions of Heaven and Hell Before Dante* (New York, 1989), 7.

122. Gardiner, *Heaven and Hell*, 38-41.

123. Gardiner, *Heaven and Hell*, 70, 140.

124. Gardiner, "Tundale's Vision," in *Heaven and Hell*, 169.

125. Dante, "The Divine Comedy," trans. L. Binyon, in *The Portable Dante*, ed. Paolo Milano (New York, 1969), 182-85.

126. Collins, *Symbolism of Animals and Birds Represented in English Church Architecture* (New York, 1913), 102.

127. M. Anderson, *Animal Carvings in British Churches* (Cambridge, 1938), 32.

128. For more on cannibalism, see G. Guzman, "Reports of Mongol Cannibalism in the Thirteenth-Century Latin Sources: Oriental Fact or Western Fiction?" in *Discovering New Worlds*, ed. S. Westrem (New York, 1991), 31-68; and P. Camporesi, *Bread of Dreams*, (Chicago, 1980), 40-55.

129. Ambrose, "On His Brother, Satyrus: II," in *Funeral Orations by Saint Gregory Nazianzen and Saint Ambrose*, trans. J. Sullivan (New York, 1953), 221.

130. Augustine, *City of God*, trans. H. Bettenson (Middlesex, 1972), 1062.

131. Augustine, "Sermon #263," in *Saint Augustine: Sermons on the Liturgical Seasons,* trans. M. Muldowney, (New York, 1959), 392.

132. The fullest explanation of this concern with the resurrected body is by Bynum, "Bodily Miracles and the Resurrection of the Body in the High Middle Ages," delivered at the International Conference on Medieval Studies in May 1988. An accessible explanation of the preoccupation with the relationship between the resurrected body and food may be found in Kiernan Nolan, *The Immortality of the Soul and the Resurrection of the Body According to Giles of Rome: A Historical Study of a Thirteenth-Century Theological Problem* (Rome, 1967), 115-22.

133. Nolan, *Giles of Rome*, 55; Aquinas, *Power of God*, II 9, 142.

134. Tertullian, "On the Soul," in *Tertullian: Apologetical Works and Minucius Felix Octavius*, trans. E. Quain (New York, 1950), 255, 257-58.

135. See, for example, Quinn, "Animals in Heaven?" in *Animals and Christianity*, ed. A. Linzey and T. Regan, 94-96.

Notes to Chapter 3: ANIMAL SEXUALITY

1. See J. Salisbury, *Church Fathers, Independent Virgins* (London: 1991) for an analysis of patristic views and definitions of human sexuality.

2. See P. Brown, *The Body and Society* (New York: 1988), 93-94 for an excellent discussion of the heretical Encratite's analysis along these lines.

3. Augustine, "Sermon 213," in *Saint Augustine: Sermons on the Liturgical Seasons* trans. M. Muldowney (New York, 1959), 127.

4. See, for example, John Climacus, *The Ladder of Divine Ascent*, trans. C. Luibheid and N. Russell (New York, 1982), 181, in which he refers to the "serpent of sensuality."

5. Clement of Alexandria, "On Marriage (Stromateis, III)," in J. Oulton and H. Chadwick, trans., *Alexandrian Christianity* (Philadelphia, 1954), 88.

6. *Midrash Rabbah: Genesis*, vol 1, trans. H. Freedman (London, 1951), 22.2, 180.

7. Augustine, *City of God*, trans. H. Bettenson (Middlesex, Eng., 1972), XIV, 16, 577.

8. Clement, "On Marriage," 89.

9. Thomas Aquinas, *Summa Theologica*, trans. the English Dominican Fathers (New York, 1947), Q. 98, 2, 493-94.

10. Augustine, *Saint Augustine: Against Julian*, trans. M. Schumacher (New York, 1957), 199-200.

11. Augustine, *Against Julian*, 148. See J. Salisbury, *Church Fathers*, 42-44 for a discus-

sion of this aspect of Augustine's thought.

12. Albertus Magnus, "Quaestiones Super de Animalibus," in *Opera Omnia I*, ed. E. Filthaut (Austria, 1955), Q 13, 89.

13. Oppian, *Cynegetica*, trans. A. Moir, Loeb Classical Library (London, 1928), lxxx, 125-27.

14. B. Rowland, *Animals with Human Faces* (Knoxville, 1973), 32.

15. Aelian, *On the Characteristics of Animals*, trans. A. Scholfield (Cambridge, Mass., 1959), vol. 1, 177, and vol. 3, 163-65. This belief continued throughout the Middle Ages, as can be seen in Bartholomaeus Anglicus's compendium of animal lore, *Medieval Lore from Bartholomaeus Anglicus*, trans. R. Steele (London, 1924), 152.

16. See, for example, Ambrose, *Saint Ambrose: Hexameron, Paradise, and Cain and Abel*, trans. J. Savage (New York, 1961), 233-34, for the association of the horse with lustfulness. See also B.Rowland, *Animals with Human Faces*, 81, 89, 103, 108, for animals associated with excess lust.

17. Oppian, *Cynegetica*, 145.

18. J. Cummings, *The Hound and the Hawk* (New York, 1988), 108.

19. See P. Payer, *Sex and the Penitentials* (Toronto, 1983), 118.

20. Alexander de Hales, *Summa Theologica*, Tomus III, Secunda Pars, Secundi Libri (Florence, 1930), 656.

21. *Midrash*, 20.3, 160.

22. Aelian, *Characteristics of Animals*, vol. 1, 45; M. Curley, trans., *Physiologus* (Austin, Tex., 1979), 52-53; and Barnabas, "The Letter of Barnabas," in *The Apostolic Fathers*, trans. F. Glimm (New York, 1948), 207.

23. J. Boswell, *Christianity, Social Tolerance and Homosexuality* (Chicago, 1980), 156; Clement of Alexandria, "Paedagogus," in Appendix 2 of Boswell, *Christianity*, 356-57.

24. Curley, *Physiologus*, 50, and Barnabas, "The Letter of Barnabas," 207.

25. Barnabas, "Letter of Barnabas," 207.

26. Clement, "Paedogogus," in Boswell, *Christianity*, 356.

27. Rowland, "Animal Imagery and the Pardoner's Abnormality," in *Neophilologus* 48 (1964), 58.

28. See D. Jacquart and C. Thomasset, *Sexuality and Medicine in the Middle Ages*, trans. M. Adamson (Princeton, 1985), 106-07.

29. Gilles de Corbeil, "Hierapigra Galeni," in *Gilles de Corbeil*, ed. C. Vieillard (Paris, 1908), 261-62.

30. See J. Boswell, *Christianity,* 319, 328, and elsewhere for an excellent analysis of the inconsistent medieval opinion on whether homosexual intercourse was against nature.

31. Boswell, *Christianity,* 389-90.

32. Curley, *Physiologus*, 29.

33. Gaston III, Count of Foix, *Livre de Chasse*, ed. G. Tilander (Karlshamm, 1971), 85.

34. Jacquart and Thomasset, *Sexuality and Medicine*, 162-63.

35. Clement of Alexandria, *Christ the Educator*, trans. S. Wood (New York, 1954), 90.

36. J. Liliequist, "Peasants against Nature: Crossing the Boundaries between Man and Animal in Seventeenth- and Eighteenth-Century Sweden," *Journal of the History of Sexuality* 1, no.3 (January 1991), 413-14.

37. A. Kinsey, *Sexual Behavior in the Human Male*, (Philadelphia, 1948), 671.

38. C. Edsman, "The Story of the Bear Wife," *Ethnos* no. 1-2 (1956), 50-51.

39. See J. Gantz, *Early Irish Myths and Sagas* (Hammondsworth, 1981), 16, for references to many such tales.

40. Aelian, *Characteristics of Animals*, vol. 1, 223.

41. Aelian, *Characteristics of Animals*, vol. 2, 59-61.

42. Aelian, *Characteristics of Animals*, vol. 2, 127.

43. Aelian, *Characteristics of Animals*, vol. 2, 31-33

44. Aelian, *Characteristics of Animals*, vol. 1, 321.

45. Aelian, *Characteristics of Animals*, vol. 1, 21.

46. Aelian, *Characteristics of Animals*, vol. 1, 321.

47. Aelian, *Characteristics of Animals*, vol. 1, 277.

48. Aelian, *Characteristics of Animals*, vol. 2, 63-65.

49. Aelian, *Characteristics of Animals*, vol. 2, 27-31.

50. Aelian, *Characteristics of Animals*, vol. 1, 279.

51. Aelian, *Characteristics of Animals*, vol. 2, 31-33.

52. Aelian, *Characteristics of Animals*, vol. 2, 195.

53. Leviticus 19:19.

54. Leviticus 18:23.

55. Augustine, *City of God*, IV, 27, 169.

56. For the influence of Aelian, see, for example, Curley, *Physiologus*, xxiv-xv: "For subsequent ages Aelian was an authority not to be neglected."

57. Aelian, *Characteristics of Animals*, I, 25, vol. 1, 45.

58. See Salisbury, *Church Fathers*, for a discussion of Christian sexuality.

59. Payer, *Sex and the Penitentials*, 45.

60. Payer, *Sex and the Penitentials*, 45.

61. Basil, "Letter 217," in *Saint Basil: The Letters*, trans. R. Deferrari (Cambridge Mass., 1962), xvi.

62. Basil, "Letter 217," 110.

63. John Climacus, *The Ladder of Divine Ascent*, trans. C. Luibheid and N. Russell (New York, 1982), 283.

64. John Climacus, *Ladder*, 175.

65. John Climacus, *Ladder*, 102.

66. E. Levin, *Sex and Society in the World of the Orthodox Slavs, 900-1700* (Ithaca, N.Y., 1989), 205-6.

67. Payer, *Sex and the Penitentials*, 5.

68. Basil, "Letter 217," 110.

69. R. Huebner, *A History of Germanic Private Law*, trans. Francis S. Philbrick (Boston, 1918), 54-55.

70. Huebner, *Germanic Private Law*, 54-55.

71. L. Bieler, ed., *The Irish Penitentials: Scriptores Latini Hiberniae*, vol. 5 (Dublin, 1963), 75.

72. Bieler, *Irish Penitentials*, 115 and 129.

73. Bieler, *Irish Penitentials*, 103.

74. Bieler, "Grove of Victory," and "Columbanus," 69 and 101.

75. Bieler, "Columbanus," in *Irish Penitentials*, 103.

76. Bieler, "Columbanus," in *Irish Penitentials*, 97.

77. Bieler, "Cummean," in *Irish Penitentials*, 115 and 129.

78. Payer, *Sex and the Penitentials*, 45.

79. "Martin's Canons" in Migne *PL* 84:585.

80. S. Gonzalez Rivas, *La Penitencia en la Primitiva Iglesia Española* (Salamanca, 1949), 177.

81. "Cap. Ab Ansegise," *PL* 97:513-14; "Benedicti Capitulam Collect Lib I," *PL* 97:712.

82. Bieler, "Bigotian Penitent," in *Irish Penitentials*, 221.

83. Payer, *Sex and the Penitentials*, 173 n. 153.

84. Gonzalez Rivas, *Penitencia*, 177.

85. Payer, *Sex and the Penitentials*, 60.

86. Levin, *Orthodox Slavs*, 205.

87. Leviticus 20:15.

88. F. Wasserschleben, *Die Bussordnungen der abendländischen Kirche* (Halle: 1851), 213. See also Payer *Sex and the Penitentials*, 45.

89. Payer, *Sex and the Penitentials*, 184 n. 91.

90. L. Larson, *The Earliest Norwegian Laws: Being the Gulathing Law and the Frostating Law* (New York, 1935), 217, 252.

91. Payer, *Sex and the Penitentials*, 173 n. 150.

92. Burchard of Worms, "Decretorum Libri Decimi Septimmi," *PL* 140:924-26, 968; Ivo of Chartres, "Decreti Pars IX," *PL* 161:682,686.

93. Ivo of Chartres, "Decreti Pars IX," *PL* 161:686.

94. Aquinas, *Summa Theologica*, Q 6, 2, 617.

95. Gerald of Wales, "The Topography of Ireland," in *The Historical Works of Giraldus Cambrensis*, ed. T. Wright (London, 1887), 87.

96. See J. Brundage, *Law, Sex, and Christian Society in Medieval Europe* (Chicago, 1987), 228 and 250.

97. Brundage, *Law, Sex, and Christian Society*, 207.

98. J. Vernet, "Los Médicos Andaluces en el *Libro de las Generacíones de Médicos, - ibn Yulyul*," *Anuario de Estudios Medievales* 5 (1968), 456-57.

99. *Njal's Saga* trans. M. Magnusson and H. Pálsson (New York, 1986), 249.

100. "Ale-Hood," in *Hrafnkel's Saga and Other Stories*, trans. H. Pálsson (New York, 1971), 90.

101. See P. Sørensen, *The Unmanly Man*, trans. J. Turvill-Petre (Odense 1983), for a full discussion of this tradition.

102. H. Janson, *Apes and Ape Lore in the Middle Ages and the Renaissance* (London, 1952), 268.

103. Gerald of Wales, *Topography of Ireland*, 85 and 124.

104. Gerald of Wales, *Topography of Ireland*, 85, 86, 87, 344.

105. Gerald of Wales, *Topography of Ireland*, 85 and 344.

106. Gerald of Wales, *Topography of Ireland*, 85.

107. Gerald of Wales, *Topography of Ireland*, 85.

108. Jacques de Vitry, *The Exempla*, ed T. Crane (New York, 1890), 157.

109. E. Gardiner, *Visions of Heaven and Hell Before Dante* (New York, 1989), 210.

110. Gardiner, *Visions of Heaven and Hell*, 169-70.

111. N. Kiessling, *The Incubus in English Literature: Provenance and Progeny* (Washington D.C., 1977), 21.

112. See J. Russell, *Lucifer: The Devil in the Middle Ages* (Ithaca, N.Y., 1984) for the development in the twelfth century of the idea of demons substantial enough for intercourse with humans. See also, Kiessling, *Incubus*, 21-28, for elaborations of the same theme.

113. Russell, *Lucifer*, 183.

114. J. LeGoff, *The Birth of Purgatory*, trans. A. Goldhammer (Chicago, 1981), 135: "Purgatory did not exist before 1170 at the earliest."

115. Thomas Aquinas, *On the Power of God*, II, 6, 8, trans. English Dominican Fathers (Westminster, Md., 1952), 211.

116. Guibert of Nogent, *Self and Society in Medieval France*, trans. J. Benton (New York, 1970), 223.

117. Guibert, *Self and Society*, 70.

118. Gerald of Wales, *Topography of Ireland*, 411.

119. Geoffrey of Monmouth, *The History of the Kings of Britain* (New York, 1966), 167-68.

120. Caesarius of Heisterbach, *Dialogue on Miracles*, trans. H. von E. Schott et al. (London, 1929), 134. See also pages 134-39 for accounts of demon intercourse.

121. Kiessling, *Incubus*, 24.

122. A. Rigault, *Le Procès de Guicard, évêque de Troyes* (Paris, 1896), 111.

123. Russell, *Lucifer*, 67, for an account of the devil's animal manifestations.

124. Brundage, *Law, Sex, and Christian Society*, 313.

125. Thomas of Chobham, *Summa Conffessorum*, ed. F. Broomfield (Paris, 1968), 402-3. See also Brundage, *Law, Sex, and Christian Society*, 400; he discusses Thomas's *Summa Theologica* as "the most detailed treatment of bestiality in the early 13th century."

126. Alexander of Hales, *Summa Theologica*, 653-55.

127. Aquinas, *Summa Theologica*, Q 154, 11, 1825.

128. Aquinas, *Summa Theologica*, Q 154, 12, 1826.

129. Brundage, *Law, Sex, and Christian Society*, 473.

130. S. Scott, ed., *Las Siete Partidas* (Chicago, 1931), 1427.

131. Rossello, *Homosexualitat a Mallorca a L'dat Mitjana* (Barcelona, 1978), 13-14.

132. K. Thomas, *Man and the Natural World* (New York, 1983), 39, and Liliequist, "Peasants against Nature," 394.

133. See Thomas, *Man and the Natural World*, 119, and Liliequist, "Peasants against Nature," 393-423, for some examples.

134. Thomas, *Man and the Natural World*, 135.

135. Liliequist, "Peasants against Nature," 397.

Notes to Chapter 4: ANIMALS AS HUMAN EXEMPLARS

1. B. Rowland, *Blind Beasts: Chaucer's Animal World* (Kent, Ohio: 1971), 10-11.

2. B. Perry, *Studies in the Text History of the Life and Fables of Aesop* (Haverford, Pa., 1936), xx.

3. L. Daly, *Aesop without Morals* (New York, 1961), 16-17.

4. Gordon, "Sumerian Animal Proverbs and Fables," *Journal of Cuneiform Studies* 12, no. 1 (1958), 4.

5. See, for example, F. Amory, "Skaufalabalkui: Its Author and Its Sources," *Scandinavian Studies* 47 (1975) 293-310, who argues that this Icelandic tale can only have had its origin in ancient Indo-European folklore.

6. Daly, *Aesop*, 21-22.

7. See Daly, *Aesop*, 29-90 for the full narrative of the *Life*.

8. Phaedrus, "Prologue to Book III," in *Babrius and Phaedrus*, ed. B. Perry (Cambridge, Mass., 1965), 255.

9. Daly, *Aesop*, 54-55, 74.

10. See N. Shapiro, *Fables from Old French: Aesop's Beasts and Bumpkins* (Middletown, Conn., 1982), xvii, in which he also observes that Aesop "resembles his own fables of beasts who present proverbial truths."

11. For good summaries of the fable tradition, see Daly, *Aesop*, 15-16.

12. A. Goldschmidt, *An Early Manuscript of the Aesop Fables of Avianus* (Princeton, 1947), 10-22.

13. Daly, *Aesop*, 19.

14. Babrius #41, in *Babrius and Phaedrus*, ed. Perry, 54-5.

15. Babrius #28, in *Babrius and Phaedrus*, ed. Perry, 41.

16. Babrius, #100, Phaedrus #7, *Babrius and Phaedrus*, ed. Perry, 129, 267-68, 456.

17. Phaedrus #7, *Babrius and Phaedrus*, ed. Perry, 381.

18. Babrius #47, *Babrius and Phaedrus*, ed. Perry, 63.

19. Babrius #34, *Babrius and Phaedrus*, ed. Perry, 49.

20. Phaedrus, #4 *Babrius and Phaedrus*, ed. Perry, 265.

21. See M. Curley, trans., *Physiologus* (Austin, Tex., 1979), xiv-xv for a description of the development of the *Physiologus*.

22. W. George and B. Yapp, *The Naming of the Beasts: Natural History in the Medieval Bestiary* (London, 1991), 6.

23. Curley, *Physiologus*, 3.

24. T. White, *The Bestiary: A Book of Beasts* (New York, 1960), 8.

25. White, *Bestiary*, 45.

26. White, *Bestiary* , 38.

27. See F. Klingender, *Animals in Art and Thought* (Cambridge, Mass., 1971), 92, for a discussion of the link between fables and bestiaries in their common use as lessons for human behavior.

28. White, *Bestiary*, 179.

29. B. Rowland, "The Relationship of St. Basil's *Hexaemeron* to the *Physiologus*," in *Épopée Animale Fable Fabliau*, ed. G. Bianciotto and M. Salvat (Paris, 1981), 489. See 491 for Rowland's discussion of Basil's preference for analogy over allegory.

30. One fable about a wolf and one about a crab. See Rowland, "St. Basil's *Hexaemeron*," 495.

31. Ambrose, *Saint Ambrose: Hexameron, Paradise, and Cain and Abel*, trans. J. Savage (New York, 1961), 235-36.

32. Ambrose, *Hexameron*, 236-37.

33. Augustine, "Contra Mendacium," in *PL* 40:538.

34. Augustine, "Christian Instruction," in *Writings of Saint Augustine* vol. 4, trans. J. Gavigan (New York, 1950), 83.

35. Ambrose *Hexameron*, 229.

36. See, M. Tilley, "Martyrs, Monds, Insects and Animals," in *The Medieval World of Nature*, ed. by J. Salisbury (New York, 1993) for a concise discussion of the competing views of the relationship between humans and animals that the Christian tradition inherited.

37. See J. Boswell, *Christianity, Social Tolerance and Homosexuality* (Chicago, 1980), 303, for a similar discussion of how "animal morality" was not a relevant philosophical construct before the twelfth century.

38. George and Yapp, *The Naming of the Beasts*, 1-5. See also White, *Bestiary*, 231-43, for a discussion of the history of bestiaries. White's translation is one of the most complete and accessible versions.

39. J. Morson, "The English Cistercians and the Bestiary," *Bulletin of the John Rylands Library* 39 (1956-57), 151-70.

40. See L. Barkan, *The Gods Made Flesh: Metamorphosis and the Pursuit of Paganism* (New Haven, 1986), 124.

41. See S. Ives, *An English 13th Century Bestiary* (New York, 1942), for a description of illumination techniques for making many copies of bestiaries.

42. White, *Bestiary*, 132.

43. White, *Bestiary*, 237.

44. See for one example, Klingender, *Animals in Art* , 339.

45. Goldschmidt, *Avianus*, 32.

46. Goldschmidt, *Avianus*, 44-47.

47. Goldschmidt, *Avianus*, 3.

48. M. Anderson, *Animal Carvings in British Churches* (Cambridge, 1938), 3.

49. W. Yapp, "Animals in Medieval Art: The Bayeux Tapestry as an Example," *Journal of Medieval History* 13 (1987), 35, 62.

50. L. Randall, *Images in the Margins of Gothic Manuscripts* (Berkeley, 1966), 4-5.

51. See K. McKenzie, "Unpublished Manuscripts of Italian Bestiaries," *Publications of the Modern Language Association* 30 (1905), 380-433, for a good description of fables that entered into Italian manuscripts. A glance at the bestiary translated by White also shows the incorporation of fables into the scientific text.

52. McKenzie, "Unpublished Manuscripts," 383.

53. McKenzie, "Unpublished Manuscripts," 381.

54. F. McCulloch, *Mediaeval Latin and French Bestiaries* (Studies in Romance Language and Literature, No. 33) (Chapel Hill, 1960), 59.

55. A. Henderson, "Medieval Beasts and Modern Cages: The Making of Meaning in Fables and Bestiaries," *Publication of the Modern Language Association* 97 (Jan. 1982), 42.

56. Shapiro, *Fables from Old French*, 74.

57. H. Spiegel, ed. and trans., *Marie de France: Fables* (Toronto, 1987), 3-5, 7.

58. G. Keidel, "The History of the French Fable Manuscripts," *Publication of the Modern Language Association* 24 (1909), 218.

59. A. Henderson, "Animal Fables as Vehicles of Social Protest and Satire: Twelfth Century to Henryson," *Proceedings/ Third International Beast Epic, Fable and Fabliau Colloquium*, ed. J. Goossens and T. Sodmann (Cologne, 1981), 163.

60. Spiegel, *Marie de France*, 103-7, 110.

61. Spiegel, *Marie de France*, 143.

62. Spiegel, *Marie de France*, 143-45.

63. Spiegel, *Marie de France*, 75.

64. Spiegel, *Marie de France*, 57.

65. Daly, *Aesop* , 257, 305.

66. Spiegel, *Marie de France*, 91.

67. Daly, *Aesop*, 133, 277.

68. Spiegel, *Marie de France*, 71.

69. Spiegel, *Marie de France*, 247.

70. Daly, *Aesop*, 151, 283.

71. Spiegel, *Marie de France*, 87.

72. See Spiegel, *Marie de France*, 133-40, for examples. Henderson, in "Animal Fables as Vehicles of Social Protest and Satire: Twelfth Century to Henryson," 164, says that even in Marie's most compassionate moments, she "betrays an upper-class condescension toward [the poor]."

73. Spiegel, *Marie de France*, 43. See also 41 and 163 for other critiques of the legal system.

74. Daly, *Aesop*, 88-89; Spiegel, *Marie de France*, 35-41.

75. Spiegel, *Marie de France*, 185.

76. Spiegel, *Marie de France*, 85. For the classical fable, see Perry, *Babrius and Phaedrus*, 401.

77. Spiegel, *Marie de France*, Fable #100, p. 253.

78. J. Ziolkowski, *Talking Animals: Medieval Latin Beast Poetry, 750-1150* (Philadelphia, 1993), 153, argues for a date of between 1043 and 1046.

79. For an analysis of the epic, see Ziolkowski, *Talking Animals*, 160-97. For a summary of the tale, see W. Rose, trans., *The Epic of the Beast* (London, n.d.), xii-xiv, xvii.

80. Nigellus Wireker, *The Book of Daun Burnel the Ass*, trans. G. Regenos (Austin, Tex., 1959), 23.

81. Wireker, *Daun Burnel*, 28.

82. See Ziolkowski, *Talking Animals*, 210-34, for an analysis of the epic. See Rose, *Epic of the Beast*, xviii-xxii, for a summary of the story.

83. Blackham, *Fable as Literature*, 42, and Rose, *Epic of the Beast*, xxiii.

84. Blackham, *Fable as Literature*, 42.

85. Editions of the full story may be found in Rose, *Epic of the Beast*, 1-151, and D. Sands, ed. *The History of Reynard the Fox* (Cambridge, Mass., 1960). For a discussion of the resolutions in the various versions, see Blackham, *Fable as Literature*, 45-48.

86. Rose, *Epic of the Beast*, 1.

87. Rose, *Epic of the Beast*, 151.

88. Sands, *History of Reynard*, 86-87, 117.

89. Sands, *History of Reynard*, 109; Isidore of Seville, *Etymologías* (Madrid, 1933), 2, 29, 75; White, *Bestiary*, 53-54.

90. Blackham, *Fable as Literature*, 41-42.

91. Blackham, *Fable as Literature*, 42.

92. Sands, *History of Reynard*, 82, 184.

93. Shapiro, *Fables from Old French*, xxxiii.

94. For Odo's biography, the best work remains A. Friend, "Master Odo of Cheriton," *Speculum* 23 (1948), 641-58.

95. "Odo of Cheriton," in *Babrius and Phaedrus*, ed. Perry, #592, 537, #595, 538; #597, 539-40.

96. A. Henderson, "Animal Fables as Vehicles of Social Protest and Satire," *Niederdevische Studiem* 30 (1981), 167.

97. J. Mosher, *The Exemplum in the Early Religious and Didactic Literature of England* (New York, 1911), 68, and see "Odo of Cheriton," in *Babrius and Phaedrus*, ed. Perry, 544.

98. Henderson, "Medieval Beasts and Modern Cages," 41-42.

99. "Odo of Cheriton," in *Babrius and Phaedrus*, ed. Perry, 548.

100. J. Salisbury, *Iberian Popular Religion, 600 B.C. to 700 A.D.* (New York, 1985), 91.

101. See J. LeGoff, *The Medieval Imagination*, trans. A. Goldhammer (Chicago, 1988), 78, for a discussion of the way the new preaching fit in with new ways of looking at the world.

102. Bernard of Clairveaux, "Sermo in Psalmis," xii, *PL* 183:234.

103. J. Mosher, *The Exemplum in the Early Religious and Didactic Literature of England*

(New York, 1911), 3, notes that examples from nature were altogether lacking in the major collections.

104. L. Randall, "Exempla and Their Influence on Gothic Marginal Art," *Art Bulletin* 39 (1957), 100.

105. Mosher, *Exemplum*, 68.

106. Jacques de Vitry, *The Exempla*, ed. T. Crane (New York, 1890), xxi.

107. Mosher, *Exemplum*, 104, and A. Henderson, "'Of Heigh or Lough Estate': Medieval Fabulists as Social Critics," *Viator: Medieval and Renaissance Studies* 9 (1978), 285.

108. F. Whitesell, "Fables in Medieval Exempla," *Journal of English and Germanic Philology* 46 (1947), 358.

109. Whitesell, "Fables in Medieval Exempla," 358.

110. Whitesell, "Fables in Medieval Exempla," 357.

111. See Jacques de Vitry, *Exempla*, liv-lvi, for the widespread use of just his collection.

112. Randall, "Exempla," 101, 107.

113. Mosher, *Exemplum*, 18.

114. I used the extensive medieval manuscript microfilm collection of the Hill Monastic Library at St. John's, Minnesota, to survey the portrayal of animals. Their Austrian collection had an art index, so I was able to draw from the index for this collection. The Austrian holdings include 3154 manuscripts, which represent the complete holdings of eight archives in Austria. The other collections were not indexed by art subject, but the catalogues did show which manuscripts in the collection had illuminations (including marginalia). I looked at all the manuscripts with illuminations in the collections from Portugal (2126 manuscripts from six archives), Cologne (260 manuscripts), and England (275 manuscripts from Queen's College in Cambridge and Lincoln Cathedral). This survey contained enough diversity from various parts of Europe for me to feel confident about the general data.

115. George and Yapp, *Naming of the Beasts*, 48.

116. Ambrose, "On Faith in the Resurrection," *Funeral Orations by Saint Gregory Nazianzen and Saint Ambrose*, trans. L. McCauley et al. (Washington, 1953), 257; Augustine, *Saint Augustine: Sermons on the Liturgical Seasons*, trans. M. Muldowney (New York, 1959), 392.

117. Spiegel, *Marie de France*, 217.

118. Spiegel, *Marie de France*, 161.

119. Spiegel, *Marie de France*, 135.

120. Spiegel, *Marie de France*, 127.

121. Bonaventure, "Life of Francis," in *Animals and Christianity: A Book of Readings*, ed. A. Linzey and T. Regan (New York, 1988), 28.

122. Spiegel, *Marie de France*, 35.

123. See B. Rowland, *Animals with Human Faces* (Knoxville, 1973), 138.

124. White, *Bestiary*, 61-65; Spiegel, *Marie de France*, 81.

125. Spiegel, *Marie de France*, 43; White, *Bestiary*, 66-67.

126. Tertullian, "On the Soul," in *Tertullian: Apologetical Works and Minucius Felix Octavius*, trans. E. Quain (New York, 1950), 255; Boethius, *The Consolation of Philosophy* (New York, 1980), 125.

127. These figures were drawn from F. Tubach, *Index Exemplorum: A Handbook of Medieval Religious Tales* (Helsinki, 1969).

128. Caesarius of Heisterbach, *Dialogue on Miracles*, trans. H. von E. Schott et al. (London, 1929), 224.

Notes to Chapter 5: HUMANS AS ANIMALS

1. E. Leach, "Anthropological Aspects of Language: Animal Categories and Verbal Abuse," in *New Directions in the Study of Language*, ed. E. Leeneberg (Cambridge, 1964), 39-40.

2. Phaedrus #566, in *Babrius and Phaedrus*, ed. B.Perry (Cambridge, Mass., 1965), 453.

3. Perry, *Babrius and Phaedrus*, 527, and H. Spiegel, ed. and trans., *Marie de France: Fables* (Toronto, 1987), 91.

4. Aristotle, *Generation of Animals*, trans. A. Peck (Cambridge, Mass., 1943), 441.

5. T. White, *The Bestiary: A Book of Beasts* (New York, 1960), 22-24, 48, 54-55. For an excellent discussion of medieval artists' creation of hybrid creatures, see J. Benton, *The Medieval Menagerie* (New York, 1992), 48-64.

6. Isidore of Seville, *Etymologías* xii, i (Madrid, 1933), 61.

7. Albert the Great, *Man and the Beasts*, trans. J. Scanlan, (Binghamton, N.Y., 1987), 149.

8. White, *Bestiary*, 32.

9. Gerald of Wales, *The Journey Through Wales/The Description of Wales* (New York, 1988), 88, 199. The story of the stag/horse hybrid was repeated in Gerald of Wales, *The History and Topography of Ireland* (New York, 1988), 75.

10. White, *Bestiary*, 31. This quality was also described in Ovid as an example of metamorphoses, thus reinforcing the notion that it falls into the category of shape-shifting. Ovid, *Metamorphoses of Ovid*, trans. M. Innes (London, 1955), 375.

11. F. Tubach, *Index Exemplorum: A Handbook of Medieval Religious Tales* (Helsinki, 1969), 79.

12. Tubach, *Index*, 92, 205.

13. Guibert of Nogent, *Self and Society in Medieval France*, trans. J. Benton (New York, 1970), 222.

14. Caesarius of Heisterbach, *Dialogue on Miracles,* trans. H. von E. Schott et al. (London, 1929), 77, 232, 293.

15. Roger of Hoveden, *The Annals of Roger de Hoveden*, trans. H. Riley (London, 1853), 486.

16. J. Russell, *Lucifer: The Devil in the Middle Ages* (Ithaca, 1984), 67 n. 10.

17. B. Woods, *The Devil in Dog Form* (Berkeley, 1959), 15-16.

18. White, *Bestiary*, 34.

19. H. Jones, *Apes and Ape Lore in the Middle Ages and the Renaissance* (London, 1952), 18, 29, 165.

20. F. Whitesell, "Fables in Medieval Exempla," *Journal of English and Germanic Philology* 46 (1947), 363.

21. Janson, *Apes and Ape Lore*, 39.

22. Janson, *Apes and Ape Lore*, 40.

23. Janson, *Apes and Ape Lore*, 33.

24. Janson, *Apes and Ape Lore*, 34-35.

25. Hildegard of Bingen, "Physica," in *PL* 197, 1329. Quoted in Janson, *Apes and Ape Lore*, 77.

26. Janson, *Apes and Ape Lore,* 85.

27. Janson, *Apes and Ape Lore*, 77.

28. J. Friedman, *The Monstrous Races in Medieval Art and Thought* (Cambridge, Mass., 1981), 108.

29. Callisthenes (Pseudo), *Alexander of Macedon*, trans. E. Haight (New York, 1955), 123-24.

30. Friedman, *Monstrous Races*, 179.

31. Augustine, *City of God*, trans. H. Bettenson (Middlesex, 1972), 662-63.

32. Friedman, *Monstrous Races*, 181.

33. Gerald of Wales, *The History and Topography of Ireland*, 73-4.

34. Described by the fourteenth-century writer Pierre Bersuire, quoted in Friedman, *Monstrous Races*, 116.

35. D. Jacquart and C. Thomasset, *Sexuality and Medicine in the Middle Ages*, trans. M. Adamson (Princeton, 1988), 163.

36. Friedman, *Monstrous Races*, 94.

37. White, *Bestiary*, 89-90.

38. Tubach, *Index*, 326.

39. See Friedman, *Monstrous Races*, 9-21, for a catalogue of the various races, including the ones described here.

40. Friedman, *Monstrous Races*, 25.

41. White, *Bestiary*, 35. See also, W. George and B. Yapp, *The Naming of the Beasts: Natural History in the Medieval Bestiary* (London, 1991), 91, who identify the Cynocephalus as the Hamadryas baboon.

42. Augustine, *City of God*, 662-63.

43. C. Bologna, ed., *Liber Monstrorum de Diversis Generibus* (Milan, 1977), 50, for example, which identifies the Sciopods as men.

44. Bologna, *Liber Monstrorum*, 34-36; and L. Whitbread, "The Liber Monstrorum and Beowulf," *Mediaeval Studies* 36 (1974), 436.

45. Friedman, *Monstrous Races*, 4.

46. White, *Bestiary*, 51, 86.

47. Callisthenes, *Alexander of Macedon*, 8-9.

48. Callisthenes, *Alexander of Macedon*, 117-19, 122.

49. M. Letts, trans., *Mandeville's Travels* (Nendeln/ Liechtenstein, 1967), xxvii-xxxvi-

ii. See J. Bennett, *The Rediscovery of Sir John Mandeville* (New York, 1954), 1. See also pages 219-43 for the immediate and extraordinary influence of the work.

50. Letts, *Mandeville's Travels*, 138, 141-43, 199.

51. Smith, "Portent Lore and Medieval Popular Culture," *Journal of Popular Culture* 14:1 (Summer 1980), 58.

52. J. Bonnell, "The Serpent with a Human Head in Art and in Mystery Play," *American Journal of Archaeology* 21 (1917), 255.

53. Bernard of Clairveaux, "Apologia ad Guillelmin," in F. Klingender, *Animals in Art and Thought* (Cambridge, Mass., 1971), 335.

54. Bologna, *Liber Monstrorum*, 50, 58-60, 62-64.

55. Friedman, *Monstrous Races*, 183, 185-87.

56. Friedman, *Monstrous Races*, 162, describes the blurring of the races into wild men in the late Middle Ages.

57. R. Bernheimer, *Wild Men in the Middle Ages: A Study in Art, Sentiment, and Demonology* (Cambridge, Mass., 1952), 42-43.

58. H. White, "The Forms of Wildness: Archaeology of an Idea," in *The Wild Man Within: An Image in Western Thought from the Renaissance to Romanticism*, ed. E. Dudley and M. Novak (Pittsburgh, 1972), 20. This figure is different from the "Green Man," who represented people's relationship with nature in general and plants in particular, not animals. See, W. Anderson, *Green Man* (London: 1990), 30-31, for the distinction between the Green Man and the Wild Man.

59. Bernheimer, *Wild Man*, 5, says that the Middle Ages was "ill prepared to answer that question [of whether these creatures were human or animal]."

60. T. Husband, *The Wild Man: Medieval Myth and Symbolism* (New York, 1980), 11.

61. M. Alexander, trans., *Beowulf* (New York, 1973), 54, 65.

62. Chrétien de Troyes, *Yvain: The Knight with the Lion* (Athens, Ga., 1975), 9.

63. Bernheimer, *Wild Man*, 21-22, 73. See also M. Anderson, *Animal Carvings in British Churches* (Cambridge, 1938), 74.

64. White, "Forms of Wildness," 5. See also Husband, *The Wild Man*, 5.

65. White, "Forms of Wildness," 7.

66. Bernheimer, *Wild Man*, 8.

67. Bernheimer, *Wild Man,* 11-12. See also David Sprunger, "Wild Folk and Lunatics in Medieval Romance," in *The Medieval World of Nature: A Book of Essays*, ed. J. Salisbury (New York, 1993), 145-63.

68. Chrétien de Troyes, *Yvain*, 79. See also, Bernheimer, *Wild Man*, 13-14, for other romances.

69. Spiegel, *Marie de France*, 135-40.

70. Andreas Capellanus, *Art of Courtly Love* (New York, 1969), 33.

71. Andreas Capellanus, *Art of Courtly Love*, 149.

72. C. Dyer, *Standards of Living in the Later Middle Ages*, (Cambridge, 1989), 57.

73. P. Camporesi, *Bread of Dreams*, trans. D. Gentilcore (Chicago, 1980).

74. Procopius, *The Gothic War*, trans. H. Dewing (London, 1924), 41-45.

75. Camporesi, *Bread of Dreams*, 87.

76. John of Salisbury, "Polycraticus," *PL* 199, 423.

77. Juvenal, *The Satires of Juvenal*, trans. R. Humphries (Bloomington, 1958), 177-78.

78. G. Macauly, ed., *The Chronicles of Froissart*, trans. Lord Berners (London, 1904), 137.

79. Jordanus Catalani, *Mirabilia Descripta: The Wonders of the East*, trans. Henry Yule (New York, 1963), 21.

80. B. Johnson, *Lady of the Beasts: Ancient Images of the Goddess and Her Sacred Animals* (San Francisco, 1988), 3.

81. See J. Salisbury, *Church Fathers, Independent Virgins* (London, 1991) for patristic views of women as more sensual and sexual than men.

82. B. Roy, "La Belle e(s)t bête: aspects du bestiaire féminin au moyen âge," *Etudes Françaises* 10 (1979), 322.

83. I. Malaxecheverria, "Le Bestiaire médiéval et l'archétype de la féminité," *Circé* 12/13 (1982), 98.

84. Malaxecheverria, "Le Bestiaire médiéval" 23.

85. C. Bynum, *Holy Feast and Holy Fast* (Berkeley, 1987), 206, 208, 260, 269.

86. N. Fiddes, *Meat: A Natural Symbol* (New York, 1991), 160.

87. J. Bonnell, "The Serpent with a Human Head in Art and in Mystery Play," *American Journal of Archaeology* 21 (1917), 257, 279.

88. Jacques de Vitry, *The Exempla*, ed. T. Crane (New York, 1890), 241, 253.

89. Juan Ruiz, *The Book of Good Love*, trans. E. Kane (Chapel Hill, 1968), 93, 120.

90. Juan Ruiz, *The Book of Good Love*, 145-46.

91. See S. Kirby, "Juan Ruiz's *Serranas*: The Archpriest—Pilgrim and Medieval Wild Women," *Hispanic Studies in Honor of Alan D. Deyermond: A North American Tribute* (Madison, 1986), 157-60, for the associations between Ruiz's descriptions and the Wild Woman folklore tradition.

92. G. Fiero, et al., *Three Medieval Views of Women* (New Haven, 1989), 124.

93. Richard de Fournival, *Master Richard's Bestiary of Love and Response*, trans. J. Beer (Berkeley, 1986), xviii.

94. Richard de Fournival, *Master Richard's Bestiary of Love*, xv.

95. Roy, "La Belle e(s)t bête," 332-33.

96. L. Barkan, *The Gods Made Flesh: Metamorphosis and the Pursuit of Paganism* (New Haven, 1986), 2-3, discusses the permeable borders of the universe that permit metamorphosis.

97. Ovid, *Metamorphoses of Ovid*, trans M. Innes (London, 1955), 31.

98. Barkan, *Gods Made Flesh*, 19-27.

99. J. Gantz, *Early Irish Myths and Sagas* (Hammondsworth, 1981), 111-12. 64, 67.

100. See Johnson, *Lady of the Beasts*, 7-98, for traditional associations of women with birds.

101. Tertullian, "On the Soul," in *Tertullian: Apologetical Works and Minucius Felix Octavius*, trans. Quain (New York, 1950), 255.

102. Ambrose, "On Faith in the Resurrection," *Funeral Orations by Saint Gregory Nazianzen and Saint Ambrose*, trans. L. McCauley et al. (Washington, 1953), 256-57.

103. Augustine, *City of God*, 782-84.

104. Thomas Aquinas, *On the Power of God*, trans. by English Dominican Fathers (Westminster, Md., 1952), 187. For Boguet, see C. Otten, *A Lycanthropy Reader: Werewolves in Western Culture* (Syracuse, 1986), 52-53.

105. See Otten, *Lycanthrophy Reader*, 31-40, for psychological analyses of cases of modern werewolves.

106. Burchard of Worms, quoted in D. Kraatz, "Fictus Lupus: The Werewolf in Christian Thought," *Classical Folia* 30 (1976) , 63.

107. L. Larson, *The Earliest Norwegian Laws: Being the Gulathing Law and the Frostating Law* (New York, 1935), 123.

108. Barkan, *Gods Made Flesh* , 104, 308 n. 17.

109. Barkan, *Gods Made Flesh*, 104.

110. See Barkan, *Gods Made Flesh*, 124-26, for the relationship between this idea and the growing popularity of metamorphosis.

111. Gerald of Wales, *The Historical Works of Giraldus Cambrensis*, ed. T. Wright (London, 1887), 84.

112. Otten, *Lycanthropy Reader*, 153.

113. Otten, *Lycanthropy Reader*, 79.

114. Edward, Duke of York, *The Master of Game*, quoted in J. Cummings, *The Hound and the Hawk* (New York: 1988), 133.

115. "*The Malleus Maleficarum*," in Otten, *Lycanthropy Reader*, 113.

116. Gerald, *Journey Through Wales*, 116.

117. Gerald, *Topography of Ireland*, 83.

118. Gerald, *Topography of Ireland*, 79-82.

119. Kraatz, "Fictus Lupus," 60.

120. Marie of France, "Bisclavret," in R. Hanning and J. Ferrante, *The Lais of Marie de France* (Durham, N.C., 1978), 92.

121 Marie de France, "Bisclavret," 94.

122. Marie of France, "Bisclavret," 96.

123. Marie of France, "Bisclavret," 100.

124. Hanning and Ferrante point out that the whole lay is a "parable about the forces of bestiality that exist within human nature and how they should (and should not) be confronted, used, or transcended;" *Lais of Marie de France*, 101.

125. "Arthur and Gorlagon," in Otten, *Lycanthropy Reader*, 234-50.

126. See Kraatz, "Fictus Lupus," 72, for an excellent analysis of the sympathetic werewolf in literature. See also Bernheimer, *Wild Man*, 164, for a summary of the story of "Guillaume de Palerne," another sympathetic tale of transformation.

Notes to Conclusion: WHAT IS A HUMAN?

1. See, for example, G. Taylor, "Shakespeare's Use of the Idea of the Beast in Man," *Studies in Philology* 42 (1945), 530-43.

2. Bonaventure, "The Life of St. Francis," in *The Soul's Journey into God. The Tree of Life. The Life of St. Francis*, trans. E. Cousins (New York, 1978), 186, Bonaventure

calls St. Francis's qualities "superhuman."

3. D. Weinstein and R. Bell, *Saints and Society* (Chicago, 1982), offer a good summary of the ways these medieval saints sought perfection in their lives and in doing so mirrored societal values. For an eloquent analysis of saints directly serving as exemplars, see P. Brown, "The Saint as Exemplar in Late Antiquity," *Representations* 1, no.2 (Spring 1983), 1-25.

4. Bonaventure, "Life of St. Francis," 182.

5. A. Elliott, *Roads to Paradise: Reading the Lives of the Early Saints* (Hanover, 1987), 196, observed that the "Legends of the saints... were one of the vehicles for the transmission of this new view [of animals]."

6. See, J.E. Salisbury, *Church Fathers, Independent Virgins* (London, 1991), for a discussion of how holy women achieved independence by following lives of sanctity. Saint Brynach typified this attitude in his refusal to offer a meal to his king, for he "wanted himself, his dependents and...his monastic foundations, to be free from any obligation...." in D. Bell, *Wholly Animals: A Book of Beastly Tales* (Kalamazoo, 1992), 33.

7. Bell, *Wholly Animals* , 17.

8. Darwin noted the importance we attach to animals as property, for he felt that this would pose one of the impediments to people's acceptance of his theory. He wrote, "Animals whom we have made our slaves, we do not like to consider our equals." Quoted in J. Rachels, *Created from Animals: The Moral Implications of Darwinism* (New York, 1991), 132.

9. Bell, *Wholly Animals*, 76-81; Waddell, *Beasts and Saints*, 25-29.

10. Bell, *Wholly Animals*, 57, 71, 73.

11. L. Delort, "Les Animaux et l'Habillement," in *L'Uomo di Fronte as Mondo Aminale Nell'Alto Medioevo: 7-13 Aprile 1983* (Spoleto, 1985), 673.

12. Ratramnus of Corbie, "Epistola 12," in E. Dümmler, ed., *Epistolae Karolini Aevi* in *MGH Epist.* 6 (Berlin, 1925), 155.

13. Salisbury, *Church Fathers, Independent Virgins*, 117-19.

14. Bell, *Wholly Animals*, 122.

15. Bell, *Wholly Animals*, 93.

16. John Witte of Hees, a fourteenth century pilgrim, quoted in J. Friedman, *The Monstrous Races in Medieval Art and Thought* (Cambridge, Mass., 1981), 143.

17. Paul the Deacon, *History of the Lombards*, trans. W. Foulke (Philadelphia, 1907), 20. L.M.C. Randall, *Images in the Margins of Gothic Mass* (Berkeley, 1966), 86, shows a Cynocephalus eating a human leg.

18. T. White, *The Bestiary: A Book of Beasts* (New York, 1960), 51.

19. "St. Brendan's Voyage," in *Visions of Heaven and Hell Before Dante*, ed. E. Gardiner (New York, 1989), 108.

20. Bonaventure, "Life of St. Francis," 218, 230.

21. Bell, *Wholly Animals*, 19-20, 106-7.

22. For an excellent discussion of Christian fasting, see C. Bynum, *Holy Feast and Holy Fast* (Berkeley, 1987), 33-47.

23. See R. Bell, *Holy Anorexia* (Chicago, 1985), for some of their stories.

24. Bynum, *Holy Feast and Holy Fast*, 300.

25. See Bell, *Holy Anorexia* and C. Bynum, *Holy Feast and Holy Fast*, 194-207, for discussions on the similarities and differences between medieval fasting and modern eating disorders.

26. The account of the plane crash in the Andes in which people survived by eating the dead drew fascinated audiences for both the book and the movie. See, P. Read, *Alive* (New York, 1974). *TIME* magazine reported stories of cannibalism during the Cultural Revolution in China under the title "Unspeakable Crimes." *Time*, Jan. 18, 1993, 35.

27. Weinstein and Bell, *Saints and Society*, 154.

28. J. Schulenburg, "Saints and Sex, ca. 500-1100: Striding Down the Nettled Path of Life," in *Sex in the Middle Ages*, ed. J. Salisbury (New York, 1991). Schulenberg recounts these and many more stories of saintly struggles for chastity, 210-12. See also Bonaventure, "Life of St. Francis, 220, for St. Francis's struggles with lust.

29. J. Boswell, *Christianity, Social Tolerance and Homosexuality* (Chicago, 1980), 303.

30. Thomas Aquinas claimed that animals were incapable of friendship because of their lack of reason. *Summa Theologica*, trans. English Dominican Fathers (New York, 1947), Q 25, 3, 1287-88.

31. Ambrose, "Concerning Virgins," in *A Select Library of Nicene and Post-Nicene Fathers*, vol. 10, ed. P. Schaff and H. Wace (New York, 1895), 376.

32. "Acta S. Vincentii Martyris," *Analecta Bollandiana*, 1 (1882), 264. For an analysis of this *Vita*, see J. Salisbury, "The Origin of the Power of Vincent the Martyr," in *Proceedings of the PMR Conference* 8 (1983), 97-107.

33. Elliott, *Roads to Paradise*, 153; H. Waddell, trans., *Beasts and Saints* (London, 1949), 50; Sulpicius Severus, "Dialogue," trans. B. Peebles, in *Fathers of the Church* vol. 7 (New York, 1949), 179.

34. Waddell, *Beasts and Saints*, 66-67.

35. Sulpicius Severus, "Dialogue," 179-80.

36. Waddell, *Beasts and Saints*, 49.

37. Elliott, *Roads to Paradise*, 159.

38. Salisbury, *Church Fathers, Independent Virgins*, 72.

39. Waddell, *Beasts and Saints*, 59.

40. Elliott, *Roads to Paradise*, 160.

41. Gerald of Wales, *The History and Topography of Ireland*, trans. J. O'Meara (London, 1988), 78, 80.

42. Waddell, *Beasts and Saints*, 94.

43. Gerald of Wales, *Topography of Ireland*, 78.

44. Waddell, *Beasts and Saints*, 87-91.

45. Waddell, *Beasts and Saints*, 53.

46. Waddell, *Beasts and Saints*, 68-70; also told in N. Bell, *Wholly Animals*, 121-22. There are a few early medieval accounts of Irish saints resurrecting animals. See

Bell, *Wholly Animals*, 34, 39, but these are unusual for the early Middle Ages. They may reflect a differing Celtic sensibility that deserves further study, or it may be that resurrection miracles are sufficiently miraculous to be worth performing on animals as well as humans.

47. J-C. Schmitt, *The Holy Greyhound: Guinefort, Healer of Children Since the Thirteenth Century* (Cambridge, 1983), 4-5. This whole work is a careful and insightful analysis of the legend and the rituals that surrounded it.

48. For the dating of the origins of the cult, see J-C. Schmitt, *Holy Greyhound*, 159.

49. J-C. Schmitt, *Holy Greyhound*, 9-36.

50. Ambrose, "The Holy Spirit," in *Saint Ambrose: Theological and Dogmatic Works*, trans. R. Deferrari (Washington, 1963), 134.

51. J. Cohen, *"Be Fertile and Increase, Fill the Earth and Master It": The Ancient and Medieval Career of a Biblical Text* (Ithaca, 1989), 227-28. See also P. Cox, "Origen and the Bestial Soul," *Vigiliae Christianae* 36 (1982), 115-140.

52. Bonaventure, "Life of St. Francis," 222.

53. Bonaventure, "Life of St. Francis," 254-55.

54. Bonaventure, "Life of St. Francis," 256-57.

55. Bonaventure, "Life of St. Francis," 255.

56. Bonaventure, "Life of St. Francis," 257-58.

57. Bonaventure, "Life of St. Francis," 261.

58. Thomas Aquinas, *Summa Theologica*, Q 64, 1, 1466.

59. See Friedman, *Monstrous Races*, 26-36, for a fine summary of the human qualities that were used to distinguish humans from monsters.

Bibliography

Aarne, Antti, and Stith Thompson. *The Types of Folktale: A Classification and Bibliography.* Helsinki: Suomalainen Tiedeakatemia, 1961.

"Acta S. Vincentii Martyris." *Analecta Bollandiana* 1 (1882): 260-64.

Adam of Bremen. *History of the Archbishops of Hamburg-Bremen.* Trans. Francis J. Ischan. New York: Columbia University Press, 1959.

Aelian. *On the Characteristics of Animals.* 3 Vols. Trans. A. F. Scholfield. Cambridge: Harvard University Press, 1959.

Aiken, Pauline. "The Animal History of Albertus Magnus." *Speculum* 22 (1947): 205-25.

Albert the Great. *Man and the Beasts.* Trans. James J. Scanlan. Binghamton, N.Y.: Medieval and Renaissance Texts and Studies, 1987.

Albertus Magnus [pseud.]. *Book of Secrets of Albertus Magnus.* Ed. by Michael R. Best and Frank H. Brightma. Oxford: Clarendon Press, 1973.

Albertus Magnus. "Quaestiones Super de Animalibus." In *Opera Omnia I*, ed. by E. Filthaut. Austria: Monasterii Westfalorum in aedibus aschendorff, 1955.

Alexander de Hales. *Summa Theologica.* Tomus III, Secunda Pars, Secundi Libri. Florence: Typographia Collegii S. Bonaventurae, 1930.

Alexander, Michael, trans. *Beowulf.* New York: Penguin, 1973.

Ambrose. "The Holy Spirit." In *Saint Ambrose: Theological and Dogmatic Works*, trans. by R. J. Deferrari. Washington, D.C.: Catholic Unversity of America Press, 1963.

————. "On Faith in the Resurrection." In *Funeral Orations by Saint Gregory Nazianzen and Saint Ambrose*, trans. Leo P. McCauley et al. Washington, D.C.: Catholic University of America Press, 1953.

————. *Saint Ambrose: Hexameron, Paradise, and Cain and Abel*. Trans. by John J. Savage. New York: Fathers of the Church, 1961.

————. "On His Brother, Satyrus: II." In *Funeral Orations by Saint Gregory Nazianzen and Saint Ambrose*, trans. J. J. Sullivan. New York: Fathers of the Church, 1953.

Amory, Fredric. "Skaufalabalkui: Its Author and Its Sources." *Scandinavian Studies* 47 (1975): 293-310.

An Illustrated World History of the Sheep and Wool Industry. Pretoria: South African Wool Board, 1970.

Anderson, M. *Animal Carvings in British Churches*. Cambridge: Cambridge University Press, 1938.

Anderson, William. *Green Man: The Archetype of Our Oneness with the Earth*. London: Harper Collins, 1990.

Andreas Capellanus. *Art of Courtly Love*. Trans. by John J. Perry. New York: W. W. Norton, 1969.

"Ansegisi abbatis capitularium collectio." Ed. by Migne, *Patrologiae Cursus Completus, Series Latina*, Belgium: Brepols, 1844-55, 97: 513ff. (Hereafter *PL*.)

Aquinas, Thomas. *On the Power of God*. Trans. by the English Dominican Fathers. Westminster, Md.: Newman Press, 1952.

————. *Summa Theologica*. Trans. by the English Dominican Fathers. New York: Benzigen Bros., 1947.

————. *Truth*. Vols. 1, 2, and 3. Chicago: Henry Regnery, 1952.

Aristotle. *Generation of Animals*. Trans. by A. L. Peck. Cambridge: Harvard University Press, 1943.

Aristotle's De Anima. Trans. by K. Foster and S. Humphries. London: Routledge and Kegan Paul, 1951.

Atil, Esin. *Kalila wa Dimna: Fables from a Fourteenth-Century Arabic Manuscript*. Washington, D.C.: Smithsonian Institution Press, 1981.

Attenborough, F. L., ed. and trans. *The Laws of the Earliest English Kings*. Cambridge: Cambridge University Press, 1922.

Augustine. *City of God*. Trans. by Henry Bettenson. Middlesex, Eng: Penguin, 1972.

————. "Contra Mendacium." *PL* 40:538.

————. "Divine Providence and the Problem of Evil." In *Writings of Saint Augustine*. Vol. 1. Trans. by Robert P. Russell. New York: CIMA Publishing Co., 1948.

————. "Faith, Hope and Charity." *Writings of Saint Augustine*. Vol. 4. Trans by Bernard M. Peebles. New York: Fathers of the Church, 1950.

————. "In Joannis Evangelium tractatus." *PL* 35:1385.

————. *On Christian Doctrine*. Trans. by D. W. Robertson. New York: Liberal Arts Press, 1958.

————. *Saint Augustine: Against Julian*. Trans. by Matthew A. Schumacher. New York: Fathers of the Church, 1957.

————. *Saint Augustine: Sermons on the Liturgical Seasons.* Trans. by Mary Sarah Muldowney. New York: Fathers of the Church, 1959.

————. *The Writings of Saint Augustine.* Vol. 4. New York: Fathers of the Church, 1947.

Bakhtin, Mikhail. *Rabelais and His World.* Trans. by Hélène Iswolsky. Cambridge: MIT Press, 1965.

Bambeck, M. "Das Werwolfmotif im Bisclavret." *Zeitschrift für romanische Philologie* 89 (1973): 123-47.

Barkan, Leonard. *The Gods Made Flesh: Metamorphosis and the Pursuit of Paganism.* New Haven: Yale University Press, 1986.

Barnabas. "The Letter of Barnabas." in *The Apostolic Fathers.* trans. by F. X. Glimm, 187-224. New York: Christian Heritage, 1948.

Bartholomaeus Anglicus. *Medieval Lore from Bartholomaeus Anglicus.* Trans. by Robert Steele. London: Chatto & Windus, 1924.

————. *On the Properties of Things: John Treviso's Translation of Batholomaeus Anglicus Proprietatibus Rerum (1495)* Vol 1 and 2. Ed. by M. C. Seymour et al. Oxford: Clarendon Press, 1975.

Basil. "Letter 217." In *Saint Basil: The Letters*, trans. by R. J. Deferrari. Cambridge: Harvard University Press, 1962.

Baum, Paul Franklin. "The Fable of Belling the Cat." *Modern Language Notes* 34 (1919): 462-70.

Beer, Jeanette. "A Fourteenth-Century 'Bestiaire d'amour'". *Reinardus*, vol. 4, 19-26. Philadelphia: John Benjamins, 1991.

————. "The New Naturalism of *Le bestiaire d'amour.*" *Reinardus*, vol. 1, 16-21. Philadelphia: John Benjamins, 1988.

————. "Richard de Fournival's Anonymous Lady: The Character of the Response to the *Bestiaire d'amour.*" *Romance Philology* 42 (1989): 267-73.

Bell, Clair Hayden. *Peasant Life in Old German Epics.* New York: W. W. Norton, 1968.

Bell, David N. *Wholly Animals: A Book of Beastly Tales.* Kalamazoo: Cistercian Publications, 1992.

Bell, Rudolph M. *Holy Anorexia.* Chicago: University of Chicago Press, 1985.

Benedict, Deacon. "Capitularum Collectio, Lib. I." *PL* 97:697-754.

Bennett, Josephine Waters. *The Rediscovery of Sir John Mandeville.* New York: Modern Language Association of America, 1954.

Benton, Janetta Rebold. *The Medieval Menagerie: Animals in the Art of the Middle Ages.* New York: Abbeville Press, 1992.

Berechiah ben Natronai. *Fables of a Jewish Aesop.* Trans. Moses Hadas. New York: Columbia University Press, 1967.

Berger, John. "Animals as Metaphor." *New Society* 39 (10 March 1977).

————. "Vanishing Animals." *New Society* 39 (31 March 1977).

Bernard of Clairveaux, "Sermo in Psalmis," xii. *PL* 183:234.

Berncovitch, Sacvan. "Clerical Satire in the 'Vox and the Wolf'". *Journal of English and German Philology* 65 (1966): 287-84.

Bernheimer, R. *Wild Men in the Middle Ages: A Study in Art, Sentiment, and Demonology*. Cambridge: Harvard University Press, 1952.

Bianciotto, Gabriel, ed. *Épopée Animale Fable, Fabliau*. Paris: Presses Universitaires de France, 1984.

Bieler, Ludwig. "Towards an Interpretation of the So Called 'Canones Wallici'". In *Medieval Studies Presented to Aubrey Gwynn*, ed. by J. A. Watt. Dublin: C. O'Lochlainn, 1961.

————, ed. *The Irish Penitentials: Scriptores Latini Hiberniae*. Vol. 5. Dublin: Dublin Institute for Advanced Studies, 1963.

Blackham, H. J. *The Fable as Literature*. London: Athlone Press, 1985.

Blake, N. F. "Reynard the Fox in England." In *Aspects of the Medieval Animal Epic*, 53-65. Louvain: Louvain University Press, 1975.

Boenig, Robert. *The Acts of Andrew in the Country of the Cannibals*. New York: Garland, 1991.

Boethius. *The Consolation of Philosophy*. New York: Penguin, 1980.

Bologna, Corrada, ed. *Liber Monstrorum de Diversis Generibus*. Milan: Bompiani, 1977.

Bonaventure. *The Soul's Journey into God. The Tree of Life. The Life of St. Francis*. Trans. by E. Cousins. New York: Paulist Press, 1978.

Bonkalo, Ervin. "Criminal Proceedings Against Animals in the Middle Ages." *Journal of Unconventional History* 3, no. 2 (1992): 25-31.

Bonnell, John K. "The Serpent with a Human Head in Art and in Mystery Play." *American Journal of Archaeology* 21 (1917): 255-91.

Boretius. "Capitularia regum francorum." In *Monumenta Germaniae Historica, Legum Sectio II*, vol. 1, no. 22, 295-96. Hanover: Impensis bibliopolii Hahniani, 1883.

Bosquet, G. H. "Des animaux et de leur traitement selon le judaïsme, le christianisme et l'islam." *Studia Islamica* 9 (1958): 31-48.

Boswell, John. *Christianity, Social Tolerance and Homosexuality*. Chicago: University of Chicago Press, 1980.

Bracton, Henry de. *On the Laws and Customs of England*. Trans. by Samuel E. Thorne. Cambridge: Selden Society, 1968.

Braudel, Fernand. *Civilization & Capitalism: 15th-18th Century*. Vol. 1, *The Structures of Everyday Life*. New York: Harper and Row, 1979.

Britton, John. *Britton*. Ed. by Francis Morgan Nichols. Oxford: Clarendon Press, 1865.

Brodeur, Arthur Gilchrist. "The Grateful Lion." *PMLA* 39 (1924): 485-524.

Brown, Peter. *The Body and Society*. New York: Columbia University Press, 1988.

————. "The Saint as Exemplar in Late Antiquity." *Representations* 1, no. 2 (Spring 1983): 1-25.

Brundage, James A. *Law, Sex, and Christian Society in Medieval Europe*. Chicago: University of Chicago Press, 1987.

Budiansky, Stephen. *The Covenant of the Wild: Why Animals Chose Domestication*. New York: William Morrow, 1991.

Burchard of Worms. "Decretorum Libri Decimi Septimmi." *PL* 140:918-34.

Bynum, Caroline Walker. *Holy Feast and Holy Fast*. Berkeley: University of California

Press, 1987.

Caesarius of Heisterbach. *Dialogue on Miracles*. Trans. by H. von E. Schott et al. London: Routledge & Sons, 1929.

Cahn, Walter. *Romanesque Bible Illumination*. Ithaca: Cornell University Press, 1982.

Calkins, Robert G. *Illuminated Books of the Middle Ages*. Ithaca: Cornell University Press, 1983.

Callisthenes [Pseud.]. *Alexander of Macedon*. Trans. by Elizabeth H. Haight. New York: Longmans, Green, 1955.

Camporesi, Piero. *Bread of Dreams*. Trans. D. Gentilcore. Chicago: University of Chicago Press, 1980.

——. *The Incorruptible Flesh: Bodily Mutation and Mortification in Religion and Folklore*. Trans. by T. Croft-Murray and H. Elson. Cambridge: Cambridge University Press, 1988.

Carey, John. "Ireland and the Antipodes: The Heterodoxy of Virgil of Salzburg." *Speculum* 64 (Jan. 1989): 1-10.

Carnes, Pack. *Fable Scholarship: An Annotated Bibliography*. New York: Garland, 1985.

"Caroli Magni Ludovici et Lotharii Imperatorum Capitularia ab Ansegiso Abbati Fontanellensi Collecta." *PL* 97:489-584.

Cary, George. *The Medieval Alexander*. Cambridge: Cambridge University Press, 1956.

Cassell, Anthony K. and Victoria Kirkham. *Diana's Hunt: Caccia di Diana—Boccaccio's First Fiction*. Philadelphia: University of Pennsylvania Press, 1991.

Cauldwell, D.O., *Animal Contact*. Girard, Kans.: Haldeman-Julius Publications, 1948.

Charbonneau-Lassay, Louis. *The Bestiary of Christ*. Trans. D. M. Dooling. New York: Viking Penguin, 1991.

Chenu, Marie-Dominique. *Nature, Man, and Society in the Twelfth Century: Essays on New Theological Perspectives in the Latin West*. Chicago: University of Chicago Press, 1968.

Chesnutt, Michael. "The Grateful Animals and The Ungrateful Man." *Fabula* 21 (1980): 24-55.

Chrétien de Troyes. *Yvain: The Knight with the Lion*. Trans. Ruth Harwood Cline. Athens, Ga.: University of Georgia Press, 1975.

Chronica Majorum. Ed. by H. R. Luard, II, 283. London: Longman and Co., 1874.

Clark, Willene B. *The Medieval Book of Birds: Hugh of Fouilloy's Aviarum*. Binghamton, N.Y., Medieval and Renaissance Texts and Studies, 1992.

Clement of Alexandria. *Christ the Educator*. Trans. by Simon P. Wood, New York: Fathers of the Church, 1954.

Clifford, Paula. *Marie de France: Lais*. London: Grant & Cutler, 1982.

Clutton-Brock, J. *Domesticated Animals from Early Times*. Austin, Tex.: University of Texas Press, 1981.

——. "The Animal Resources." In *The Archaeology of Anglo-Saxon England*, ed. by D. M. Wilson, 373-92. London: Methuen, 1976.

Cohen, Jeremy. *"Be Fertile and Increase, Fill the Earth and Master It": The Ancient and Medieval Career of a Biblical Text*. Ithaca: Cornell University Press, 1989.

Coleman, Janet. "The Owl and the Nightingale and Papal Theories of Marriage." *Journal of Ecclesiastical History* 38, no. 4 (Oct. 1987): 517-68.

Collins, Arthur. *Symbolism of Animals and Birds Represented in English Church Architecture.* New York: McBride, Nast, 1913.

Cook, Albert S. *Old English Physiologus.* New Haven: Yale University Press, 1921.

"Council of Ancyra," canon 16. *PL* 67:154.

Cox, Patricia. "Origen and the Bestial Soul." *Vigiliae Christianae* 36 (1982): 115-40.

Coy, J. "The Animal Bones." In J. Haslam, "A Middle Saxon Iron Smelting Site at Ramsbury, Wiltshire." *Medieval Archaeology* 24 (1980): 41-51.

Crabtree, Pam Jean. "Zooarchaeology at Early Anglo-Saxon West Stow." In *Medieval Archaeology*, ed. by Charles L. Redman. Binghamton, N.Y.: Medieval & Renaissance Texts & Studies, 1989.

Cronin, G. "The Bestiary and the Medieval Mind—Some Complexities." *Modern Language Quarterly* (1941): 191-98.

Cross, Tom Pette, and C. H. Slover, eds. *Ancient Irish Tales.* New York: Henry Holt, 1936.

Cummings, John. *The Hound and the Hawk.* New York: St. Martin's Press, 1988.

Curley, Michael J., trans. *Physiologus.* Austin, Tex.: University of Texas Press, 1979.

Dahlberg, C. "Chaucer's Cock and Fox." *Journal of English and German Philology* 53 (1954): 277-90.

Dale-Green, Patricia. *The Cult of the Cat.* London: Heinemann, 1963.

Daly, L. W. *Aesop without Morals.* New York: Thomas Yoseloff, 1961.

Dante, "The Divine Comedy." Trans. by L. Binyon. In *The Portable Dante*, ed. by Paolo Milano. New York: Viking Press, 1969.

Dasent, G. W. *Popular Tales from the Norse.* Edinburgh: D. Douglas, 1903.

Davis, R. H. C. *The Medieval Warhorse.* London: Thames and Hudson, 1989.

de Vos, Antoon. *Deer Farming: Guidelines on Practical Aspects.* Rome: Food and Agriculture Organization of the United Nations, 1982.

Delort, Lezione. "Les Animaux et l'Habillement." In *L'Uomo di Fronte as Mondo Aminale Nell'Alto Medioevo: 7-13 Aprile 1983*, 673-700. Spoleto: Presso La Sede Del Centro, 1985.

Detienne, Marcel. "Between Beasts and Gods." In *Myth, Religion and Society*, ed. by R. L. Godeon, 215-28. Cambridge: Cambridge University Press, 1981.

Doherty, Dennis. *The Sexual Doctrine of Cardinal Cajetan.* Regensburg: Verlag Friedrich Pustet, 1966.

Donovan, M. J. "The Moralite of the Nun's Priest's Sermon." *Journal of English and German Philology* 52 (1953): 498-508.

Doob, Penelope B. R. *Nebuchadnezzar's Children: Conventions of Madness in Middle English Literature.* New Haven: Yale University Press, 1974.

Douglas, Mary. *Purity and Danger.* Middlesex: Penguin, 1966.

Drew, Katherine Fischer, trans. *The Burgundian Code.* Philadelphia: University of Pennsylvania Press, 1972.

———, trans. *The Laws of the Salian Franks.* Philadelphia: University of Pennsylvania Press, 1991.

————, trans. *The Lombard Laws*. Philadelphia: University of Pennsylvania Press, 1973.

Druce, G. C. "The Mediaeval Bestiaries and Their Influence on English Ecclesiastical Decorative Art." *Journal of the British Archaeological Association* 25 (Dec. 1919): 40-82.

————. "Some Abnormal and Composite Human Forms in English Church Architecture." *Archaeological Journal* 72 (1915): 168-69.

Dyer, Christopher. *Standards of Living in the Later Middle Ages*. Cambridge: Cambridge University Press, 1989.

————. "English Diet in the Later Middle Ages." In *Social Relations and Ideas: Essays in Honour of R. H. Hilton*. Cambridge: Cambridge University Press, 1983.

Edward, Duke of York. *The Master of Game*. Ed. W. A. and F. Baille-Grohman. London: Balantine, Hanson, 1904.

Elliott, Alison Goddard. *Roads to Paradise: Reading the Lives of the Early Saints*. Hanover: Brown University Press, 1987.

English Rural Life in the Middle Ages. Bodlein Picture Book no. 14. Oxford: Oxford University Press, 1965.

Farmer, D. L. "Some Livestock Price Movements in 13th Century England." *Economic Historical Review* 2d ser., 22 (1969): 1-16.

Ferguson, Everett. *Demonology of the Early Christian World*. New York: Edwin Mellen Press, 1984.

Fiddes, Nick. *Meat: A Natural Symbol*. New York: Routledge, 1991.

Fiero, Gloria K., et al. *Three Medieval Views of Women*. New Haven: Yale University Press, 1989.

Fleming. *Animal Plagues*. London: Chapman & Hall, 1871-74.

Fornasari, M., ed. *Collectio Canonum in V Libris (Lib. I-III)*. *Corpus Christianorum VI*. Turnholt: Brepols, 1970.

Frederick II. *The Art of Falconry: Being the De Arte venandi cum avibus of Frederick II of Hohenstaufen*. Trans. and ed. by Casey A. Wood and F. M. Fyfe. Stanford: Stanford University Press, 1969.

Freeman, Michelle. "Dual Natures and Subverted Glosses: Marie de France's 'Bisclavret.'" *Romance Notes* 25, no. 3 (Spring 1985): 288-301.

Friedman, John Block. *The Monstrous Races in Medieval Art and Thought*. Cambridge: Harvard University Press, 1981.

Friedmann, Herbert. *A Bestiary for Saint Jerome*. Washington D.C.: Smithsonian Institution Press, 1980.

Friend, Albert C. "Master Odo of Cheriton." *Speculum* 23 (1948): 641-58.

————. "The Proverbs of Serlo of Wilton." *Mediaeval Studies* 16, (1954): 179-80.

Gantz, Jeffrey. *Early Irish Myths and Sagas*. Hammondsworth: Penguin, 1981.

Gardiner, Eileen. *Visions of Heaven and Hell Before Dante*. New York: Italica Press, 1989.

Geoffrey of Monmouth. *The History of the Kings of Britain*. New York: Penguin, 1966.

George, Wilma and Brunsdon Yapp. *The Naming of the Beasts: Natural History in the Medieval Bestiary*. London: Gerald Duckworth, 1991.

Gerald of Wales. *The Historical Works of Giraldus Cambrensis*. Ed. by Thomas Wright.

London: George Bell, 1887.

————. *The History and Topography of Ireland*. Trans. by J. J. O'Meara. London: Penguin Books, 1988.

————. *The Journey Through Wales/The Description of Wales*. New York: Penguin, 1988.

Ghisalberti, F. "Medieval Biographies of Ovid." *Journal of the Warburg and Courtauld Institutes* 9 (1946): 10-59.

Gilles de Corbeil. "Hierapigra Galeni." *Gilles de Corbeil*. Ed. by C. Vieillard. Paris: H. Campion, 1909.

Goldschmidt, A. *An Early Manuscript of the Aesop Fables of Avianus*. Princeton: Princeton University Press, 1947.

Gonzalez Rivas, Severino. *La Penitencia en la Primitiva Iglesia Española*. Salamanca: Consejo Superior de Investigaciones Científicas, 1949.

Goody, Jack. *Cooking, Cuisine and Class*. Cambridge: Cambridge University Press, 1982.

Gordon, Edmund I. "Sumerian Animal Proverbs and Fables." *Journal of Cuneiform Studies* 12, nos. 1 & 2 (1958): 1-21, 43-75.

Gottfried von Strassburg. *Tristan*. Baltimore: Penguin Classics, 1960.

Gregory of Tours. *History of the Franks*. Trans. by E. Brehaut. New York: W. W. Norton, 1969.

Guibert of Nogent. *Self and Society in Medieval France*. Trans by J. F. Benton. New York: Harper and Row, 1970.

Hamel, Frank. *Human Animals: Werewolves and Other Transformations*. New Hyde Park: University Books, 1969.

Hanning, Robert and Joan Ferrante. *The Lais of Marie de France*. Durham, N.C.: Labyrinth Press, 1978.

Harrod, Henry. "Some Details of a Murrain of the 14th Century, from the Court Rolls of a Norfolk Manor." *Archaeologia* (1866): 41.

Harthan, J. P. "Animals in Art: Mediaeval Bestiaries." *Geographical Magazine* 22 (1949): 182-90.

Harwood, Dix. *Love for Animals and How It Developed in Great Britain*. New York: Columbia University Press, 1928.

Henderson, Arnold Clayton. "Animal Fables as Vehicles of Social Protest and Satire: Twelfth Century to Henryson." In *Proceedings/ Third International Beast Epic, Fable and Fabliau Colloquium*, ed. by Jan Goossens and Timothy Sodmann. Cologne: Bohlam, 1981.

————. "Animal Fables as Vehicles of Social Protest and Satire." *Niederdevische Studiem* 30 (1981): 161-73.

————. "Medieval Beasts and Modern Cages: The Making of Meaning in Fables and Bestiaries." *Publication of the Modern Language Association* 97 (Jan. 1982): 40-49.

————. "'Of Heigh or Lough Estate': Medieval Fabulists as Social Critics." *Viator: Medieval and Renaissance Studies* 9 (1978): 265-90.

Henisch, Bridget. *Fast and Feast: Food in Medieval Society*. University Park: Pennsylvania State University Press, 1976.

Henry, Françoise. *The Book of Kells*. New York: Alfred A. Knopf, 1974.

Henryson, Robert. *The Moral Fables of Aesop.* Ed. and trans. by George D. Gopen. Notre Dame, Ind.: University of Notre Dame Press, 1987.

Hernandez, Ludovico. *Les procès de bestialité aux XVIe at XVIIe siècles: documents judiciares inédits publiés avec un avant-propos.* Paris: Bibliotheque des curieux, 1920.

Heusler, Andreas. "The Story of the Völsi, an Old Norse Anecdote of Conversion." Trans. by Peter Nelson. In *Sex in the Middle Ages*, ed. by Joyce E. Salisbury, 187-200. New York: Garland, 1991.

Holmes, Urban T. "Gerald the Naturalist." *Speculum* 11 (Jan. 1936): 110-21.

Hook, David. "Some Observations upon the Episode of the Cid's Lion." *MLR* 71 (1976): 553-64.

Hoveden, Roger of. *The Annals of Roger de Hoveden.* Trans. H. T. Riley. London: H.G. Bohn, 1853.

Huebner, Rudolf. *A History of Germanic Private Law.* Trans. by Francis S. Philbrick. Boston: Little, Brown, 1918.

Husband, Timothy. *The Wild Man: Medieval Myth and Symbolism.* New York: Metropolitan Museum of Art, 1980.

Ignatius of Antioch. *Epistle to the Romans.* Trans. by A. Roberts and J. Donaldson. In *Ante-Nicene Fathers*, vol. 1. Edinburgh: Ante-Nicene Christian Library, 1885.

Irving, P.M.C. Forbes. *Metamorphosis in Greek Myths.* London: Oxford University Press, 1990.

Isidore [pseud.]. "Benedictus Levita." *PL* 97:699-912.

Isidore of Seville. *Etymologías.* Madrid: Biblioteca de Autores Cristianos, 1933.

Ives, Samuel A. *An English 13th Century Bestiary.* New York, H.P. Kraus, 1942.

Ivo of Chartres. "Decreti Pars IX." *PL* 161:655-690.

Jacquart, Danielle, and Claude Thomasset. *Sexuality and Medicine in the Middle Ages.* Trans. by Matthew Adamson. Princeton: Princeton University Press, 1988.

Jacques de Vitry. *The Exempla.* Edited by Thomas F. Crane. New York: Burt Franklin, 1890.

James, Montague Rhodes. *The Bestiary...and a Preliminary Study of the Latin Bestiary as Current in England.* Oxford: Oxford University Press, 1928.

————, *Marvels of the East.* Oxford: Oxford University Press, 1929.

Janson, H. W. *Apes and Ape Lore in the Middle Ages and the Renaissance.* Vol. 20 of Studies of the Warburg Institute. London: Warburg Institute, 1952.

John Climacus. *The Ladder of Divine Ascent.* Trans. by C. Luibheid and N. Russell. New York: Paulist Press, 1982.

John of Salisbury. "Polycraticus." *PL* 199:423.

Johnson, Buffie. *Lady of the Beasts: Ancient Images of the Goddess and Her Sacred Animals.* San Francisco: Harper & Row, 1988.

Jordanus Catalani. *Mirabilia Descripta: The Wonders of the East.* Trans. Henry Yule. New York: Burt Franklin, 1963.

Juvenal. *The Satires of Juvenal.* Trans. by R. Humphries. Bloomington: Indiana University Press, 1958.

Keidel, George C. " The History of the French Fable Manuscripts." *Publication of the*

Modern Language Association 24 (1909): 207-19.

Keller, John Esten. *Motif-Index of Mediaeval Spanish Exempla*. Knoxville: University of Tennessee Press, 1949.

Kiessling, Nicolas. *The Incubus in English Literature: Provenance and Progeny*. Washington State University Press, 1977.

Kinsey, Alfred C. *Sexual Behavior in the Human Male*. Philadelphia: W.B. Saunders, 1948.

Kirby, Steven D. "Juan Ruiz's *Serranas*: The Archpriest—Pilgrim and Medieval Wild Women." *Hispanic Studies in Honor of Alan D. Deyermond: A North American Tribute*, 151-69. Madison: Hispanic Seminary of Medieval Studies, 1986.

Klein, J. *The Mesta*. Cambridge: Harvard University Press, 1920.

Klingender, Francis. *Animals in Art and Thought*. Cambridge: MIT Press, 1971.

Knock, Ann. "The 'Liber Monstrorum': An Unpublished Manuscript and Some Reconsiderations." *Scriptorium* 32 (1978): 19-28.

Kosmer, Ellen. "The 'noyous humoure of lecherie.'" *Art Bulletin* 57 (1975): 1-8.

Kraatz, D. "Fictus Lupus: The Werewolf in Christian Thought." *Classical Folia* 30 (1976): 57-79.

Krappe, Alexander H. "Guiding Animals." *Journal of American Folklore* 55 (1942): 228-46.

Lamond, Elizabeth, trans. *Walter of Henley's Husbandry*. London: Longmans, Green, 1890.

Langdon, John. *Horses, Oxen and Technological Innovation: The Use of Draught Animals in English Farming from 1066 to 1500*. Cambridge: Cambridge University Press, 1986.

Larson, Laurence M. *The Earliest Norwegian Laws: Being the Gulathing Law and the Frostating Law*. New York: Columbia University Press, 1935.

Leach, Edmund. "Anthropological Aspects of Language: Animal Categories and Verbal Abuse." In *New Directions in the Study of Language*, ed. E. M. Leeneberg. Cambridge: MIT Press, 1964.

Lees, B. A., ed. *Records of the Templars in England in the Twelfth Century*. London: Oxford University Press, 1935.

Leges Burgundionum. *Monumenta Germaniae Historica. Legum Section I. Legum Nationum Germanicarum. Tomi II. Pars I*. Hanover: Impensis Bibliopolii Hahniani, 1842.

LeGoff, Jacques. *The Birth of Purgatory*. Trans. by Arthur Goldhammer. Chicago: University of Chicago Press, 1981.

——. *The Medieval Imagination*. Trans. by Arthur Goldhammer. Chicago: University of Chicago Press, 1988.

Lehnert, Martin. *Poetry and Prose of the Anglo-Saxons*. Halle (Saale): Vebmax niemeyer Verlag, 1960.

Letts, Malcolm, trans. *Mandeville's Travels*. Nendeln/Liechtenstein: Kraus Reprint, 1967.

Levin, Eve. *Sex and Society in the World of the Orthodox Slavs, 900-1700*. Ithaca: Cornell University Press, 1989.

Levy, Brian, and Paul Wackers, eds. *Reynardus*. Vol. 4. Philadelphia: John Benjamins, 1991.

Linzey, Andrew, and Tom Regan. *Animals and Christianity: A Book of Readings*. New York: Crossroad, 1988

Lloyd, T. H. *The English Wool Trade in the Middle Ages*. Cambridge: Cambridge University Press, 1977.

Macauly, G. C., ed. *The Chronicles of Froissart*. Trans. by Lord Berners. London: Macmillan, 1904.

MacBeth, George. *The Penguin Book of Animal Verse*. Harmondsworth: Penguin, 1965.

McCloy, Dorothy F. "From Celibacy to Sexuality. An Examination of some Medieval and Early Renaissance Versions of the Story of Robert the Devil." In *Human Sexuality in the Middle Ages and Renaissance*, ed. by Douglas Radcliff-Umstead. Pittsburgh: University of Pittsburgh Press, 1978.

McCulloch, F. *Mediaeval Latin and French Bestiaries*. Studies in Romance Language and Literature, no. 33. Chapel Hill: University of North Carolina Press, 1960.

McKenzie, Kenneth. "Unpublished Manuscripts of Italian Bestiaries." *Publications of the Modern Language Association* 30 (1905): 380-433.

Maimonides, Moses. *Guide for the Perplexed*. Trans. by Shlomo Pines. Chicago: University of Chicago Press, 1963.

Malaxecheverria, Ignacio. "Le Bestiaire médiéval et l'archétype de la féminité." *Circé* 12/13 (1982).

Masters, R.E.L. *Forbidden Sexual Behavior and Morality*. New York: Julian Press, 1962.

————. *Eros and Evil: The Sexual Psychopathology of Witchcraft*. New York: The Julian Press, 1962.

Matten, Marie. *Las Siete Partidas*. Chicago: University of Chicago Press, 1931.

Mellinkoff, Ruth. "Riding Backwards." *Viator* 4 (1973): 153-76.

Merwin, W. S., trans., *Poem of the Cid*. New York: Mentor, 1959.

Midrash Rabbah: Genesis. Trans. by H. Freedman. Vol. 1. London: Soncino Press, 1951.

Montanari, Massimo. "Rural Food in Late Medieval Italy." In *Bauerliche Sachkultur des Spatmittelalters: Internationaler Kongress Krems an der Donau 21 Bis 24. September 1982*. Vienna: Osterreichischen Akademie der Wissenschaften, 1984.

Montanari, Lezione. "Gli animali e l'alimentazione umana." In *L'Uomo di Fronte as Mondo Aminale Nell'Alto Medioevo: 7-13 Aprile 1983*, 619-63. Spoleto: Presso La Sede Del Centro, 1985.

Moore, J. H. "The Ox in the Middle Ages," *Agricultural History* 35, no. 2 (1961): 90-93.

Morson, J. "The English Cistercians and the Bestiary." *Bulletin of the John Rylands Library* 39 (1956-57): 146-70.

Mosher, Joseph Albert. *The Exemplum in the Early Religious and Didactic Literature of England*. New York: Columbia University Press, 1911.

Murray, Alexander. *Reason and Society in the Middle Ages*. Oxford, Oxford University Press, 1978.

Neckam, Alexander. *De Naturis Rerum*. Ed. by T. Wright. London: Longman, Green, Longman and Roberts, and Green, 1863.

Newlyn, Evelyn S. "Robert Henryson and the Popular Fable Tradition in the Middle Ages." *Journal of Popular Culture* 14 (1980): 108-18.

Newman, Barbara. "The *Cattes Tale*: A Chaucer Apocryphon." *The Chaucer Review* 26, no. 4 (1992): 411-23.

Nigel de Longchamps. *Speculum Stultorum*. Ed. by J. N. Mozley and R. R. Rayme. Berkeley: University of California Press, 1960.

Nigellus Wireker. *The Book of Daun Burnel the Ass*. Trans by Graydon W. Regenos. Austin: University of Texas Press, 1959.

Njal's Saga. Trans. by Magnus Magnusson and Hermann Pálsson. New York: Penguin, 1986.

Nolan, Kiernan. *The Immortality of the Soul and the Resurrection of the Body According to Giles of Rome: A Historical Study of a Thirteenth-Century Theological Problem*. Rome: Studium Theologicum "Augustinianum," 1967.

Nordenfalk, Carl. *Celtic and Anglo-Saxon Painting*. New York: George Braziller, 1977.

O'Callaghan, Joseph F. *A History of Medieval Spain*. Ithaca: Cornell University Press, 1975.

Oppian. *Cynegetica*. Trans. by A. W. Moir. London: Loeb Classical Library, 1928.

Otten, Charlotte F. *A Lycanthropy Reader: Werewolves in Western Culture*. Syracuse: Syracuse University Press, 1986.

Oulton, John Ernest Leonard, and Henry Chadwick, trans. *Alexandrian Christianity*. Philadelphia: Westminster Press, 1954.

Ovid. *Metamorphoses of Ovid*. Trans. by Mary M. Innes. London: Penguin, 1955.

Pálsson, Hermann, trans. *Hrafnkel's Saga and other Stories*. New York: Penguin, 1971.

Paul the Deacon. *History of the Lombards*. Trans. by William Dudley Foulke. Philadelphia: University of Pennsylvania Press, 1907.

Payer, Pierre J. *Sex and the Penitentials*. Toronto: University of Toronto Press, 1983.

Payne, Ann. *Medieval Beasts*. New York: New Amsterdam Books, 1990.

Perry, Ben Edwin, trans. *Babrius and Phaedrus*. Cambridge: Harvard University Press, 1965.

————. *Studies in the Text History of the Life and Fables of Aesop*. Haverford, Pa.: American Philological Association, 1936.

Pick, Franz, and René Sédillot. *All the Monies of the World: A Chronicle of Currency Values*. New York: Pick Publishing Co., 1971.

Pierre de Beauvais. *A Medieval Book of Beasts: Pierre de Beauvais' Bestiary*. Trans. by Guy R. Mermier. Lewiston, N.Y.: Edwin Mellon Press, 1991.

Piggott, Stuart. *Ancient Europe*. Chicago: Aldine Publishing Co., 1965.

Plous, S. "The Role of Animals in Human Society," *Journal of Social Issues* 49, no. 1 (1993): 6.

Ponting, Kenneth. *Sheep of the World*. Dorset: Blandford Press, 1980.

Poole, Austin Lane. "Live Stock Prices in the Twelfth Century." *English Historical Review* 55 (April 1940): 284-95.

Postan, M. M. *Cambridge Economic History of Europe*. Vol. 1. Cambridge: Cambridge University Press, 1966.

————. "Village Livestock in the 13th Century." In *Essays on Medieval Agriculture and General Problems of the Medieval Economy*, 214-48. Cambridge: Cambridge University Press, 1973.

Power, Eileen. *The Wool Trade in English Medieval History*. Oxford: Oxford University

Press, 1941.

Procopius. *The Gothic War*. Trans. by H. B. Dewing. London: Loeb Classical Library, 1924.

Rachels, James. *Created from Animals: The Moral Implications of Darwinism*. New York: Oxford University Press, 1991.

Randall, Lilian M. C. "Exempla and Their Influence on Gothic Marginal Art." *Art Bulletin* 39 (1957): 97-107.

———. *Images in the Margins of Gothic Mss*. Berkeley: University of California Press, 1966.

———. "The Snail in Gothic Marginal Warfare." *Speculum* 37 (1962): 358-67.

Ratramnus of Corbie. "Epistola 12." In *Epistolae Karolini Aevi*, ed. by E. Dümmler, in *MGH Epist*. 6, i55. Berlin: 1925.

Read, Piers Paul. *Alive*. New York: Avon, 1974.

Reed, R. *Ancient Skins, Parchments and Leathers*. New York: Seminar Press, 1972.

Rendell, Alan Wood. *Physiologus: A Metrical Bestiary of Twelve Chapters by Bishop Theobald*. London: John & Edward Bumpus, 1928.

Riccobono, S., and Johannes Baviera, eds. *Fontes Juris Romani Antejustiniani*. Florence: S.A.G. Barbéra, 1940.

Richard de Fournival. *Master Richard's Bestiary of Love and Response*. Trans. by Jeanette Beer. Berkeley: University of California Press, 1986.

Rickard, Peter, et al. *Medieval Comic Tales*. Totowa, N.J.: Rowman and Littlefield, 1973.

Rigault, A. *Le Procès de Guicard, évêque de Troyes*. Paris: A. Picard, 1896.

Ritvo, Harriet. *The Animal Estate: The English and Other Creatures in the Victorian Age*. Cambridge: Harvard University Press ,1987.

Rivers, Theodore John. *Laws of the Alamans and Bavarians*. Philadephia: University of Pennsylvania Press, 1977.

Rooney, Anne. *Hunting in Middle English Literature*. Rochester: Boydell Press, 1993.

Rose, William, trans. *The Epic of the Beast*. London: George Routledge, n.d.

Rosenfield, Leonora Cohen. *From Beast-Machine to Man-Machine*. New York: Octagon Books, 1968.

Rossello, Ramon. *Homosexualitat a Mallorca a L'dat Mitjana*. Barcelona: Calamus Scriptorius, 1978.

Rouselle, Aline. *Porneia: On Desire and the Body in Antiquity*. Trans. by Felicia Pheasant. New York: Basil Blackwell, 1988.

Rowland, Beryl. "Animal Imagery and the Pardoner's Abnormality." *Neophilologus* 48 (1964): 56-60.

———. *Animals with Human Faces*. Knoxville: University of Tennessee Press, 1973.

———. *Blind Beasts: Chaucer's Animal World*. Kent: Kent State University Press, 1971.

———. "The Relationship of St. Basil's *Hexaemeron* to the *Physiologus*." In *Épopée Animale Fable Fabliau*, ed. by G. Bianciotto and Michel Salvat, 489-98. Paris: Presses Universitaires de France, 1981.

Roy, Bruno. "La Belle e(s)t bête: aspects du bestiaire féminin au moyen âge." *Etudes Francaises* 10 (1979): 319-34.

Ruiz, Juan. *The Book of Good Love*. Trans. by Elisha Kent Kane. Chapel Hill: University of North Carolina Press, 1968.

Russell, Jeffrey Burton. *Lucifer: The Devil in the Middle Ages*. Ithaca: Cornell University Press, 1984.

Sabine, E. L. "Butchering in Medieval London." *Speculum* 8 (1933): 335-53.

Salisbury, Joyce E. *Church Fathers, Independent Virgins*. London: Verso, 1991.

―――. *Iberian Popular Religion, 600 B.C. to 700 A.D.* New York: Edwin Mellen Press, 1985.

―――, ed. *The Medieval World of Nature: A Book of Essays*. New York: Garland, 1993.

―――. "The Origin of the Power of Vincent the Martyr." In *Proceedings of the PMR Conference* 8 (1983): 97-107.

Sands, Donald B., ed. *The History of Reynard the Fox*. Cambridge: Harvard University Press, 1960.

Sayers, Dorothy L., trans. *The Song of Roland*. New York: Penguin, 1957.

Schmitt, Jean-Claude. *The Holy Greyhound: Guinefort, Healer of Children Since the Thirteenth Century*. Cambridge: Cambridge University Press, 1983.

Schulenburg, Jane. "Saints and Sex." In *Sex in the Middle Ages*, ed. by Joyce E. Salisbury, 203-31. New York: Garland Publishing Co., 1991.

Scott, S. P. *Visigothic Code*. Littleton, Colorado: Fred B. Rothman & Co., 1982.

Shapiro, Norman R. *Fables from Old French: Aesop's Beasts and Bumpkins*. Middletown, Conn.: Wesleyan University Press, 1982.

Shapiro, Norman R. *The Fabulist French: Verse Fables of Nine Centuries*. Chicago: University of Illinois Press, 1992.

Sir Gawain and the Green Knight. Trans. by Burton Raffel. New York: Mentor, 1970.

Smith, Norman R. "Portent Lore and Medieval Popular Culture." *Journal of Popular Culture* 14, no. 1 (Summer, 1980): 47-59.

Sophocles. "Antigone." In *The Theban Plays*, trans. by E. F. Watting, 126-62. New York, Penguin, 1980.

Sørensen, Preben M. *The Unmanly Man*. Trans. by Joan Turvill-Petre. Odense: Odense University Press, 1983.

Spiegel, Harriet, ed. and trans. *Marie de France: Fables*. Toronto: University of Toronto Press, 1987.

Stevenson, J., ed. "The Book of Hyde." In *The Church Historians of England*, vol. 2, part 2, 483–520. London: Seelys, 1854.

Sturluson, Snorri. *King Harald's Saga*. Trans. by Magnus Magnusson and H. Pálsson. New York: Penguin, 1982.

Sulpicius Severus. *Writings of Sulpicius Severus*. Trans. by Bernard Peebles. New York: Fathers of the Church, 1949.

Taylor, George Coffin. "Shakespeare's Use of the Idea of the Beast in Man." *Studies in Philology* 42 (1945): 530-43.

Te Velde, H. "A Few Remarks upon the Religious Significance of Animals in Ancient Egypt." *Numen* 27 (1980): 76-82.

Tertullian. "On the Soul." In *Tertullian: Apologetical Works and Minucius Felix Octavius*.

Trans. by Edwin A. Quain. New York: Fathers of the Church, 1950.

Theobald. *Physiologus: A Metrical Bestiary of Twelve Chapters by Bishop Theobald.* London: John & Edward Bumpus, 1928.

Thiébaux, Marcelle. *The Stag of Love.* Ithaca: Cornell University Press, 1974.

Thiele, Georg. *Der illustrierte lateinische Aesop in der Handschrift des Ademar.* Leiden: Verlag von A.W. Sijthoff, 1905.

Thiolier-Mejean, Suzanne. *Les Poésies Satiriques et Morales des Troubadours du XIIe siècle a la Fin du XIIIe siècle.* Paris: A. G. Nizet, 1978.

Thomas, Keith. *Man and the Natural World.* New York: Pantheon Books, 1983.

Thomas of Chobham. *Summa Conffessorum.* Ed. by F. Broomfield. Paris: Béatrice-Nauwelaerts, 1968.

Thompson, E. M. "The Grotesque and the Humorous in Illumination of the Middle Ages." *Bibliographica* 2, part 7 (1896): 309-32.

Thompson, Stith. *Motif-Index of Folk-Literature.* Bloomington: Indiana University Press, 1955-58.

Thorpe, Benjamin. *Ancient Laws and Institutes of England.* London: G. Eyre and A. Spottiswoode, 1840.

Tilley, Maureen A. "Martyrs, Monks, Insects and Animals." In *The Medieval World of Nature,* ed. by Joyce E. Salisbury, 93-107. New York: Garland, 1993.

Tinker, Edward. *Centaurs of Many Lands.* Austin: University of Texas Press, 1964.

Toynbee, J.M.C. *Animals in Roman Life and Art.* Ithaca: Cornell University Press, 1973.

Triolo, Alfred. "Matta bestialita in Dante's 'Inferno': Theory and Image" *Traditio* 24 (1968): 247-92.

Trow-Smith, R. *A History of British Livestock Husbandry to 1700.* London: Routledge & Kegan Paul, 1957.

Tubach, Frederic. *Index Exemplorum: A Handbook of Medieval Religious Tales.* Helsinki: Suomalainen Tiedeakatemia, 1969.

Vernet, J. "Los Médicos Andaluces en el *Libro de las Generacíones de Médicos, -ibn Yulyul.*" *Anuario de Estudios Medievales* 5 (1968): 456-57.

Vogel, Cyrille, ed. *Le Pecheur et la Penitence au Moyen-Age.* Paris: Les éditions du Cerf, 1969.

Waddell, Helen, trans. *Beasts and Saints.* London: Constable, 1949.

Wasserschleben, F. W. H. *Die Bussordnungen der abendländischen Kirche.* Halle: Verlag von Ch. Graeger, 1851.

Weinstein, Donald, and Rudolph M. Bell. *Saints and Society.* Chicago: University of Chicago Press, 1982.

Weitzmann, Kurt. *Late Antique and Early Christian Book Illumination.* New York: George Braziller, 1977.

Westrem, Scott D. *Discovering New Worlds: Essays on Medieval Exploration and Imagination.* New York: Garland, 1991.

Whitbread, Leslie. "The Liber Monstrorum and Beowulf." *Mediaeval Studies* 36 (1974): 434-71.

White, Beatrice. "Medieval Animal Lore." *Anglia* 72 (1954): 21-30.

White, Hayden. "The Forms of Wildness: Archaeology of an Idea." In *The Wild Man Within: An Image in Western Thought from the Renaissance to Romanticism*, ed. by Edward Dudley and Maximillian E. Novak. Pittsburgh: University of Pittsburgh Press, 1972.

White, Lynn, Jr. "Continuing the Conversation." In *Western Man and Environmental Ethics: Attitudes Towards Nature and Technology*, ed. by Ian G. Barbour, 55-65. Reading, Mass.: Addison-Wesley, 1973.

―――. "The Historic Roots of Our Ecologic Crises." *Science* 155 (1967): 1203-7.

―――. *Medieval Technology and Social Change*. London: Oxford University Press, 1964.

White, T. H. *The Bestiary: A Book of Beasts*. New York: G. P. Putnam's Sons, 1960.

Whitesell, Frederick R. "Fables in Medieval Exempla." *Journal of English and Germanic Philology* 46 (1947): 348-66.

Whiting, B. J. "Proverbial Material in Old-French Poems on Reynard the Fox." *Harvard Studies and Notes in Philology and Literature* 18 (1935): 235-70.

Williams, Charles Allyn. *The Oriental Affinities of the Legend of the Hairy Anchorite*. Urbana: University of Illinois Press, 1925, 1927.

Williamson, J. B. "Elyas as a Wild Man in *Li Estoire del Chevalier au Cisne*." *Essays in Honor of L. F. Solano*, 193-202. Chapel Hill: University of North Carolina Press, 1970.

Wittkower, Rudolph. "Marvels of the East: A Study in the History of Monsters." *Journal of the Warburg and Courtland Institute* 5 (1942): 159-97.

Wolfson, Harry. "The Internal Senses in Latin, Arabic, and Hebrew Philosophic Texts." *Harvard Theological Review* 28 (1935): 69-133.

Woodruff, Helen. "The Physiologus of Bern." *Art Bulletin* 12 (1930): 226-50.

Woods, Barbara Allen. *The Devil in Dog Form*. Berkeley: University of California Press, 1959.

Yapp, W. Beundson. "Animals in Medieval Art: The Bayeux Tapestry as an Example." *Journal of Medieval History* 13 (1987): 15-73.

Ziolkowski, Jan M. "Avatars of Ugliness in Medieval Literature." *Modern Language Review* 79 (1984): 1-20.

―――. "A Fairy Tale from before Fairy Tales: Egbert of Liège's 'De puella a lupellis seruata' and the Medieval Background of 'Little Red Riding Hood.'" *Speculum* 67 (July 1992): 549-75.

―――. *Talking Animals: Medieval Latin Beast Poetry, 750-1150*. Philadelphia: University of Pennsylvania Press, 1993.

Index